TRADITION AS SELECTIVITY
Scripture, Mishnah, Tosefta, and Midrash in the Talmud of Babylonia

The Case of Tractate Arakhin

SOUTH FLORIDA STUDIES IN THE HISTORY OF JUDAISM

Edited by
Jacob Neusner
William Scott Green, James Strange

Number 09
Tradition as Selectivity
Scripture, Mishna, Tosefta, and Midrash
in the Talmud of Babylonia

by
Jacob Neusner

TRADITION AS SELECTIVITY

Scripture, Mishnah, Tosefta, and Midrash in the Talmud of Babylonia

The Case of Tractate Arakhin

by

Jacob Neusner

Scholars Press
Atlanta, Georgia

TRADITION AS SELECTIVITY
Scripture, Mishnah, Tosefta, and Midrash in the Talmud of Babylonia

The Case of Tractate Arakhin

Publication of this book was made possible by a grant from the Tisch Family Foundation, New York City. The University of South Florida acknowledges with thanks this important support for its scholarly projects.

Library of Congress Cataloging in Publication Data
Neusner, Jacob, 1932-
    Tradition as selectivity : scripture, Mishnah, Tosefta, and
    Midrash in the Talmud of Babylonia : the case of Tractate Arakhin /
    by Jacob Neusner.
    p.   cm. -- (South Florida studies in the history of Judaism :
    09)
    Includes index.
    ISBN 1-55540-478-2 (alk. paper)
    1. Talmud. Arakhin--Criticism, interpretation, etc. I. Title.
II. Series.
BM506.A73N48   1990
296.1'25--dc20   90-37012
                                    CIP

Printed in the United States of America
on acid-free paper

There is a Jewish proclivity for vindicatory law, for law that is justified, against law that is autocratically prescribed...a Jewish inclination for the vindicatory.

David W. Halivni

The Talmud...deals with an overwhelmingly broad subject – the nature of all things according to the Torah. Therefore its contours are a reflection of life itself. It has no formal external order, but is bound by a strong inner connection between [sic!] its many diverse subjects....The authority of the Talmud lies in its use of this rigorous method in its search for truth with regard to the entire Torah – in other words, with regard to all possible subjects in the world, both physical and spiritual.

Adin Steinsaltz

The Talmud is, in truth, about all things. There is no corner of human life and no corner of Jewish life into which the fastidious rabbis did not peer.

Leon Wieseltier

FOR

MY FRIEND AND COLLEAGUE

AS MEMBER OF THE INSTITUTE FOR ADVANCED STUDY

PROFESSOR BENJAMIN ARNOLD

UNIVERSITY OF READING

Table of Contents

Part One
"ITS CONTOURS ARE A REFLECTION OF LIFE ITSELF"
Steinsaltz
"...THE TALMUD IS, IN TRUTH, ABOUT ALL THINGS"
Wieseltier
TRUE FOR TOSEFTA TO TRACTATE ARAKHIN

Part Two
"ITS CONTOURS ARE A REFLECTION OF LIFE ITSELF"
Steinsaltz
"...THE TALMUD IS, IN TRUTH, ABOUT ALL THINGS"
Wieseltier
FALSE FOR BABYLONIAN TALMUD TRACTATE ARAKHIN
CHAPTERS ONE, FOUR, AND FIVE

Part Three
"THE JEWISH PREDELICTION FOR JUSTIFIED LAW"
Halivni
TRUE FOR SIFRA AND (THEREFORE) ALSO FALSE FOR
BABYLONIAN TALMUD TRACTATE ARAKHIN CHAPTER SEVEN

Part Four
CONCLUSION

Preface

Since all inquiry begins with some one document and its material traits, I conduct a simple, empirical experiment on tractate Arakhin in the Mishnah, Tosefta, and Talmud of Babylonia (a.k.a. the Bavli), and on its counterpart, Lev. 27:1-8 and Lev. 27:16-25, in Sifra. The specific research problem of this book is how the Bavli (the Talmud of Babylonia), as exemplified in one tractate, relates to its sources, by which I mean, materials it shares with other and (by definition) earlier-redacted documents. In this instance what I want to know is how Bavli Arakhin deals with the topic and facts set forth at [1] Lev. 27:1-8, 16-25, the prior reading of [2] Sifra to those verses, [3] the received version of those same facts set forth by [3] Mishnah-tractate Arakhin, and the exegesis of Mishnah-tractate Arakhin by [4] Tosefta Arakhin. What is at stake is an account of just how "traditional" the Bavli is. The question that defines the problem is how the Bavli has formed of available writings (redacted in documents now in hand) a single, cogent, and coherent statement presented by the Bavli's authorship as summary and authoritative: a canonical statement on a given subject. In what ways does a Bavli tractate frame such a (theologically canonical) statement out of what (as attested in extant writings) its authorship has in hand? In the exercise of which the present work is a continuation, *The Bavli and its Sources*, the prior source was the Talmud of the Land of Israel. The prior sources in this book are the Tosefta and Sifra.

If I have chosen as the proximate target of this analysis two discrete positions on the character of the Talmud of Babylonia as a whole, it is only because I want readers to recognize that the position I propose to demonstrate within the data at hand – while here obviously correct and fully in conformity with the character of the sources – competes with other views of the documents and how they are to be read. In Chapter One I spell out why I think the Steinsaltz-Wieseltier position on the relationship of the Bavli to its received writings, and the Halivni position on the relationship of the Bavli to Scripture, present an important challenge. The positions of these several colleagues prove absurd, alas, and having read this book, readers will suppose that I have set up a straw man to demolish. But the contrary is the case. While erroneous and essentially uninformed, Steinsaltz's and Wieseltier's characterization of the Bavli enjoys the status of self-evidence; while stated in a clumsy, nearly incomprehensible manner, Halivni's proposition is found congenial in broad circles as well. So it is important time and again to test their allegations against the evidence. That is what I do here, in a very systematic way.

It may prove of interest if I place into the context of the present period in my ongoing research an entire sequence of books that I completed in my year as Member of the Institute for Advanced Study, of which this *Beistudie* forms an important component. First, my long-term scholarly research program, which began around 1960 and will conclude around 2000 or so, aims at uncovering the history of the formation of Judaism in the first six centuries A.D. The work that has delineated each stage in that formative process has moved from literary, to historical, to religions-historical study. I differentiate the stages in the canonical writings that attest to the formative history of Judaism through the systematic comparison of the Judaic systems – worldview, way of life, definition of the social entity – adumbrated by the documents of each period. I have already finished my characterization of the literary evidence for the first and second phases in the formative history of Judaism. The comparison of the Judaic systems attested by the documents of those first and second phases, respectively, is in *The Transformation of Judaism. From Philosophy to Religion.* In that book – briefly dealt with in Chapter One – I trace the transformation of the Judaic system put forth in the Mishnah, which I classify as philosophical, to the Judaic system adumbrated in the Talmud of the Land of Israel, Genesis Rabbah, and Leviticus Rabbah, which I classify as religious. Two prior projects now brought to completion are *Judaism as Philosophy: The Method and Message of the Mishnah* and also *Rabbinic Political Theory: Religion and Politics in the Mishnah.*

Three *Beistudien* of the present phase in my work have involved experiments on methodological problems. These are first, *Symbol and Theology in Judaism* on the problem of deciphering the symbolic vocabulary of Judaism in the first seven centuries A.D., as that vocabulary came to expression in both iconic and written media. What I wished to find out was how to make sense of data in two media. The first are conventional representations of the same objects, in the same combination, in iconography of synagogues. The second are what seemed to me conventional lists of persons, events, or conceptions, which surface in various combinations for various purposes in literary form. These seemed to me comparable, since the conventional lists use words as opaque symbols, taking on meaning only in combination with other such opaque symbols. Future work on the larger-scale structures of theological character in the documents of Judaism in the first seven centuries A.D. will be guided by these methodological results. The second of these *Beistudien* of the present period in my research is *The Canonical History of Ideas. The Place of the So-called Tannaite Midrashim, Mekhilta Attributed to R. Ishmael, Sifra, Sifré to Numbers, and Sifré to Deuteronomy.* This is an experiment in dating documents by appeal to the presence or absence of indicative conceptions and other approaches to finding a location of a document. I took as my givens the indicative conceptions of the Mishnah as against those of the Talmud of the Land of Israel, and tried to find out where, in relationship to those poles, the named documents situate themselves. The third is the present book.

The works of systematic *haute vulgarisation* of my own ideas for a larger scholarly audience produced at the same time as this *Beistudie* are [1] *Jews and Christians: The Myth of a Common Tradition;* [2] *Studying Classical Judaism: A Primer,* which answers the question, What do we know, and how do we know it? with reference to the history, literature, religion, and theology of the Judaism portrayed in the canonical writings of the first six centuries A.D.; [3] *Ancient Judaism. Debates and Disputes. Second Series.*[1]

Current *Vorstudien,* in preparation for the third phase in the study of the formation of Judaism, have brought me to the earliest stages in the next major chapter of my work, the literary phase of the description, analysis, and interpretation of the talmudic component of the history of Judaism, which involves a major translation project, on the one side, and an analytical study of already translated tractates, on the other. These items form prolegomena to the description of the Talmud of Babylonia: [1] *The Bavli. The Talmud of Babylonia. An Introduction;* [2] *The Talmud: Close Encounters.* In addition, I now have to carry forward my translation of the Bavli, to set the stage for a variety of further inquires. The work accomplished along with the present book is as follows: *The Talmud of Babylonia. An American Translation. XXI. Bava Mesia,* in four volumes; *The Talmud of Babylonia. An American Translation. XXXIII. Temurah; The Talmud*

---

[1]The publishers are Trinity Press International and SCM.

of Babylonia. An American Translation. XXXVI. *Niddah; The Talmud of Babylonia. An American Translation.* XXXIV. *Keritot; The Talmud of Babylonia. An American Translation.* XXVIII. *Zebahim;* and *The Talmud of Babylonia. An American Translation.* XXXI. *Bekhorot.* On the basis of the sample made ready for analytical purposes by my analytical re-translation of the ten tractates, out of the thirty-seven, of the Talmud of Babylonia, I shall undertake the next step in my scholarly program.

This is the first account of the rules of literary and logical composition of the Talmud of Babylonia and is tentatively titled, *The Bavli's One Voice: Types of Analytical Discourse in the Babylonian Talmud, their Proportions, and their Fixed Order.* This mainly statistical study of types of forms and the order in which the forms are utilized will open the way to a broader inquiry Specifically, in *Transformation* I take the two sets of documents as evidence of systems to which they refer or attest, and it is the systems that I claim exhibit traits I can describe and connections – comparisons and contrasts – I can analyze and interpret. So that work formed an exercise in the study of category formation, following upon a rather protracted labor of description of texts, analysis of the systems adumbrated or attested by them, and then interpretation of the systems within a single context of comparison and contrast. So much for the literature that conveys to us the first and the second stages in the formation of Judaism, the philosophical and the religious, respectively.

This book was born in a discussion with Professor William Scott Green, University of Rochester, about the critical reception of Steinsaltz's *The Talmud. The Steinsaltz Edition* (New York, 1989: Random House). I had originally dismissed as nonsense the thought that Steinsaltz and others really claimed – or meant to say – that "everything is in the Talmud." Green showed me that that exaggerated and ignorant conception is broadly held, and that both Steinsaltz and his arch-critic, Wieseltier, express it in quite explicit language. I then imagined that the allegation derives only from a clumsy and inexact knowledge of English on Steinsaltz's part, and a neophyte journalist's slovenly use of language on Wieseltier's. But Green insisted that the same conception circulates broadly, and in diverse forms. A review of other recent writing about the document showed he was right; for a third example, I selected my student, Professor Robert Goldenberg, State University of New York at Stony Brook, whose writing on the Talmud shows an unjustified self-assurance, a confidence with slight basis on genuine scholarly achievement; in the dreadful essay cited in context, readers will see how he retails opinions of others, rather than conducts scholarship in original sources. I then concurred that an address to the notion of the Talmud's universal agenda ("its contours are a reflection of life itself..." "...about all things") was called for. Halivni's quite distinct error seemed to me to derive from the same misconception of the character of the Talmud of Babylonia. It then appeared worth the time and effort to compose a sequel to *The Bavli and its Sources* – the issues being the same, though the data quite distinct – and this book is the outcome. I thank Professor Green for insisting that the work be done and demonstrating that much is at stake in the outcome.

I owe thanks to three agencies. I wrote this book and all the sixteen others – seventeen in all – to which reference has here been made during the year in which I was supported in part by a Senior Fellowship of the National Endowment for the Humanities (FA 28396-89), and I take much pride in offering to that agency in the support of humanistic learning my very hearty thanks for the recognition and material support that the Fellowship afforded to me. I found the Endowment, particularly the Division of Fellowships and Seminars, always helpful and courteous in dealing with my application and express my admiration and appreciation to that thoroughly professional staff of public servants. Brown University complemented that Fellowship with substantial funds to make it possible for me to spend the entire academic year, 1989-1990, in full-time research. In my twenty-two years at Brown University, now concluded, I always enjoyed the University's generous support for every research initiative that I undertook, and it was a welcome challenge to be worthy of the unusual opportunities accorded to me as a research scholar at that University. I never took for granted the commitment of the University's scarce resources to my work in particular and now express the thanks commensurate to it. The Institute for Advanced Study, where I wrote this book, afforded a pleasant setting in which to pursue full-time research. I thank all those who made it so, particularly the Members for 1989-1990. I dedicate this book to one of the best of the lot, to whose wit, charm, and erudition I owe many engaging hours of conversation.

JACOB NEUSNER

Graduate Research Professor of Humanities and Religious Studies
UNIVERSITY OF SOUTH FLORIDA
TAMPA
and
Martin Buber Professor of Judaic Studies
UNIVERSITY OF FRANKFURT

June 30, 1990

The Institute for Advanced Study
Princeton, New Jersey

Prologue

The Talmud of Babylonia (a.k.a. Babylonian Talmud, Bavli), ca. 600, comes at the end of a set of writings produced by sages of Judaism over a period of four hundred years, starting with the Mishnah in ca. 200. These writings, produced over a period of four centuries, related in various ways both to Scripture and to the Mishnah, as well as to one another. Consequently, the formation of the Judaic system attested by the Talmud of Babylonia is described as traditional, in the sense that later sages received from earlier ones traditions to be preserved, refined, and handed on, in an ongoing and continuous process of a linear, harmonious, and one dimensional, connected manner. The Judaism that came to expression in the Talmud of Babylonia therefore is portrayed as traditional, the result of a sustained process of tradition. That view of the formation of Judaism is not sustained by the character of the Talmud of Babylonia and, it follows, the Judaic system set forth, in written form, by that Talmud is to be classified as not tradition or the result of a process of tradition but as autonomous, free-standing, and fully autocephalic – the result of a process of selection. But the literary form given to that system was indeed traditional, hence the long-standing misreading of the matter by people familiar with the classical writings of that Judaism.

In this book through the analysis of the qualities of literary evidence in Tosefta, Sifra, and the Talmud of Babylonia (the first two highly traditional in form and intent, the third quite different from the others, for the case at hand, tractate Arakhin/Lev. Chapter Twenty-Seven) I propose to show, in dialogue with the opinions of others, that the Bavli took shape through a process of not tradition but selectivity. If Tosefta in relationship to the Mishnah, and Sifra in relationship to Scripture, prove both formally and programmatically quite traditional, then the Bavli in relationship to the entire

1

inherited corpus of writing is not at all traditional. Its authorship, moreover, scarcely pretended to do more than select and recast whatever they wished out of a received body of writings in such a way as to make the statement that they, for their part, chose to make.

To grasp what is at stake, a brief account of the prior documents will prove helpful to the reader. These writings rest on two types of base documents, compilations of exegesis of Scripture called Midrash collections, which refer to the Scriptures of ancient Israel (to Christianity, the Old Testament, to Judaism, the Written Torah), and the Tosefta, or supplements, and the two Talmuds, the one of the Land of Israel or the Yerushalmi, the other of Babylonia, which refer to the Mishnah (in Judaism, the first component of the Oral Torah ultimately encompassing all the literature at hand). All of the writings of Judaism in late antiquity copiously cite Scripture. More important, some of them serve (or are presented and organized) as commentaries on the former, the Written Torah, others as amplifications of the latter, the Mishnah as the beginning of the transcription of the Oral Torah. Since Judaism treats all of these writings as a single, seamless Torah, the one whole Torah revealed by God to Moses, our rabbi, at Mount Sinai, the received hermeneutic naturally does the same. All of the writings are read in light of all others, and words and phrases are treated as autonomous units of tradition, rather than as components of particular writings, for example, paragraphs or units of discourse and books, composite units of sustained and cogent thought.

My method, worked out in the shank of the book, is to survey a tractate and read it as I think it should be read. I also compare the traits of the tractate with what people have said about the Bavli as a whole. In this way readers will grasp what is at stake in the argument of this book. I want the reader to see very graphically and precisely the extent and character of the utilization or neglect, by the authorship of the Bavli, of the antecedent documents. That is why I reprint an enormous selection. But I took a large sample, rather than the whole, for two reasons, first, because of the essential uniformity of the talmudic literature, which allows even a modest sample to tell us the shape and structure of the editorial conventions that apply throughout, and also simply because the sheer bulk of the entire tractate would demand more space than is necessary graphically to make the point I wish in my study to establish. I survey my sample to find out how the "tradition," namely, the Bavli, in the case of Bavli tractate Arakhin (a choice I explain in Chapter One), relates to its "sources," namely, the prior literature on the same subject as is treated in our tractate, Tosefta and Sifra in particular. That survey is meant to yield a set of facts pertinent to the larger question I seek to investigate, the issue of continuities among documents, or, in terms of history of religions, the definition of the canon and – more to the point – the exegesis of exegesis.

The result of pursuing these questions should yield the answer to yet another: can we discern within the Bavli's treatment of a subject documentary traits of *traditionality*, that is, laying down a summary, final and experienced judgment for all time? And can we see within the Bavli elements of a program to turn sources into a single tradition, on a given topic? When I can answer that program of questions, I can form a hypothesis, resting on literary facts, concerning the literary and doctrinal traditionality of a sample item within the rabbinic corpus of late antiquity. The issue is drawn in the title of this book: selectivity or traditionality.

That is to say, I can frame a theory on – to state with emphasis – *how the Judaism of the Dual Torah speaking through the Bavli in conclusion constituted of its received materials a whole and proportioned system – way of life, worldview, addressed to a defined Israel – and turned into a systemic statement, that is,* a statement of the tradition *handed down in and formed out of prior sources, a variety of available writings on any given subject.*

Let me explain the context in which I was motivated to conduct this experiment. This work continues one program among the four that I ordinarily carry on at one time. As my work proceeds, I generally think through and often also work on [1] a principal project; [2] ancillary studies *(Beistudien)*, very often experiments in method or try-outs on new ideas, not ready for exploration and exposition in major monographs; [3] *haute vulgarisation* of my own scholarly work, to speak to a broader audience in the humanities than my rather technical studies are likely to serve; [4] *Vorstudien*, or preliminary studies, aimed at preparing texts, through translation and analysis, for later use in my principal work in the history of religion. This exercise falls into the second category and also carries forward a prior work of the same kind, which is *The Bavli and its Sources: The Question of Tradition in the Case of Tractate Sukkah.*[1] Specifically, here and in related works I am forming a bridge between my studies on the first two principal stages in the formative history of Judaism in late antiquity, those marked, in literary terms, by the Mishnah and so-called Tannaite Midrash compilations, on the one side, and the Talmud of the Land of Israel and some of the Rabbah Midrash compilations, Genesis

---

[1] Atlanta, 1987: Scholars Press for Brown Judaic Studies.

Rabbah and Leviticus Rabbah, on the other, and a project that is now well underway, concerning the third and final stage in that same formation, marked, in documents, by the Talmud of Babylonia and some later Rabbah Midrash compilations, Ruth Rabbah, Song of Songs Rabbah, Esther Rabbah I, and Lamentations Rabbati.

Now in this further exercise among my *Beistudien*, I treat two distinct questions, spelled out in greater detail in Chapter One. First, is it so, as David W. Halivni has maintained, that there is a "Jewish predilection" to what he calls (in his somewhat awkward and private language) "vindicatory law"? As I said just now, what he means is that the norm in Jewish culture (a term left undefined by him and otherwise not used by me at all) is to derive law by exegesis from Scripture. He further maintains that that "predilection" is set aside in the Mishnah but reaffirmed in the Talmud of Babylonia. Certainly if the Judaism adumbrated by the Talmud of Babylonia is a traditional system, then Halivni's characterization will prove congruent to its fundamental characteristics; participants in a traditional system will prefer to tease out of a received authoritative text whatever they wish to say on their own, and discussions will exhibit a strongly exegetical character. I expand upon the character of this test in Chapter One. Part Three of this book addresses data that afford very little support for Halivni's view.

Second, is it true, as Adin Steinsaltz and Leon Wieseltier (among a great many) maintain, that the Talmud of Babylonia contains "everything"? That allegation, in the intellectually rather vulgar form in which we receive it, of course is unanswerable, indeed, untenable. How would we know whether or not "everything" is there, absent a conception of what would form a definitive exception? And of what, in or out of cultural context, does "everything" consist? Still, we may rephrase matters in such a way as to make possible an exercise of verification or falsification. To do so, we (charitably) limit the claim advanced by Steinsaltz and his critic, Wieseltier, to a more modest scale. We ask this question: Do the framers of the final document mean to take over and rehash *everything on the topic of a given tractate* they have received out of the past? We have ample evidence on precisely what they had in hand, covering the Mishnah, the Tosefta, the Tannaite Midrash compilations, the earlier amoraic Midrash compilations, and (where pertinent, which is not so with our tractate), the Talmud of the Land of Israel. That claim that "everything" is in the document that comes at the end of a process of tradition (a drastically limited revision of the Steinsaltz-Wieseltier characterization) should surely find support or meet refutation. Support would prove probative if we can show that the authorship of the Talmud of Babylonia intended to provide a reprise of the entirety (or at least the greater part) of the received tradition. Refutation then consists in showing that that is not the so. We have a model for a genuinely capacious document, containing "everything" on a given topic, which is the Tosefta. Here, too, the Tosefta will give us a fine example of what such a document, holding "everything" a prior document has presented, would accomplish. And, by comparison, the Bavli will differ so materially as to accord to the Steinsaltz-Wieseltier theory the status of an intellectual solecism, an instance of words used with no special sense or meaning in mind. Parts One and Two of the book examine evidence that pertains to the conceptions of Steinsaltz and Wieseltier: one document that, within its limits, would conform to their characterization, in Part One, another document that hardly validates their claim. Unfortunately, they speak of that other document – the Bavli – when they ask us to believe that "the Talmud's contours are a reflection of life itself....There is no corner of human life and no corner of Jewish life into which the fastidious rabbis did not peer," and so forth.

Now the broader issue, for which these unfortunate characterizations require more sustained attention than, on their own, they deserve, should be made explicit. Nothing will so distinctively characterize writers of a traditional document than the importance of preserving "everything." For the task of tradition begins with the act of lovingly rehearsing the self-evidently valid, received facts: repeating them, clarifying them, vindicating them. So the appearance of an effort to include everything and omit nothing (again, in all charity, we have to allege that Steinsaltz and Wieseltier have added the word "relevant") will form part of the claim upon plausibility of a piece of writing that should be classified as traditional. Since, as a matter of fact, we have in hand in the Tosefta a major treatment of the subject dealt with in every tractate of the Talmud of Babylonia, we have a perfectly simple way of finding out whether that fundamental, received (therefore "traditional") writing has defined the program of the successors. If ˙˙ has, then they are guided by the considerations of tradition, and if ˌas not, then, in this aspect of their work, they are not. Further discussion of these issues is in Chapter One.

As I shall explain in Chapter One, I have in mind now to find out whether or not we may characterize the third and last stage as the theological. In the next decade or so, beginning with now-completed studies of the Bavli and the related Midrash compilations, particularly Lamentations Rabbah, Song of Songs Rabbah, Esther Rabbah I, and Ruth Rabbah, as well as my Babylonian-Talmud analytical studies now fully designed and in progress, I shall accomplish the same work for the third and final stage in the formation of Judaism, from ca. 450 to ca. 600. Some of the descriptive and analytical work is now complete, but – as indicated above, in my plan for a statement, on a sound statistical and literary-analytical foundation, of the rules of composition of the Talmud of Babylonia – a fair amount of descriptive study of texts and a still larger labor of analytical study of contexts stands between this work and the third and final interpretive enterprise I have in mind at this time, which is the passage from religion to theology. The ten tractates of the Bavli that I have translated will form the sample for the analysis of some of the problems associated with the coming inquiry. Some years from now I hope to reach a study tentatively titled, the transformation of Judaism: from religion to theology. And that will inaugurate a period of analysis of the theological (conceptual, methodological alike) substrate of the documents of Judaism in the formative age: what all writings take for granted, but none expresses.

To undertake systemic analysis on the strength of written evidence, I have systemically to complete the rereading of the classic documents of the Judaism that took shape in the first to the seventh centuries A.D. and that has predominated since then, the Judaism of the Dual Torah. These documents – the Mishnah, Midrash compilations, the two Talmuds – represent the collective statement and consensus of authorships and show us how those authorships proposed to make a statement upon their situation – and, I argue, upon the human condition. It is in that context that the present work finds its larger place and purpose.

1

Scripture, Mishnah, Tosefta, and Midrash in the Talmud of Babylonia: What Is at Stake?

There is a Jewish proclivity for vindicatory law, for law that is justified, against law that is autocratically prescribed...a Jewish inclination for the vindicatory.

David W. Halivni

The Talmud...deals with an overwhelmingly broad subject – the nature of all things according to the Torah. Therefore its contours are a reflection of life itself. It has no formal external order, but is bound by a strong inner connection between [sic!] its many diverse subjects....The authority of the Talmud lies in its use of this rigorous method in its search for truth with regard to the entire Torah – in other words, with regard to all possible subjects in the world, both physical and spiritual.

Adin Steinsaltz

The Talmud is, in truth, about all things. There is no corner of human life and no corner of Jewish life into which the fastidious rabbis did not peer.

Leon Wieseltier

i. The Ignorance of the Learned: Two Commonplace Errors

Halivni claims what the evidence does not sustain, Steinsaltz is wrong, and Wieseltier simply uninformed. The first-named is having difficulty with the English language, and what he means is scarcely obvious. The second does not grasp what he knows well but grasps imperfectly, the third exaggerates, his language being out of control. The work of describing the Talmud of Babylonia in an intelligible and accurate way is impeded by the misleading impressions formed of the

7

document by persons who have studied the document piecemeal but never as a whole. Such persons, often (as in Steinsaltz's case) with years of study in yeshivas to their credit, describe the document as disjointed, or disorganized, or dialectical (meaning, merely, meandering), but it is only the modes of their own confused processes of learning that they describe. Unaware of the character of the whole and confused by their encounter with bits and pieces, read out of all literary context, persons who have studied the document proceed to describe it in such a way as utterly to misrepresent its character. A catalogue of errors, broadly circulated, in the description of the Talmud of Babylonia would fill many pages; this book tests the validity of two of them. Specifically, I propose to address these quite distinct, but commonly held propositions concerning the Talmud of Babylonia:

1. the Bavli expresses a deeply held cultural "predilection" of Jews for finding a foundation in Scripture for beliefs and rules;
2. the Bavli is a compendium of a vast amount of information, more or less haphazardly collected over centuries of accumulation and agglutination, so "everything" is in it.

Each proposition stands by itself, and neither depends upon the other. Some maintain that the Talmud of Babylonia brings to the surface a deep-seated "predeliction" that Jews in general are supposed to have for "justified law," a term defined presently. It is that "proclivity" or "predeliction" that explains the character of the documents that followed the Mishnah, documents that emerge out of an essentially exegetical process in dialogue with Scripture. The upshot is that the the law of the Talmud is supposed to emerge from a long process of scriptural exegesis, a process short circuited by the Mishnah, the second century law code that overall failed to justify its laws, for example, by appeal to scriptural proof or antecedent or, at least, exegesis. Then the Bavli should appear to follow a program of Scripture exegesis, at least where Scripture is pertinent to its topic and program. We have a document that does organize around Scripture and its exegesis whatever it wishes to set forth, but it is not the Bavli, and the Bavli is not like that other document at all. So Halivni is wrong, not merely because there is no evidence that sustains his allegations as to the character of long centuries of the history of the Judaism of the Dual Torah prior to the redaction of the earliest of its documents, which is the Mishnah. He is wrong because the evidence of how things ought to be in documents that we do have conflicts with his theory of how matters were. To state the matter simply, an accurate perspective upon the document as a whole yields very little evidence of a "Jewish proclivity for vindicatory law," and none whatsoever that the law derived, to begin with, from a protracted and systematic exegetical process.

The other broadly held error, made by learned people bewildered by processes of study that have confused them, is unrelated to Halivni's. Represented by Steinsaltz and Wieseltier,[1] many maintain that we can find pretty much everything and its opposite in the Talmud. As I shall point out, precisely what people mean when they say that "everything is in it" is very difficult to define, and hence how to test the accuracy of such a characterization is not at all obvious. After all, if we do not know what people are saying, how are we (or they) going to show that they are right or wrong? But we cannot dismiss so weighty a figure as Steinsaltz with the observation that he seems to be making things up as he goes along, and, if Wieseltier is hardly a scholar to begin with, he can at least claim with justice that lots of people say what he says, so he is, in any event, a reliable reporter of a broadly held opinion. His sole error is to record as fact, without inquiry of his own, a widespread mistake.

One can affirm one of these views of the document without conceding the accuracy of the other, but, as a matter of fact, both derive from a rather impressionistic and superficial understanding of the document and its roots. A grasp of the document seen whole will have forestalled arrant nonsense about how "no corner of human life" is left unexamined by the Talmud's sages. So the two quite distinct errors of description derive from one and the same failure of scholarship, which is, confusing bits and pieces, seen out of documentary context, with the whole. In the pages of this book I test and show to be false both characterizations of the Talmud of Babylonia, with special reference to a single tractate, Arakhin.[2]

---

[1]I choose these two because of Steinsaltz's recent (if transient) prominence in the U. S. mass media and because of Wieseltier's strong criticism of Steinsaltz. I have therefore two exemplars who agree on nothing else but upon the proposition at hand. Later on I shall point to a third figure who says pretty much the same thing. In point of fact, nearly all accounts of the Bavli concur, all being equally oblivious to the literary structure of the document that the simplest analysis reveals.

[2]Readers are invited to outline and analyze any other tractate, or chapter of some size, because wherever they turn, they will replicate my results. The importance of Arakhin is explained presently. I am in process of completing the translation of ten Bavli tractates, which will form the foundation for my *The Bavli's One Voice*, introduced below. I plan, then, to analyze through re-translation another five or ten tractates, to lay the foundation for the next synthetic study, which will be my *The Bavli's One Message: The Proposition of the Process*. The program of these books is self-evident from their titles, and

My test of the Halivni's proposition, in Part Three,[3] requires an answer to this question: Does Scripture, properly explained, define for the framers of the tractate what is important in the topic at hand? That question addresses a more subtle question than whether or not our authors find prooftexts for their propositions. We may stipulate at the outset that, when they can, they do. What is claimed is something quite different and more profound, and that is, the framers of the Talmud take as a principal task the investigation of the law through Scripture, not merely tying law to Scripture (though that is part of it) but reading the law in dialogue with Scripture. So in Part Three I ask, is the program of our tractate defined by a sustained encounter with Scripture. I find the answer by comparing our tractate with the framing of issues concerning the topic of our tractate by Scripture exegetes. That seems to me a simple and direct approach to finding the answer. If there is a Jewish prediliction for "justified law," a term set forth presently, then Jewish law should be formed out of the reading of Scripture. But here we shall see that the program defined in the reading of Scripture pertaining to our subject and the program of our tractate bear no relationship to each other at all.

My test of Steinsaltz's and Wieseltier's proposition, in Parts One and Two of the book, is, of course, made complicated by the difficulty of explaining what people mean when they claim that everything is in the Talmud. It is manifestly absurd to claim that "the Talmud is about all things," simply because if we made a list of everything, or, at least, everything about which various writers in the first seven centuries C.E. write, we could readily show that the Talmud is only about some of them. If, for instance, we compare the Bavli with the Denkart, the important Iranian law code, which is more or less contemporary, the Denkart is "about" more things than the Bavli is. But it is hardly fair to serious colleagues to treat a journalist's mere exaggeration for effect (if that was what was Wieseltier intended) as a serious claim about the character of a piece of writing. Nor shall I score points by making an elaborate proof of the absurdity of a claim that is beyond demonstration. If someone wishes to demonstrate that the Talmud is about "all things," how in the world would he undertake to falsify his proposition? Take, for example, a list of the things about which

---

where they are meant to lead is equally obvious. But of course the work has to be done.

[3]I wanted to keep the chapters of Bavli tractate Arakhin in their given order, so I treat the chapter that ought to sustain Halivni's proposition in Part Three, though it comes later than the three chapters that allow me to find out whether, as Steinsaltz and Wieseltier allege, "everything" is in the Talmud. This ought not to cause confusion, since the issues are kept separate.

Aristotle and Plato concern themselves, or (as I said) the things paramount in the Denkart, of Zoroastrian Iran, or the Quran, of Muslim Arabia, before and after the formation of the document, respectively. If these writings cover things that the Talmud of Babylonia does not, then we should assuredly know that the Talmud is not only not about "everything" but it is not even about everything that engaged other important writers of the same time and place.

This excursion into the absurdities of a loose formulation of a proposition should not divert attention from a serious claim, which is, in the language of another contemporary, that the Talmud's "contours are a reflection of life itself." What that must mean is that, in dealing with any given subject, the Talmud will wander expansively across the outer limits of a topic – and beyond. But that too is a somewhat murky claim, since how are we to know, beyond the pages before us, just what those outer limits might have been? There is yet another formulation of matters, and this one does make possible a serious test. It is that "the Talmud...deals with...the nature of all things *according to the Torah*." This language, given by me in italics, limits what is claimed. Is it the fact, then, that the Talmud of Babylonia takes over and sets forth everything that the prior documents, received by that point as "the Torah," have said about a given subject? Now that question seems to me a fair one, since what is claimed is not that the Talmud has everything about everything (the "contours are a reflection of life itself" indeed!), but that the Talmud has everything that the Torah has handed down: "the nature of all things according to the Torah."[4]

What happens if I can show, however, that in treating a given topic the prior Torah – Scripture, the Mishnah, the Tosefta, the Midrash compilation – has set forth a fair number of facts, propositions, and conceptions, that prove of no consequence to the framers of the Talmud in their formulation of their statement about that same topic? Then it turns out that the Talmud in fact does not deal with "the nature of all things according to the Torah," but, rather, the framers of the Talmud formulate a given topic in line with what they think important, and they set forth that topic in line with the facts

---

[4]Since the Bavli ignores twenty-five of the Mishnah's sixty-two tractates, treating only thirty-seven of them, and completely by-passes two of the Mishnah's six divisions, except for a single (unrepresentative) tractate in each, Steinsaltz's claim is exceedingly difficult to interpret. The Bavli, as a matter of fact, most certainly does not "deal with...the nature of all things *according to the Torah*." – it does not even deal with the nature of all things that the Mishnah's (part of the Torah) takes up. This leads me to wonder whether Steinsaltz has given much thought to these matters that he announces with such certainty.

that suit their framing of matters, and, finally, they then select from
the inherited holy books – Scripture, Midrash, Tosefta, and Midrash
alike – whatever suits their purpose. They simply neglect the rest. If I
can show that that process of selectivity characterizes the Babylonian
Talmud's authors' reading of the prior writings, then I can show that it
is false to describe the Talmud as an account of "all things according to
the Torah."

The test undertaken in these pages can have taken any tractate
among the thirty-seven that make up the Talmud of Babylonia. For
the testing of the second proposition, certainly, all are equally
serviceable. But if we wish to know how the framers of the Babylonian
Talmud's treatment of a given topic in relationship to Scripture works
itself out, then to begin with we had better select a tractate that rests
upon solid foundations in Scripture (and many do not). I have chosen
tractate Arakhin because it does, indeed, call upon Scripture, and,
moreover, the scriptural books that supply its topic and rules are
subjected to not one but two very important Midrash exercises, contained
in Sifra and Leviticus Rabbah. Hence if those responsible for the
Bavli's materials – authors of compositions, editors of composites alike
– do exhibit the traits that people commonly assign to them, it is in a
tractate that to begin with appeals for topic, rule, and principle to
Scripture that we should be able to demonstrate that fact. If the law of
the Talmud of Babylonia derives from a long process of systematic
exegesis, or if the sages of the Talmud of Babylonia expound the topic
at hand through an essentially exegetical medium of thought, then
that tractate more than most others should demonstrate it. As to the
second proposition, if it is the case that the Bavli talks about pretty
much everything, then any tractate should be as suitable as any other
to find out precisely the contours and character of a document of such a
promiscuous topical program as to cover pretty much anything.

Lest I give reason to form the impression that I have invented
propositions no one really maintains – the difficulty in grasping
precisely what people mean by them will already have struck the
reader – let me specify in their exact language the immediately
contemporary figures who adopt both propositions I shall show are
false.

ii. Halivni's Misunderstanding

The principal current exponent of the first proposition, which as a
matter of fact comes to us from ancient times, is David W. Halivni, who
in his *Midrash, Mishnah, and Gemara. The Jewish Predilection for
Justified Law,* states that the Mishnah and associated materials

consist "almost entirely of fixed law; they contain very little discursive material."[5] In their view, "law was to be officially transmitted only in the apodictic form." Argument and discussion would be neglected and not preserved. He further maintains that "this state also prevailed throughout the amoraic period (200-427), until the redactors of the Talmud...came to the aid of the discursive material and affirmed it worthy to be preserved." The role of the redactors of the Talmud, called by Halivni "Stammaim," was "to provide lengthy explanatory notes, complete defective statements, [which] supplement the text with passages of their own." These conclusions, reached in his commentary to half of the Talmud of Babylonia, led Halivni to suppose that in casting matters as they did, the *Stammaim* reverted to the practice of the authorship of collections of biblical commentaries on legal passages of Scripture. Specifically, Halivni inquires into what he calls "midrashic form," "the form used when law is tied to Scripture." Using as the subtitle of his book "the Jewish predilection for justified law," he argues that there is a Jewish "proclivity for vindicatory law, for law that is justified, against law that is autocratically prescribed." This distinction leads him to take the view that what he calls mishnaic form, that is, law without exegetical foundation linking law to Scripture, was exceptional: "Mishnaic form initially emerged as a response to the particular political and religious conditions that prevailed in Palestine during the period following the destruction of the Temple." He further maintains that there is a "Jewish inclination for the vindicatory. "The discovery that Jewish apperception since the time of the Bible favored justificatory law was an unexpected result of this study." The book then is divided by periods: biblical, post-biblical, mishnaic, amoraic, stammaitic, then the Gemara as successor of Midrash, and the legacy of the Stammaim.

Halivni's proposition, then, provides a contemporary statement of the first of the two false characterizations of the document. But reading his book in its own framework and not for purposes of an experiment, we note that the work rests on three premises. First, Halivni takes for granted the unity of all sources in a single "Judaism," joined to the axiom that the talmudic literature speaks for all Jews of the time and the postulate of a cogent "Jewish mentality." That is why he can fabricate a single "Jewish apperception." Second, he takes for granted the reliability of all attributions of sayings. Third, Halivni takes as historical fact the accuracy of what is attributed. Whether a differentiated and critical reading of the same sources would lead to

---

[5]*Midrash, Mishnah, and Gemara. The Jewish Predilection for Justified Law.* David Weiss Halivni (Cambridge, 1986: Harvard University Press). 164 pp.

the same conclusions no one can say. In all, it is rather naive and intellectually retrograde, but very, very learned – if not very critical or persuasive.

iii. Steinsaltz's and Wieseltier's Misrepresentation of the Character of the Bavli

Among the numerous versions of the second proposition, most current and choice are those of Adin Steinsaltz and his leading U.S. critic, Leon Wieseltier. I have selected Steinsaltz and Wieseltier because they stand at opposite corners. Since Wieseltier reviewed Steinsaltz's re-presentation of the Talmud of Babylonia, he has presented himself as an expert in these matters; it is not unfair, therefore, to hold him to his word. Steinsaltz, for his part, allows himself to be compared to various exemplary figures in the history of talmudic study, even to Rashi. So both figures may be assumed to think they know that about which they make pronouncements. Then we cannot dismiss as uninformed or merely impressionistic what Steinsaltz says when he states, "The Talmud...deals with an overwhelmingly broad subject – the nature of all things according to the Torah. Therefore its contours are a reflection of life itself. It has no formal external order, but is bound by a strong inner connection between [sic!] its many diverse subjects."[6] He further states, "The authority of the Talmud lies in its use of this rigorous method in its search for truth with regard to the entire Torah – in other words, with regard to all possible subjects in the world, both physical and spiritual."[7] Nor can we treat as uninformed mumbling what Wieseltier alleges when he says, "The Talmud is, in truth, about all things. There is no corner of human life and no corner of Jewish life into which the fastidious rabbis did not peer."[8] Both figures, and others too numerous to list, see the Talmud of Babylonia as disorganized, promiscuous in its agenda, and concerned with everything and its opposite.

What we shall see when we pursue the two propositions under study in our analysis of a tractate is that Wieseltier and Steinsaltz simply have not grasped in an accurate and detailed way the character of the document. Lest I be thought to misrepresent the weightier of the two (Wieseltier not being a scholar in this area to begin with), let me

---

[6]*The Talmud. The Steinsaltz Edition* (New York, 1989). *A Reference Guide*, p. 7.
[7]*Ibid.*, p. 3.
[8]Leon Wieseltier, "Unlocking the rabbis' secrets," *New York Times Book Review*, December 17, 1989, p. 3. There are other choice errors in that supercilious review, to which a scholar of Steinsaltz's standing ought not to have been subjected, but this seems to me the most blatant.

pursue the matter further. Steinsaltz is explicit in alleging that the Talmud of Babylonia is disorganized. For example, he says, "One of the principal difficulties in studying the Talmud is that it is not written in a systematic fashion; it does not move from simple to weighty material, from the definition of terms to their use. In almost every passage of the Talmud, discussion is based on ideas that have been discussed elsewhere, and on terms that are not necessarily defined on the page where they appear."[9] He further states,

> Viewed superficially, the Talmud seems to lack inner order....The arrangement of the Talmud is not systematic, nor does it follow familiar didactic principles. It does not proceed from the simple to the complex, or from the general to the particular...It has no formal external order, but is bound by a strong inner connection between its many diverse subjects. The structure of the Talmud is associative. The material of the Talmud was memorized and transmitted orally for centuries, its ideas are joined to each other by inner links, and the order often reflects the needs of memorization. Talmudic discourse shifts from one subject to a related subject, or to a second that brings the first to mind in an associative way."[10]

It is hardly surprising that Steinsaltz will find everything in the document, as he says, "It has no formal external order, but is bound by a strong inner connection between its many diverse subjects."

The sedimentary theory of the document, premised upon its utter disorganization, is also expressed by Robert Goldenberg, who claims to describe the character of the Talmud when he says, "Evidence suggests that various centers of rabbinic study developed their own such collections [of Mishnah commentary], though in the end only one overall collection was redacted...for Babylonia. For several generations, the collections remained fluid. Materials were added, revised, or shifted. Free association led to the production of extended discourses or sets of sayings that at times had little to do with the mishnaic passage serving as point of departure."[11] The protracted passages of the Talmud of Babylonia, tractate Arakhin that we shall examine hardly sustain these descriptions of the Talmud in general but contradict them, point by point. That is not to suggest Steinsaltz's and Goldenberg's characterizations overall invariably misrepresent the

---

[9]Adin Steinsaltz, *The Talmud. The Steinsaltz Edition. A Reference Guide* (New York, 1989: Random House), p. vii.

[10]*Ibid.*, p. 7.

[11]Robert Goldenberg, "Talmud," in Robert M. Seltzer, ed., *Judaism. A People and Its History. Religion, History, and Culture. Selections from The Encyclopaedia of Religion*. Mircea Eliade, editor in chief (New York, 1989: Macmillan), p. 102.

character of the document, only that they represent matters in a way that suggests insufficient consideration, on their part, of the facts of the matter. In the case of so substantial and diverse a document as the Talmud, mere impressions can sustain every opinion and its opposite. But sustained consideration of representative passages yields definitive evidence for only a single view.

It is that the Talmud is not a mere compilation of this and that, the result of centuries of the accumulation, in a haphazard way, of the detritus of various schools or opinions. The four chapters we shall follow, beginning to end, show us a sample of the Talmud that is exceedingly carefully and well crafted, a sustained and cogent inquiry. Scarcely a single line is out of place; not a sentence in the entire passage sustains the view of a document that is an agglutinative compilation. We can state very simply how the Talmud analyzes our Mishnah passage. We ordinarily begin with the clarification of the Mishnah paragraph, turn then to the examination of the principles of law implicit in the Mishnah paragraph, and then broaden the discussion to introduce what I call analogies from case to law and law to case. These are the three stages of numerous discourses. Within a protracted discussion, we note numerous cross-references, a point made much earlier and reconsidered in a fresh context. The various propositions were systematically tested and examined. If the passage was orally formulated and orally transmitted, we can discern, moreover, no indications of a mnemonic; the whole seems to presuppose the possibility of referring later on to an earlier passage, and other indications of the premise of a written document or at least notes. It would be very easy to outline the discussion of innumerable sustained discourses, beginning to end, and to produce a reasoned account of the position and order of every completed composition and the ordering of the several compositions into a composite. And that composite really does provide a beginning and an end.[12]

---

[12]In my forthcoming work, *The Bavli's One Voice: The Types of Discourse of the Talmud of Babylonia*. Atlanta, 1991: Scholars Press for South Florida Studies in the History of Judaism, I set forth what I can show to be the Bavli's rules for setting forth a complete discussion; the choices people faced; the selections they made; the reasons for them. Any conception that a document for which, entirely inductively, we can specify the rules of composition and the available types of discourse is confused, disorganized, chaotic, promiscuous in its topical program ("everything is in it") derives from ignorance, and it is the ignorance that requires explanation. For the evidence of the document is one-sided and overwhelmingly confirms the claims made here and refutes the characterizations of Wieseltier, Steinsaltz, and, in another context altogether, Goldenberg.

The facts before us do not indicate a haphazard, episodic, sedimentary process of agglutation and conglomeration – a document that can contain everything in general, as Wieseltier and Steinsaltz represent matters, because it concerns itself with nothing in particular. They point, quite to the contrary, to a well-considered and orderly composition, planned from beginning to end and following an outline that is definitive throughout. That outline has told the framers of the passage what comes first – the simplest matters of language, then the more complex matters of analysis of content, then secondary development of analogous principles and cases. In this passage, as we shall see, Wieseltier and Steinsaltz are simply wrong: we do move from simple criticism of language to weighty analysis of parallels. True, we invoke facts treated elsewhere; but reference is always verbatim, so, with a modicum of information, we can follow the discussion. True, the Talmud is not an elementary primer of the law, but it does not pretend to be. It claims to discuss the Mishnah paragraph that it cites, and it discusses that Mishnah paragraph. Perhaps Steinsaltz had in mind some other document when, as his premise, he admits that the document does not move from the definition of terms to their use. True enough, but that is not the only way in which a systematic discourse can be undertaken, and, in the context at hand, that is not even a way that would have proved relevant to the tasks undertaken by our authorship. In any event, his representation of the Bavli contradicts even the chapter that he translated and presented in the book from which these quotations are taken.

When Steinsaltz says that a superficial view of the document yields the judgment that it lacks "inner order," he is entirely correct: that is a very *superficial* view indeed. It is also wrong and has already been shown to be wrong. Readers who compare what they will see in Bavli-tractate Arakhin with the words just now quoted will find his judgment astonishing. And the remainder of his remarks about how the document does not proceed from the simple to the complex or from the general to the particular, how it lacks formal external order, simply do not find justification in the pages we are going to review. His conception that the structure of the Talmud is associative is wrong for our protracted passage, but right for the organization and composition of the tractates overall – hence, irrelevant at any given line of the writing.[13] Steinsaltz's presentation of his ideas is confusing; it is

---

[13]Steinsaltz is remarkably reticent to explain what he means here. He does not appear to have done much homework in reading the vast, available scholarly literature, and his account bears the stench of indolence, if not mere ignorance. The list of books of which Steinsaltz remains blissfully ignorant (at

sufficient to observe that the discourse at hand in no way suggests that
the ideas are joined to each other only by inner links, and if as
Steinsaltz claims, the needs of memorization dictate the formulation or
even the order of the materials at hand on a single page of the Talmud,
viewed as a composition, I cannot point to a single piece of evidence for
that fact.

Goldenberg's description is equally puzzling. No one doubts that
some indeterminate period of time was characterized by the confusion
that he imputes. Who knows, after all, how and where materials were
added, revised, or shifted, when in hand is only the result of that
allegedly agglutinative process? But the pages we shall study shows
us no examples of "free association" – and we shall see no capacity to
throw in, promiscuously, everything about anything. Goldenberg's
characterization itself may be found guided by free association; it
certainly is confused and out of all relationship with the documents he
claims to describe. Why unimportant figures such as Wieseltier and
Goldenberg have so vastly misrepresented matters is a matter of no
consequence, since neither is a significant figure in the contemporary
study of the Talmud. But Steinsaltz is, and we have to explain why he
has misunderstood a document that he knows so well. A clue to what
has gone wrong is the character of the notes and background discussion

---

least, by his silence, by his failure to respond to ideas of others, by his failure
even to credit prior scholars with the discovery of scholarly commonplaces that
he represents as his own discoveries), is not a short one. Mine are not the only
books he has read. But it suffices to note that I have discussed these
problems at some length in various books, including the following: *Judaism:
The Classical Statement. The Evidence of the Bavli.* Chicago, 1986: University
of Chicago Press; *The Integrity of Leviticus Rabbah. The Problem of the
Autonomy of a Rabbinic Document.* Chico, 1985: Scholars Press for Brown
Judaic Studies; *The Talmud of the Land of Israel. A Preliminary Translation
and Explanation.* Chicago: The University of Chicago Press: 1983; XXXV.
*Introduction. Taxonomy, The Bavli and its Sources: The Question of Tradition
in the Case of Tractate Sukkah.* Atlanta, 1987: Scholars Press for Brown Judaic
Studies; *Sifré to Deuteronomy. An Introduction to the Rhetorical, Logical, and
Topical Program.* Atlanta, 1987: Scholars Press for Brown Judaic Studies; *The
Making of the Mind of Judaism.* Atlanta, 1987: Scholars Press for Brown Judaic
Studies; *The Formation of the Jewish Intellect. Making Connections and
Drawing Conclusions in the Traditional System of Judaism.* Atlanta, 1988:
Scholars Press for Brown Judaic Studies; *Judaism as Philosophy. The Method
and Message of the Mishnah;* and other books. Steinsaltz's bibliographical
apparatus is so casual that we cannot tell what he may or may not have read; he
adheres to the canons of scholarship of some realm other than the academy
and does not seem to have done much homework on the various problems he
purports to treat. That is not to suggest he makes things up as he goes along,
only that he is remarkably uneven in his reading of available discussions of
these same problems. That is not a mark of scholarship of an ambitious sort.

in Steinsaltz's translation of the chapter of the tractate he has presented in English, which is Bava Mesia Chapter One. These prove diverting and unfocused, so that they lead attention away from the center of discourse into peripheral and essentially tangential issues. And that is precisely how Steinsaltz represents the Talmud: you throw in whatever comes to mind about whatever subject catches your fancy. Steinsaltz does not seem to want to allow the Bavli to speak in whole thoughts: paragraphs and propositions. Steinsaltz's unit of discourse is formed by phrases and sentences, and that explains why more often than not it is difficult to see the main point. So it would appear that Steinsaltz does not see the whole, and when he reports that what he does see is disorganized and confused, associative rather than propositional, unsystematic and not well-crafted into whole arguments, it is an entirely honest report. The Talmud is not unsystematic and confused, Steinsaltz is.

Nor does Steinsaltz make it easy to discern any point at all in the text – associative if not propositional. Take, for example, his note on "This one shall swear." It provides sprightly information about false oaths in the Ten Commandments, perjury and the like. The note serves the exercise of show and tell, rather than sustained discourse on some one subject, the text at hand. The provision of the legal decision emerging from the passage addresses a world in which English readers find themselves alien. Here, too, we are given information of rather limited relevance. The background sidebar is a kind of learned mumbling too. All that we have of the entire page that pertains to the talmudic passage before us, then, are the translation and commentary – everything else is filler.

Now this is not to suggest there is no evidence, in the document itself, that can be read to sustain the descriptions of Steinsaltz and Goldenberg on the superficially confused and certainly confusing principles of selection and ordering that governed the layout of the Talmud.

To the contrary, we can point to some passages that hardly support my claim of a well-crafted and beautifully articulated document. But properly understood, these passages show clear adherence to a well-considered principle of agglutination. It is because Steinsaltz and Goldenberg and others do not understand the principles of discourse of the document that they find some passages confusing. Here is a case in point, drawn from Bavli Bava Mesia 105A-B.

9:5

A.   He who leases a field from his fellow,

B.   and it did not produce [a crop],

C.   if there was in it [nonetheless sufficient growth] to produce a heap [of grain],

D.   [the lessee] is liable to tend it.

E.   Said R. Judah, "What sort of measure is 'a heap'?

F.   "But: if [the field yields only] so much [grain as had been] sown [there, for reseeding next year, he is liable to tend it]."

I.1   A   *Our rabbis have taught on Tannaite authority:*

B.   He who leases a field from his fellow, and it did not produce [a crop], if there was in it [nonetheless sufficient growth] to produce a heap [of grain], [the lessee] is liable to tend it. For thus he writes in the lease: "I shall plow, sow, weed, cut, and make a pile of grain before you, and you will then come and take half of the grain and straw. And for my work and expenses, I shall take the other half" [T. B.M. 9:13A-D].

2.   A   And how much is meant by **sufficient growth] to produce a heap [of grain]?**

B.   Said R. Yosé b. R. Hanina, "Enough to set up the winnowing fan in it."

C.   *The question was raised: "What if the winnowing fan protrudes from both sides?"*

D.   *Come and take note: said R. Abbahu, "For my part, I had an explanation from R. Yosé b. R. Hanina, 'Enough so that [Freedman:] the receiver does not see the sun.'"*

3.   A   *It has been stated:*

B.   Levi said, "It is three *seahs* of wheat."

C.   The household of R. Yannai say, 'Two *seahs.*"

D.   Said R. Simeon b. Laqish, "The two *seahs* of which they spoke exclude expenses."

4.   A   *There we have learned in the Mishnah:*

B.   Wild olives and grapes –

C.   the House of Shammai declare susceptible to uncleanness.

D.   And the House of Hillel declare insusceptible to uncleanness [M. Uqs. 3:6D-F].

E.   *What is meant by "wild olives"?*

F.   Said R. Huna, "Thieving olives [the ones that yield little oil]."

G.   *Said R. Joseph, "And what verse of Scripture sustains that view? 'Also the thieves of your people shall exalt themselves to establish the vision, but they shall fail' (Dan. 11:14)."*

H.   *R. Nahman b. Isaac said, "It is from here: 'If he beget a son that is a robber, a shedder of blood' (Ezek. 18:10)."*

I.   *And what is the volume of oil of such negligible volume that the olives are classed as "thieving olives"?*

J.   *R. Eleazar said, "Four qabs per loading [up the beam of the olive press. If the olives then do not yield more than four qabs, they are so classified]."*

K.   The household of R. Yannai say, "Two *seahs* per loading of the beam."

L.   *But they really do not differ. The one speaks of a locale in which
      they put one* kor *into the press at a time, the other, where they put
      three* kors *into the press at a time.*

5.   A.   *Our rabbis have taught on Tannaite authority:*

      B.   [105B] [**The** zab **and the clean person who] climbed up on a
            tree which was shaky, or on a branch that was shaky on a
            firm tree, [the clean person, having been on an object that
            has been shaken by a person afflicted by flux, such as is
            described in Lev. 15] [M. Zab. 3:1G-H].**

      C.   *What, then, would be a tree that was shaky?*

      D.   The household of R. Yannai say, "Any tree the roots of which lack
            sufficient strength for a quarter-*qab* to be hollowed out of it."

      E.   *And what is a shaky branch?*

      F.   R. Simeon b. Laqish said, "[Freedman:] That which is hidden in
            the grip of the hand."

6.   A.   *There we have learned on Tannaite authority:*

      B.   **He who walks through a grave area on stones that he
            cannot move, on a man, or on a strong cow, is clean. He
            who walks through a grave area on stones that he can
            dislodge, on a weak man, or on a weak cow, is unclean [M.
            Oh. 18:6A-B].**

      C.   *What is the definition of a weak man?*

      D.   R. Simeon b. Laqish said, "[Freedman:] Anyone whose knees
            knock together because of the weight of the rider on him."

      E.   *What is the definition of a weak cow?*

      F.   The household of R. Yannai say, "Any one on which the weight of
            the rider causes the cow to drop pieces of shit."

7.   A.   Said the household of R. Yannai, "For the purposes of prayer and
            for phylacteries, the limit of a burden is four *qabs*."

      B.   *What is the context in which the limit is specified as to prayer?*

      C.   *It is in line with that which is taught on Tannaite authority:*

      D.   He who is carrying a burden on his shoulder and the time for
            reciting the Prayer has come – if it is a weight of less than four
            qabs, he throws it over his shoulder and recites the Prayer. If it is
            of four *qabs'* weight, he puts it on the ground and then says his
            prayer.

      E.   *What is the context in which the limit is specified as to tefillin?*

      F.   *It is in line with that which is taught on Tannaite authority:*

      G.   If on one's head one was carrying a load, and had tefillin on his
            head as well, if the phylacteries are crushed on the burden, it is
            forbidden; if not, it is permitted.

      H.   And what is the weight of the burden that is in mind?

      I.   Four *qabs*.

8.   A.   *R. Hiyya taught on Tannaite authority:*

      B.   He who is carrying out loads of manure on his head and has his
            tefillin on his head, lo, this one should not put them off to the side
            nor put them on his loins, because that would be disrespectful;
            but he must bind them on his hand where he normally puts the
            tefillin of the arm.

      C.   In behalf of the household of Shila they said, "Even their wrapper may not be placed on the head as a burden while one is wearing tefillin."

      D.   *And how much [a burden on the head is forbidden if one is wearing tefillin]?*

      E.   *Said Abayye, "Even a sixteenth of a Pumbeditan weight."*

II.1 A.   **Said R. Judah, "What sort of measure is 'a heap'? But: if [the field yields only] so much [grain as had been] sown [there, for reseeding next year, he is liable to tend it]:"**

      B.   And how much is required for reseeding?

      C.   *R. Ammi said R. Yohanan said, "Four seahs to a kor of land."*

      D.   *R. Ammi in his own name said, "Eight seahs to a kor."*

      E.   *An old man said to R. Hama son of Rabbah bar Abbahu, "I'll explain the difference to you. In the time of R. Yohanan, the land was fertile, and in the time of R. Ammi, it was poor."*

2.   A.   *There we have learned in the Mishnah:*

      B.   As for wind that has scattered sheaves over an area from which gleanings have not been collected, with the result that it is not clear what produce belongs to the householder, and what produce belongs to the poor – they estimate how much of the field's produce is likely to be subject to the restrictions of gleanings and the householder gives this amount of the produce to the poor. Rabban Simeon b. Gamaliel says, "He gives to the poor the amount of produce that is thrown to the ground when sowing the field" [M. Peah 5:1D-F].

      C.   *And how much is the amount of produce that is thrown to the ground when sowing the field?*

      D.   *When R. Dimi came, he said R. Yohanan [said], and some say, it was in the name of R. Yohanan, "For qabs per kor."*

      E.   *R. Jeremiah raised the question, "Is it per kor that is sown or per kor that is harvested? And if it means for a kor that is sown, is it a kor that is sown by hand or by oxen?"*

      F.   *Come and take note: when Rabin came, he said in the name of R. Abbahu in the name of R. Eleazar – others say, in the name of R. Yohanan, "Four qabs per kor of seed."*

      G.   *But the question is, Is it a kor that is sown by hand or by oxen?"*

      H.   *That question stands.*

I.1-3 cite and gloss the Tosefta's treatment of our Mishnah paragraph. Nos. 4-8, continued by II.1-2, would lend strong support to the opinion of those who characterize the Talmud of Babylonia as disorganized and lacking a well-crafted program of exposition, were it not for the simple fact that the whole forms a conglomeration of autonomous compositions on the problem of defining various quantities to which discrete passages of the Mishnah or other Tannaite teachings make reference. Once we realize that II.1 forms an integral part of this essay on quantities, we understand that the whole was formulated within its own, clear logical principle of agglutination and then inserted here for obvious reasons. True enough, we have something other than sequential exposition of passages of the Mishnah. But the principle of forming the composite is perfectly clear and there is no problem in understanding why the framer of the Talmud has selected the passage for inclusion here. This brings us to the claims of Adin Steinsaltz and Robert Goldenberg that the Talmud is disorganized. For example, as noted earlier, Steinsaltz states,

> Viewed superficially, the Talmud seems to lack inner order....The arrangement of the Talmud is not systematic, nor does it follow familiar didactic principles. It does not proceed from the simple to the complex, or from the general to the particular...It has no formal external order, but is bound by a strong inner connection between its many diverse subjects. The structure of the Talmud is associative. The material of the Talmud was memorized and transmitted orally for centuries, its ideas are joined to each other by inner links, and the order often reflects the needs of memorization. Talmudic discourse shifts from one subject to a related subject, or to a second that brings the first to mind in an associative way."[14]

It is hardly surprising that Steinsaltz will find everything in the document, as he says, "It has no formal external order, but is bound by a strong inner connection between its many diverse subjects." The sedimentary theory of the document, premised upon its utter disorganization, is expressed by Robert Goldenberg, who claims to describe the character of the Talmud when he says, "Evidence suggests that various centers of rabbinic study developed their own such collections [of Mishnah commentary], though in the end only one overall collection was redacted...for Babylonia. For several generations, the collections remained fluid. Materials were added, revised, or shifted. Free association led to the production of extended discourses or sets of sayings that at times had little to do with the mishnaic passage serving as point of departure."[15]

But the passage before us shows only that the framers of the Talmud of Babylonia resort to a variety of agglutinative principles; it does not sustain the view that they lacked a sense of what they were doing, that they just threw in everything and its opposite, that they covered everything because they had in mind nothing in particular, that they worked on a principle of promiscuous free association, or that their document did not follow rules of structure and order that we can

---

[14]*Ibid.*, p. 7.
[15]Robert Goldenberg, "Talmud, " in Robert M. Seltzer, ed., *Judaism. A People and Its History. Religion, History, and Culture. Selections from The Encyclopaedia of Religion.* Mircea Eliade, editor in chief (New York, 1989: Macmillan), p. 102.

grasp and expound. Here we see quite to the contrary that when the Talmud appears to talk about a variety of unrelated subjects, the reason is that the relationship among compositions of a composite derives from a different principle or relevance from the one we ordinarily anticipate – and, as a matter of fact, discern in the vast stretches of the document overall. Steinsaltz and Goldenberg describe the Talmud in the way they do because they do not understand the document's structure and order and principles of cogent discourse, which is to say, seeing the Bavli only as a mélange of phrases and sentences, they really do not understand the document.

iv. What Is at Stake in the Accurate Characterization of the Bavli

So much for the blunders of others. Let me now place into the context of my research the very particular questions that engage me in this particular book. This exercise in comparing what people say about the Talmud of Babylonia with the actual traits of that document forms part of my long-term inquiry into whether or not the Talmud of Babylonia is a traditional or a free-standing document. And that protracted study, as I shall presently explain, plays an important role in a still larger inquiry that is now underway into the characterization of the Judaism to which the Talmud of Babylonia and associated Midrash compilations attests. This monograph in particular carries forward the experiment conducted in my *The Bavli and its Sources: The Question of Tradition in the Case of Tractate Sukkah.*[16] In that work I investigated the question of how the Talmud of Babylonia relates to the Talmud of the Land of Israel. My premise is that in a traditional literature, authors of a later work will choose to take over and improve upon the program of an earlier one. That choice will certainly govern characteristics of their writing in form and perhaps also in substance. In a writing that is essentially autonomous, among authors intending to set forth a free-standing system of their own, by contrast, a prior work may supply an occasional *aperçu* but it will define no paramount program of thought and inquiry. The specific set of propositions to be clarified and refined will find their definition entirely within the generative conceptions of the framers of the writing. The present book works on the same general question.

My question is this: does the Talmud of Babylonia adumbrate a traditional system formed out of prior sources, making a cogent and authoritative statement in common and forming a continuous set of writings, or does it attest to a different sort of system altogether? But

---

[16]Atlanta, 1987: Scholars Press for Brown Judaic Studies.

the specific subset of questions derives from a fresh source. As I spell out in Chapter One, I address two widely circulated allegations as to the character of the Talmud of Babylonia. I have invented a test of falsification and validation of these allegations, and with special reference to tractate Arakhin, I show that the claims widely made as to the character of the Talmud of Babylonia are false, but these same allegations do characterize another document, the Tosefta. It follows that, if the Tosefta is accurately described, then it is (within the definitions just now given) to be classified as a traditional writing, and, if the Talmud of Babylonia is falsely described, then, within that same framework, it is to be classified as an other than traditional writing.

The traditional type of religious system in its literary expression – such as its documents permit us to analyze – will give evidence of having been formed out of prior sources. It will be understood to derive from a continuous process of tradition, with sayings handed on from an earlier generation to a later one until a complete and final statement came to full expression. Now, as a matter of fact, the Bavli is widely alleged to stand in relationship to prior writings as a summary statement stands to the sources that are summarized. It is supposed to respond to a received program and to restate a vast corpus of already circulating and traditional materials. That characterization of matters in point of fact does not prove symmetrical with the Bavli, but it does apply quite neatly to the Tosefta. The latter sort of system – the free-standing and autonomous one – assuredly recognizes and draws upon a received corpus of authoritative writings. But the literary evidence of such a system does not give evidence that the system forms a tradition shaped out of prior sources. In *The Bavli and its Sources*, I argued that that document and the system that it brings to literary expression viewed in relationship to the immediately prior Talmud, the one of the Land of Israel, do not fall into the classification formed by books that take over from the predecessors' materials to be handed on continuators, materials that therefore are continuous with one another. The Bavli is not part of a traditional literature, each of the documents of which stand in close relationship with its neighbors, fore and aft, each borrowing from its predecessor, handing on to its successor a nourishing tradition. It uses what it chooses – a mark not of traditionality but of autonomy.

v. The Experiment Conducted Here

To test the two notions, first, that the Talmud is fundamentally exegetical of Scripture (by reason of that "Jewish proclivity" and "predeliction that Halivni has posited), and, second, that "everything" is in the Talmud (a charitable revision of the exaggerations of Steinsaltz and Wieseltier), I turn to the Tosefta, which is a document that contains "everything," that it has received from the Mishnah. This permits us to do two things. First, it shows us what a document that really forms itself around an exegetical program actually looks like. Second, it establishes a stunning contrast between the Tosefta's "everything" with the Bavli's "some things, carefully chosen." That is to say, I appeal, for my null hypothesis, to the model of the Tosefta, which does conform in a curious way to the traits we should assign to a document to be classified as traditional and not free-standing. With the Mishnah seen as base, the Tosefta emerges as Halvini would want it, as essentially exegetical. Second, with the Mishnah defined as "the tradition," the Tosefta proves to be defined within the programmatic and even redactional framework of the tradition, wholly depending upon the prior writing for its program of thought and exposition.

Hence, in a very exact sense, the Tosefta may be classified as not free-standing and conceivably systemic in intent, but traditional and wholly exegetical in its plan and program. Having defined what would characterize a rabbinic document such as the Talmud of Babylonia if that writing was traditional – thus, in Halivni's term, exhibiting a predilection to "vindicated law," and in Steinsaltz's and Wieseltier's term, containing everything (within the definition appropriate to the data at hand), we examine that document in its own terms. What we find is that Halivni is wrong about an alleged "Jewish predeliction," since the program of the tractate examined here of the Talmud of Babylonia vis-à-vis Scripture in no way is governed by the exegesis of Scripture; Steinsaltz and Wieseltier are wrong about the Talmud's supposedly containing "everything." When Steinsaltz and Wieseltier say about the coverage of the Talmud that it extends to "the nature of all things according to the Torah," that "the authority of the Talmud lies in its use of this rigorous method in its search for truth with regard to the entire Torah – in other words, with regard to all possible subjects in the world, both physical and spiritual," that "the Talmud is, in truth, about all things," and that "there is no corner of human life and no corner of Jewish life into which the fastidious rabbis did not peer" – in these wild and impressionistic allegations of theirs, they simply contradict the simple facts of the matter.

The contrast between the Tosefta, which does exhibit the traits imputed by Halivni, Steinsaltz, and Wieseltier to the Bavli, with the Bavli, will strike the reader on every page. Negative results in both cases – an indifference to an exegetically based program, a disinterest in repeating "pretty much everything (relevant)" received from prior generations on a given topic – will point once more toward the quality of mind of the framers of the Talmud of Babylonia and, it goes without saying, the character of the system their writing attests. And what we shall see, when we reach the Talmud of Babylonia, is two things. First, its authorship has not found in the exegetical reading of the law, such as is set forth in Sifra, a principal source interest. Second, any claim of traditionality demonstrated by the Talmud's systematic rehearsal of a received exegetical program is unsubstantiated. To repeat the claim in the fantastic language of Adin Steinsaltz, "The Talmud...deals with an overwhelmingly broad subject – the nature of all things according to the Torah. Therefore its contours are a reflection of life itself. It has no formal external order, but is bound by a strong inner connection between [sic!] its many diverse subjects....The authority of the Talmud lies in its use of this rigorous method in its search for truth with regard to the entire Torah – in other words, with regard to all possible subjects in the world, both physical and spiritual"; and in the extraordinary and off-hand exaggeration of Leon Wieseltier, "the Talmud is, in truth, about all things. There is no corner of human life and no corner of Jewish life into which the fastidious rabbis did not peer." I do not think that a too demanding test of the accuracy of these allegations is comprised by the result of a simple comparison between a document inherited by the framers of the Talmud of Babylonia and the place and use of that document within their writing. The choice, then, is simple: is everything they received within their document, some things, or nothing? If everything, then Steinsaltz and Wieseltier in this particular case have solid foundations for their broader (if in its own terms incomprehensible) judgment; if something, then their characterization simply is false; if nothing, then the matter is under the judgment, *non liquet*.

vi. The Importance of the Results of this Experiment
for a Broader Inquiry

Since this work forms a *Beistudie* within a much larger and protracted inquiry, let me show how these two distinct issues pertain to a larger enterprise in which I am presently engaged. Having worked out [1] the description of texts, read one by one, in such works as my *Judaism: The Evidence of the Mishnah, The Integrity of Leviticus Rabbah*, and parallel studies, to [2] the analysis of those same texts seen in relationship to one another, that is, to comparison and contrast among a set of documents, hence to connection, as in *Judaism: The Classical Statement. The Evidence of the Bavli*, on the relationship of the Yerushalmi and the Bavli, *Comparative Midrash: The Plan and Program of Genesis Rabbah and Leviticus Rabbah,* and *From Tradition to Imitation: The Plan and Program of Pesiqta deRab Kahana and Pesiqta Rabbati,* I here proceed to [3] the interpretation of texts. What concerns me in particular is how the Talmud of Babylonia relates to prior writings, because, as is now clear, when I know how its authorship respond to the received documents, I can determine whether they for their part set forth a statement that is traditional or free-standing, and, in my language, "systemic." This exercise begins with literature, but points toward a sequel addressing the systemic traits of the Judaism to which the Talmud of Babylonia and its closely associated Midrash compilations attest or adumbrate.

Let me point to what I conceive to be at stake in solving the problem of traditionality and spell out what is at stake in the problem of literary description with which this sizable exercise commences. Theologians of the tradition formed out of prior sources of Judaism correctly identify as the premise of all exegesis deep connections between one document and the next, so that all documents impose meanings upon each, and each demands a reading in the setting of the whole literature. The position at hand addresses the *entirety* of the writings of the ancient rabbis, all together, all at once, everywhere and all the time. Here I begin to investigate the continuities among all documents, thus a textual community. Issues of the relationships among – the continuity of – documents form a first step toward the much larger description of the whole of canonical Judaism: the Judaism of the Dual Torah. That is a Judaism that to begin with invokes its tradition formed out of prior sources to define itself: a Judaism of the Dual Torah as against a Judaism that appeals to a different symbol altogether from a canonical one, for example, the Judaic system of the Essenes of Qumran, with its teacher of righteousness as its critical symbolic expression. Each document in the corpus of the rabbinic writings of late antiquity bears points in common with others. They form a tradition, and each document constitutes a partial statement of that complete tradition. But in the final document that emerges from the canonical literature, which is the Talmud of Babylonia, they also make a statement. I mean to characterize that statement.

What is at stake in doing so? To understand the answer, we have to note that between 200 and 400 Judaism changed from a philosophy to a religion. And between 400 and 600, a set of positions, attitudes, and beliefs, forming a religion, came to expression in a cogent and coherent way in a statement that conforms to the definition of a theology: a fully exposed set of doctrines and norms – whether in the expression of what we are to do or how we are to think, whether in law or in lore (*halakhah, aggadah,* in the categories that are often invoked). That set of doctrines and norms represented the transformation of a Judaism from a religion to a theology, and the Talmud of Babylonia and closely related Midrash compilations convey that theology. Specifically, what we learn in those writings are the how of the making of normative decisions and statements and the what of a coherent intellectual system that makes of religious attitudes a formation of theological truths.

Now, as a matter of fact, in prior research, culminating in *The Transformation of Judaism: From Philosophy to Religion,* I have been able to demonstrate the way in which an essentially philosophical system was recast and reworked into a fresh and free-standing one, which I classify as religious. I classify a system as fundamentally religious or essentially philosophical by appeal to objective indicative traits. A philosophical system forms its learning inductively and syllogistically, by appeal to the neutral evidence of the rules shown to apply to all things by the observation of the order of universally accessible nature and society. A religious system frames its propositions deductively and exegetically by appeal to the privileged evidence of a corpus of truths deemed revealed by God.

The classification of the successor system – the one that took up the Mishnah and recast it into the form that it is given in the Talmud of the Land of Israel – is religious and not philosophical. Precisely what I mean must be made clear, since the mishnaic system also was a religious one. But the Mishnah's was a religious system of a philosophical character, and the successor system was not of a philosophical character. What I mean by a religious system of a philosophical character is readily explained: these worldly data are classified according to rules that apply consistently throughout, so that we may always predict with a fair degree of accuracy what will happen and why. And a philosophical system of religion, then, systematically demonstrates out of the data of the world order of nature and society the governance of God in nature and supernature: this world's data pointing toward God above and beyond. The God of the philosophical Judaism, then, sat enthroned at the apex of all things, all being hierarchically classified. Just as philosophy seeks the explanation of things, so a philosophy of religion (in the context at hand) will propose orderly explanations in accord with prevailing and cogent rules. The profoundly philosophical character of the Mishnah has already provided ample evidence of the shape, structure, and character of that philosophical system in the Judaic context. The rule-seeking character of mishnaic discourse marks it as a philosophical system of religion. But the successor system saw the world differently.

The difference pertains not to detail but to the fundamental facts deemed to matter. Some of those facts lie at the very surface, in the nature of the writings that express the system. These writings were not free-standing but contingent, and that in two ways. First, they served as commentaries to prior documents, the Mishnah and Scripture, for the Talmud and Midrash compilations, respectively. Second, and more consequential, the authorships insisted upon citing Scripture passages or Mishnah sentences as the centerpiece of proof, on the one side, and program of discourse, on the other. But the differences that prove indicative are not merely formal. More to the point, while the Mishnah's system is steady-state and ahistorical, admitting no movement or change, the successor system of the Yerushalmi and associated Midrash compilations tells tales, speaks of change, accommodates and responds to historical moments. It formulates a theory of continuity within change, of the moral connections between generations, of the way in which one's deeds shape one's destiny – and that of the future as well. If what the framers of the Mishnah want more than anything else is to explain the order and structure of being, then their successors have rejected their generative concern. For what they, for their part, intensely desire to sort out is the currents and streams of time and change, as these flow toward an unknown ocean.

But these large-scale characterizations in well-crafted systems do not provide the only pertinent evidence. Details, too, deliver the message. The indicators for each type of system, as these are attested in their written testimonies, derive from the character of the rhetorical, logical, and propositional-topical traits of those writings. The shift from the philosophical to the religious modes of thought and media of expression – logical and rhetorical indicators, respectively – come to realization in the recasting of the generative categories of the system as well. These categories are transformed, and the transformation proved so thorough-going as to validate the characterization of the change as "counterpart categories." The result of the formation of such counterpart categories in the aggregate was to encompass not only the natural but also the supernatural realms of the social order.

That is how philosophical thinking gave way to religious thinking. An economics, based on prime value assigned to real wealth, now encompassed wealth of an intangible, impalpable, and supernatural order, but valued resource nonetheless. A politics, formerly serving to legitimate and hierarchize power and differentiate among sanctions by appeal to fixed principles, now introduced the variable of God's valuation of the victim and the antipolitical conception of the illegitimacy of worldly power, the opposite of the

Mishnah's this-worldly political system altogether. In all three ways the upshot is the same: the social system, in the theory of its framers, now extends its boundaries upward to Heaven, drawing into a whole the formerly distinct, if counterpoised, realms of Israel on earth and the heavenly court above. So if I had to specify the fundamental difference between the philosophical and the religious versions of the social order, it would fall, quite specifically, upon the broadening of the systemic boundaries to encompass Heaven. The formation of counterpart categories, therefore, signals not a reformation of the received system but the formation of an essentially new one.

But the critical issue addressed by the new system – the one I classify as religion and not philosophical – and the central point of tension and mode of remission thereof, the exegetical focus – these remain to be identified. And, as a matter of fact, the Yerushalmi's counterpart categories in hand themselves do not help to identify the generative problematic that defined the new system and integrated its components. For the issues I locate as the systemic economics and politics – Torah in place of land, the illegitimacy of power and the priority of the absence thereof – while present and indicative in the documentary expression of the system, assuredly do not occupy a principal position within those documents. For the successor documents' categories are not those of philosophy, on the one side, and a politics disembedded from economics, on the other.

In the nature of systemic analysis, therefore, in my *Transformation of Judaism*, I have brought the categories of one system to the data of another, those of the initial system to the ones of the successor system, and the result is to discover only how different are the latter from the former. So concerning the transformed Judaism of the late fourth and fifth century we now know everything but the main thing. True, since we compare the given to the new, I had no choice but to proceed as I have. But what I have done thus far is ask only my questions – that is, the systemic questions of philosophy and political economy or philosophical economics and politics – to a literature that dealt with such questions essentially by dismissing them. For the upshot of the formation of counterpart categories turns out to be the destruction of the received categories, now turned on their heads and emptied of all material and palpable content, refilled then with intangibles of intellect and virtuous attitude alone. Knowing how a system has revalued value and reconstructed the sense of legitimate power by deeming legitimate only the victim and never the actor, does not tell us what the system locates at its center.

If I ask myself, then, how am I to identify the systemic foci, its sources of the exegetical problematic and its definition of its generative issues, I must propose as the answer not a subjective judgment as to what is dominant and commonplace, but rather, an objective claim as to what is essential and definitive and integrating (which, as a matter of fact, in this context also happens to be commonplace). By objective I mean simply, my results should emerge for anyone else examining the same evidence in accord with the same principles of description and analysis (interpretation is always subjective). Where to begin? In general, historians of religion concur, the power of religion lies in its capacity to integrate, to hold together discrete components of the social order and explain how they all fit together. And, in general, it seems to me a simple fact that the power of philosophy lies in its capacity to differentiate, discriminate, make distinctions and clarify the complex by showing its distinct parts. Then a successor system, connected to but autonomous of its antecedent, will prove philosophical if it continues the labor of differentiation, religious if it undertakes a work of integration. And the Judaism before us addresses the principal, and striking, distinctive characteristic of the philosophical system it had inherited, the one between economics and politics, (re)integrating what had been kept apart in a theory of political economy such as the Pentateuch and Aristotle had laid out, but the framers of the Mishnah had not composed at all.

Let me spell out what I conceive to be the principal success of integration, within a supernatural framework that must be deemed religious and only religion, accomplished by our sages of blessed memory in the Yerushalmi and related writings. We recall,[17] the one striking contrast between the social system put forth by Aristotle and that set out by the framers of the Mishnah lay in the superior systematization of politics within the frame of economics accomplished by Aristotle and not achieved at all by the Mishnah's social system. Aristotle's systemic message, delivered through his philosophy, economics, and politics, was carried equally by economics and politics in such a way that the two formed a single statement, one of political economy. To state the matter very simply: the principal economic actor of Aristotle's social system, the householder (in the language of our sources, the landholder or farmer for Aristotle and Xenophon) also constituted the principal political figure, the one who exercised legitimate power, and the joining of the landholder and the civic actor in a single person, moreover, accounted for Aristotle for the formation of society: the *polis* or lowest whole and indivisible social unit of society.

---

[17] I refer to my *Rabbinic Political Theory: Religion and Politics in the Mishnah.* Chicago, 1991: University of Chicago Press.

But for the framers of the Mishnah, the economic actor, the one who controlled the means of production, was the householder, while the householder never played a political role or formed part of the political classes at all. That fact is shown by the simple distinction of usage, in which the subject of most sentences involving the disposition of scarce resources was the householder, while that same social entity (class) never made an appearance in any of the political tractates and their discourses, which choose, for the subjects of their sentences, such political figures as the king, high priest, (sages') court, and the like. These usages signal the disembeddedness of economics from politics, a fact further highlighted by the Mishnah's separation of the economic entity – the village or town made up of householders – from the political entities – royal government, temple authority, sages' court; none of these, as a matter of fact, correspond with the village or town, that is, the *polis*, in the Mishnah's philosophical system.

What the philosophical Judaism kept apart, the religious Judaism now joined together, and it is just there, at that critical joining, that we identify the key to the system: its reversal of a received point of differentiation,[18] its introduction of new points of differentiation altogether. The source of generative problems for the Mishnah's politics is simply not the same as the source that served the successor system's politics, and, systemic analysis being what it is, it is the union of what was formerly asunder that identifies for us in quite objective terms the critical point of tension, the sources of problems, the centerpiece of systemic concern throughout. And one fundamental point of reversal, uniting what had been divided, is the joining of economics and politics into a political economy, through the conception of *zekhut*, a term defined presently.

The other point at which, we find, what the one system treated as distinct, the next and connected system chose to address as one and whole, is less easily discerned, since to do so we have to ask a question the framers of the Mishnah did not raise in the Mishnah at all. That concerns the character and source of virtue, specifically, the affect, upon the individual, of knowledge, specifically, knowledge of the Torah or Torah study. To frame the question very simply, if we ask ourselves, what happens to me if I study the Torah, the answer, for the Mishnah, predictably is, my standing and status change. Torah study and its effects form a principal systemic indicator in matters of

---

[18]For, after all, the problematic of the Mishnah's politics is the principle of differentiation among legitimate political agencies, first between Heaven's and humanity's, second, among the three political institutions of the Mishnah's "Israel."

hierarchical classification, joining the *mamzer* disciple of sages in a mixture of opposites, for one self-evident example.

But am I changed within? In vain we look in the hundreds of chapters of the Mishnah for an answer to that question. Virtue and learning form distinct categories and, overall, I am not changed as to my virtue, my character and conscience, by my mastery of the Torah. And still more strikingly, if we ask, does my Torah study affect my fate in this world and in the life to come, the Mishnah's authorship is strikingly silent about that matter too. Specifically, we find in the pages of that document no claim that studying the Torah either changes me or assures my salvation. But the separation of knowledge and the human condition is set aside, and studying the Torah deemed the source of salvation, in the successor system. The philosophical system, with its interest in *homo hierarchicus*, proved remarkably silent about the affect of the Torah upon the inner man. The upshot is at the critical points of bonding, the received system proved flawed in its separation of learning from virtue and legitimate power from valued resources. So to the simple conclusion: *What philosophy kept distinct, religion joined together: that defines the transformation of Judaism from philosophy to religion.*

The reliable rules of sanctification – to invoke theological categories – are joined with the unpredictable event of salvation, and the routine – to call upon the classification of Max Weber – meets the spontaneous. Not to be gainsaid, the social order is made to acknowledge what, if disorderly, also is immediate and therefore necessary. History, that omnipresent but carefully ignored presence in the philosophical Judaism, in the form of not change but crisis, regains its rightful place at the systemic center. So, it must follow, the comparison between one system and its connected, but distinct, successor points to quite objective evidence on the basis of which we may characterize the successor in its own terms. For the categories that present themselves now derive from the system subjected to description, and not from those of the prior system (let alone from my own theory of the components of a theory of the social order). They emerge at that very point – the joining place of differentiation or its opposite, integration – at which systemic description begins, the exegesis of the system's exegesis. Why virtue joins knowledge, politics links to economics, in the religious system but not in the philosophical one is of course obvious. Philosophy differentiates, seeking the rules that join diverse data; religion integrates, proposing to see the whole all together and all at once, thus (for an anthropology, for example) seeing humanity whole: "in our image, after our likeness." Religion by its nature (so it would seem from the case at hand) asks the questions of integration, such as the theory intended to hold together within a single boundary earth and Heaven, this world and the other, should lead us to anticipate. So our observations about the broadening of the frontiers of the social order turn out to signal a deeper characteristic of the analysis at hand.

Why should we have taken the route that has led us to this mode of analysis? The reason is that of special interest in the work of systemic description is not so much theology or doctrine or belief as the interplay of religion and society, that is, the relationship between contents and context, conviction and circumstance, each viewed as distinct and autonomous, an independent variable. Religion is a decisive fact of social reality, and not merely a set of beliefs on questions viewed in an abstract and ahistorical setting. Our task is now to identify the system that the successor documents' authorships formed, and this we do by proposing to define the questions they pursued, the self-evidently valid answers they set forth, in making a single and coherent statement about their own condition. But when, as in the case of Judaism of the Dual Torah in its formative age, a religion does set forth a statement received as coherent, whole, authoritative, encompassing ("everything is in it" indeed!), then we have not only a set of attitudes and doctrines and required actions, we have something that is stable, cogent, coherent – a theology. In many ways, the history of the formation of Judaism is the story of how a philosophical mode of thought was joined to a religious mode of understanding human existence in a coherent theology: the Talmud of Babylonia and its related Midrash compilations. The method, then, was that of the Mishnah, the content, of the Talmud of the Land of Israel and associated Midrash compilations, and the result, a Judaic system in pure and perfect balance, proportion, order, worthy of being classified as a theological system and not merely a religious one.

But how to investigate the proposition that the major transformation of Judaism accomplished by the Talmud of Babylonia was the transformation of a religious system into a theological one? In the next decade or so I hope to accomplish the same work for the third and final stage in the formation of Judaism, from ca. 450 to ca. 600[19] that I have already set forth for the second and intermediate stage. Some of the descriptive and analytical work is now complete, but a fair

---

[19]Michael G. Morony, "Teleology and the Significance of Change," in F. M. Clover and R. S. Humphreys, *Tradition and Innovation in Late Antiquity* (Madison, 1989: The University of Wisconsin Press), pp. 21-27, seems to me right on target in his arguments on the character of the final centuries of late antiquity. My work on the period at hand presupposes Morony's periodization.

amount of descriptive study of texts and a still larger labor of analytical study of contexts stands between this work and the third and final interpretive enterprise I have in mind at this time, which is the passage from religion to theology. I hardly need say that – as is my way – the theoretical labor is now well underway for the final stage. As I said at the outset, I generally write in my mind my major theoretical work, only afterward putting the whole down on paper – and catching up, in research, with the results of my abstraction, imagination, and sheer day-dreaming.

Catching up means another go-around in the literary evidence. So to undertake systemic analysis on the strength of written evidence, I have systemically reread the classic documents of the Judaism that took shape in the first to the seventh centuries A.D. and that has predominated since then, the Judaism of the Dual Torah. These documents – the Mishnah, Midrash compilations, the two Talmuds – represent the collective statement and consensus of authorships (none is credibly assigned to a single author and all are preserved because they are deemed canonical and authoritative) and show us how those authorships proposed to make a statement to their situation – and, I argue, upon the human condition. Now I undertake the interpretation of a principal component of the entire corpus of writing. Characterizing the Talmud of Babylonia, its modes of expression and thought, its media for conveying final decisions, and signaling its message set forth whole and complete – these form the tasks of the larger project of which this book, although a *Beistudie* addressing some very limited questions of correct description of a piece of writing, forms an important component. So we turn to the work itself, beginning with a demonstration that there are documents that conform to the description, "...in truth, about all things," at least, pertinent to a given subject. I shall now show that the Steinsaltz-Wieseltier thesis (revised for sense) does describe the Tosefta.

vii. Why Arakhin in Particular?

Halivni is the more important of the two scholars treated here, Steinsaltz being essentially a popularizer and at best capable of merely workmanlike paraphrase, so I chose Arakhin to set up a fair test of Halivni's proposition on the centrality of exegesis in the formation, and representation, of the law. The reason is that among the thirty-seven tractates of the Mishnah's sixty-two that are treated in the Talmud of Babylonia, Arakhin falls into the category of a not very philosophical, but very scriptural, tractate. That is to say, important philosophical issues, expressed in concrete details but deriving from abstract principles, for example, of being and becoming, the nature of mixtures, the resolution of doubts, the principles of classification and speciation, predominate in some tractates. In others, we find a strong interest in the exposition of scriptural laws. It seemed to me that a fair test of Halivni's conception of the inner and definitive traits of the law required a close reading of the latter, and not the form, type of tractate. It is very easy to prove on the basis of numerous tractates that altogether lack a scriptural foundation – for example, that treat topics unknown to the Pentateuch – that he is wrong in his allegations about the nature of the law and its origins. It is equally simple to show that he is under a profound misapprehension as to the character of the law when we open tractates that take up facts set forth in Scripture but address to those facts issues of no consequence in Scripture. But what about the tractates in which at issue are principally Scripture's laws and the issues Scripture brings to bear upon those laws? Arakhin is one such tractate.

At the outset let me characterize the tractate, and we shall see that at its deepest layers it is scriptural and not philosophical. Mishnah-tractate Arakhin Chapters One through Six deal with pledges to contribute the value of persons or property to the Temple, in line with Lev. 27:1-8. Chapter Seven moves on to Lev. 27:16-25, the distinction between a field which one purchases and one which is received through inheritance ("a field of possession"). Chapter Eight proceeds to Lev. 27:26, the declaration that something is *herem* or devoted. Chapter Nine addresses Lev. 25:13-17, 25:25-28, and 25:29-34. Now to leave no doubt that Arakhin is correctly classified as a scriptural, not a philosophical, tractate, let me catalogue what I conceive to be all those pericopes that entirely lack a philosophical program. They are as follows:

M. 2:1-6: formal composition on lower and upper limits of various classes of things; M. 3:1-6: formal composition on possibilities of lenient and strict rulings in various, diverse classes of law; M. 4:1-4 spell out the difference between the one who vows and the one whose Valuation is vowed with reference to assessing the amount that is owing; Scripture's specifications generate the exercise; M. 5:1-6 work out the difference between pledging a Valuation and vowing value as that difference applies to the estate of one who makes such a pledge or vow; M. 6:1-5 deal with collecting what is owing to the Temple when there are various claimants to the same goods or property; M. 7:1-4 contain nothing of philosophical interest, working on the exposition of a distinction imposed by Scripture;

M. 8:1-4 expound the matter of the devoted thing as Scripture
defines it; M. 8:6-7 work out secondary questions; M. 9:1-8 apply
the rules of redeeming in the Jubilee year property that has
been sold but that returns at that time, then sale of a dwelling
house in a walled city, in line with Lev. 25:29-34.

Is Arakhin philosophical? No, neither in important details nor, all
the more so, as a whole, does this tractate formulate philosophical
issues in legal form. Such philosophical discourse as I can identify is
episodic and ad hoc. To the contrary, the tractate is deeply scriptural
in its organization and structure, expounding and articulating rules of
Scripture. The tractate works out the application of rules of Leviticus
Chapters Twenty-Five and Twenty-Seven. Of 50 pericopes, I count 45
that bear no philosophical interest, or 90 percent of the whole. At the
beginning of the coming chapter we shall see precisely where and how
Scripture dictates the program of the document: topic and treatment of
the topic alike.

Then, to the contrary, what are the (few) pericopes of the tractate
that do deal with issues I classify as philosophical? M. Ar. 1:1-4 work
out the classification of interstitial persons, by showing that the
distinction between pledging Valuation and having one's Valuation
pledged allows us to assign classes in the excluded middle to one
category or another. As to how we deal with the relationship between
the potential and the actual, at M. Ar. 7:5 we have the issue of
whether we deem what is going to happen as if it already has
happened. The case is simple. If a person purchases a field from his
father, is this deemed a field of possession, that is, one received by
inheritance, at the point that the father dies? Yes, it is. All concur
that if the father died and the man then sanctified the field, it falls
under the rule of the field of possession. But if the man purchased the
field and sanctified it and only afterward the father died, is it a field
of possession? Meir holds that it is a field that has been bought, Judah
and Simeon maintain that what is going to happen is deemed already
to have happened. Therefore the field is deemed a field of possession.
On the interplay of intentionality and deed, M. Ar. 8:5 sets forth the
limitation on the affects of intentionality. One cannot affect the status,
for example, by the declaration of one's attitude, of something that
does not fall within one's own domain. That limitation on attitude or
intentionality is important here because one cannot declare oneself
obligated to pay the Valuation or the worth of another person. That is
because one controls one's own property, which is what is at stake. But
here one cannot change the status of someone else or that person's
property. As to the resolution of doubts (which on its own can hardly be

labelled distinctively philosophical), M. Arakhin 9:7 deals with the excluded middle. We classify the case by reference to the traits applying to both of the poles at the extremes. It follows that this tractate has no philosophical program of any substance. The entire program of the tractate is dictated by Lev. 25:27, and the purpose is to spell out and apply or amplify the rules of those passages.

To place these observations into context, among all the tractates of the Mishnah, there is in fact a correlation between the high philosophical quotient of a tractate and the low utilization of scriptural propositions or even facts in that same tractate – and vice versa. The correlation between the philosophical focus and the absence of a scriptural foundation is indicated by the use of **boldface type**. The correlation between the non-philosophical discourse characteristic of a tractate and elaborate representation of scriptural rules is indicated in *italics*. Scribal tractates, neither philosophical nor scriptural, are indicated in *italicized boldface type*.

1. Mainly philosophical	1. Not scriptural at all
Abodah Zarah	Abodah Zarah
Berakhot	Erubin
Bikkurim	Gittin
Demai	Hallah
Erubin	Horayot
Hallah	Hullin
Hagigah	Keritot
Horayot	Kilayim
Kelim	Maaser Sheni
Keritot	Maaserot
Kilayim	Makhshirin
Maaser Sheni	Meilah
Maaserot	Miqvaot
Makhshirin	Nazir
Meilah	Nedarim
Miqvaot	Negaim
Moed Qatan	Niddah
Nazir	Ohalot
Nedarim	Orlah
Negaim	Parah
Niddah	Peah
Ohalot	Qinnim
Orlah	Rosh Hashshanah
Parah	Sanhedrin
Peah	Shabbat

Qiddushin
Qinnim
Sanhedrin
Shabbat
Shabuot
Shebiit
Tebul Yom
Terumot
Tohorot
Uqsin
Yadayim
Yebamot
Zabim
Zebahim

Shabuot
Shebiit
Tebul Yom
Terumot
Tohorot
Uqsin
Yadayim
Yebamot
Zabim

2. Philosophical use of Scripture

Bava Batra
Menahot

2. Scripture supplies facts, but not the tractate's problematic or program

Bava Batra
Bava Mesia
Berakhot
Bikkurim
Demai
Hagigah
Kelim
Ketubot
Menahot
Maaser Sheni
Middot
Moed Qatan
Qiddushin
Taanit
Tamid

3. Not philosophical at all

Arakhin
Bava Mesia
Bava Qamma
Bekhorot
Gittin
Ketubot
Makkot
Megillah

3. Essentially scriptural

Arakhin
Bava Batra
Bava Mesia
Bava Qamma
Bekhorot
Bikkurim
Hagigah
Makkot

Middot	Megillah
Pesahim	Menahot
Rosh Hashshanah	Pesahim
Sheqalim	Sotah
Sotah	Sukkah
Sukkah	Temurah
Temurah	Yoma
Yoma	

In the aggregate, it would appear that where there is a deeply philosophical treatment of a topic, Scripture supplies no facts or no facts that generate important problems. Scripture commonly supplies facts that are treated in a philosophical way. Some tractates rest wholly on scriptural facts and undertake no philosophical inquiry, for example, into problems of classification and interstitiality. A few tractates are neither scriptural nor philosophical; these are classed as either scribal or priestly, for example, Gittin, on the one side, Middot, on the other. But, in the main, we now see with great clarity, most tractates of the Mishnah pursue a philosophical program. I count 41 essentially philosophical tractates, 13 essentially scriptural ones, so that the proposed correlation covers 54 of the 61 tractates. Among the correlated tractates, 76% are fundamentally philosophical, 24% are essentially not philosophical, and among all of the 61 tractates (again omitting all reference to Abot and Eduyot), 89% fall into one classification or the other, and only 11% prove anomalous. These are rough figures, of course, but a review of my detailed account of the tractates[20] will strengthen the argument that the Mishnah is to be described as philosophical, but not only philosophical, in its basic mode and structure of thought and discourse. It suffices now to observe that no fairer test of Halivni's proposed characterization of the law as we find it in the Mishnah and Talmuds alike can be provided by any other tractate.[21]

---

[20]For the evidence to which I make reference see my *The Philosophical Mishnah. Volume I. The Initial Probe.* Atlanta, 1989: Scholars Press for Brown Judaic Studies; *The Philosophical Mishnah. Volume II. The Tractates' Agenda. From Abodah Zarah to Moed Qatan.* Atlanta, 1989: Scholars Press for Brown Judaic Studies; *The Philosophical Mishnah. Volume III. The Tractates' Agenda. From Nazir to Zebahim.* Atlanta, 1989: Scholars Press for Brown Judaic Studies; *The Philosophical Mishnah. Volume IV. The Repertoire.* Atlanta, 1989: Scholars Press for Brown Judaic Studies, and *Judaism as Philosophy. The Method and Message of the Mishnah.* Columbia, 1991: University of South Carolina Press.

[21]A problem in dealing with Halivni and Steinsaltz (among others) is that they do not appear to read scholarship of colleagues, so it is difficult to know how

they solve problems that others discern in their own work. They seem to imagine that silence forms an appropriate reply to criticism. That suggests, to be sure, that they are writing only for believers. In any event, without clear evidence as to their response to criticism, we have no way of knowing what, if anything, they might wish to say in reply to sustained and serious efforts to examine their findings, their reasoning, their use of evidence, and even their grasp of the texts they claim to adduce in behalf of their propositions. That is not to suggest they do not know how to read the Talmud of Babylonia (or other rabbinic writings) in an accurate and informed way. They assuredly have given ample evidence that they do. It is to say that, if they do grasp things accurately, then exactly how their processes of analysis and reasoning lead them to propositions so blatantly contrary to the character of the evidence – so we shall see in full measure – is not easy to discern. Because of Halivni's silence on other approaches, besides his, to the problems on which he works, it is especially important to choose a tractate that is on the surface most likely to sustain his hypothesis to be correct – or at least not contradict it at the outset, as so many Mishnah tractates do. Because Steinsaltz appears simply ignorant of most of scholarship on the Bavli in the nineteenth and twentieth centuries, and because he provides in his "Steinsaltz edition" no bibliography whatsoever, it is still more important to show precisely how the program of the Bavli carefully chooses, out of the received heritage, what its framers wish to treat. I cannot imagine a more persuasive argument against his conception that pretty much everything is there.

Part One

"ITS CONTOURS ARE A REFLECTION OF LIFE ITSELF"
Steinsaltz

"...THE TALMUD IS, IN TRUTH, ABOUT ALL THINGS"
Wieseltier

TRUE FOR TOSEFTA TO TRACTATE ARAKHIN

2

The Tosefta as a Traditional Writing: The Tosefta and the Mishnah

i. The Physiognomy of a Traditional Document

We shall now see that Steinsaltz and Wieseltier are right in claiming that there is a document of the Judaism of the Torah that covers "everything," or, at least (to rephrase their claim in more comprehensible terms), "everything important in the Torah, by the criterion of what is in the Mishnah." That, of course, claims considerably less than they wish to allege, but it is a proposition that we can test, and as a matter of fact it can be shown to be true of one document, therefore false for documents unlike that one. I refer, of course, to the Tosefta, which follows the entire program of the Mishnah and treats nearly every chapter of the Mishnah – if not "everything" then, at least, most things.[1] We therefore can show a

---

[1]Though it is not critical to my argument, we shall further observe a document that conforms to Halivni's claim that the exegesis of a prior text forms a principal impetus and motivation in the formation of a posterior one (a much more abstract formulation of Halivni's thesis, to be sure, but we need not be forever paralyzed by his rather clumsy language). The Tosefta is a document that formulates its thought – in form and in message alike – in entirely exegetical terms. So its framers clearly concur with Halivni that it is better to state one's ideas as exegesis of a received text than as free-standing conceptions; and it is best of all to state whatever one has in mind only through the instrumentality of clarifying a received text. Then the received text provides the outline, the agenda, and the issues, and the traditional text that follows responds to these: a true "proclivity" and "predeliction" to a "justified

document that covers "everything important in the Torah" pertinent to the subject(s) treated there. When, in Part Two, we turn to the Bavli and ask, by the criteria met by the Tosefta, whether there, too, we find "everything important in the Torah" on the topic at hand, we shall see that we do not.

In the terms of Steinsaltz and Wieseltier, the Tosefta vis-à-vis the Mishnah does contain (almost) "everything," and it does treat everything that has gone before; it omits very little of the Mishnah's sentences, less still of its whole paragraphs. So the authorship of the Tosefta takes responsibility to include in its document "everything" that the Mishnah treats, or nearly everything. While Wieseltier's statement has no relationship to the Tosefta (or to any other document of Judaism, short of the *Encyclopaedia Judaica* or perhaps Maimonides' *Mishneh-Torah*), Steinsaltz could well be describing the Tosefta when he says of the Talmud of Babylonia, "The Talmud...deals with...the nature of all things according to the Torah. Therefore its contours are a reflection of life itself. It has no formal external order, but is bound by a strong inner connection between [sic!] its many diverse subjects." If we modify his statement and say, "[the Tosefta's] contours are a reflection of the Mishnah;...it is bound by a strong inner connection among [the Mishnah's] many diverse subjects," that statement would approximate the facts of this document. When, by contrast, we examine the Babylonian Talmud, which is notoriously choosy in assessing what it will discuss within the Mishnah and the Tosefta alike, it will quickly become clear, Steinsaltz's description of that document is hopelessly out of touch with the facts.

Let us now turn to Mishnah-tractate Arakhin in the context of the Written Torah's statement of its topical program and of the facts that that program means to delineate. This protracted exercise lays out four chapters of Mishnah-tractate Arakhin together with the counterpart materials of Tosefta-tractate Arakhin. We see that the Tosefta's treatment of the topic depends in every way upon the Mishnah's. The Tosefta in general contains materials of three kinds: direct citation and gloss of the Mishnah's sentences; exegesis, without direct citation, of the Mishnah's sentences, in discussions that are fully comprehensible only by reference to the Mishnah; and statements that deal with the subject matter of the Mishnah but that are fully comprehensible

---

law," in that the received and traditional text is supposed to justify and vindicate the laws laid down later on. But since Halivni's formulation is specifically within the setting of Scripture, we shall consider a document that concurs and that discusses the topic, Arakhin, wholly within a scriptural context.

without reference to the Mishnah. The first two types vastly predominate throughout the Tosefta's treatment of the Mishnah. The reason that the Tosefta is to be classified as a traditional document is simple. The Tosefta appeals for order, structure, and program to the Mishnah's tractate. It has no plan or agenda of its own. So – conforming more or less to what Steinsaltz says about the Bavli – the Tosefta's authorship sets forth nearly all of its materials in relationship to the Mishnah, and it has faithfully conformed to nearly the whole of a received agenda.

ii. Leviticus on Valuations and Mishnah-Tractate Arakhin

The principal, but not sole, theme of the tractate is gifts of the value of persons, or of property, to the Temple. Paramount is the pledge of a person's Valuation, Lev. 27:1-8, which is treated in Chapters One through Six, inclusive of attention to how these funds are collected by the Temple. Then we deal with the dedication and redemption of a field of possession, that is, a field which one has received by inheritance, Lev. 27:16-25, dealt with in Chapters Seven and Eight, and with the devoted thing *(herem)*, Lev. 27:28-29, which occurs in Chapter Eight. Chapter Nine's first two pericopae return us to the field received as an inheritance. The remainder of Chapter Nine brings us to Lev. 25:25-34, on the sale of a house in a walled city and how it is redeemed. It follows that the tractate really attends to two quite separate matters, the Valuation, and certain rules regarding property rights. What justifies including the latter in the present tractate is that the priests have a claim on property which is not redeemed in the Jubilee and that the cause of having to redeem the property is the fact that the land was sanctified to begin with. Let us first consider how Maimonides *(Valuations* 1:1-3, 9 and 8:12-13, Klien, pp. 171-172, 210) provides an introduction to the laws of Valuations and of vowing one's worth to the Temple:

> 1:1. Valuations are vows belonging to the class of vows of consecration, for Scripture says, *When a man shall clearly utter a vow of persons unto the Lord, according to thy valuation* (Lev. 27:2). Hence liability for them is based on *He shall not break his word* (Num. 30:3), *Thou shalt not be slack to pay it* (Deut. 23:22), and *He shall do according to all that proceedeth out of his mouth* (Num. 30:3).
>
> 1:2. It is a positive Scriptural commandment that cases of valuation must be decided in the manner prescribed by Scripture. Whether one says, "I pledge my own valuation," or "I pledge the valuation of this person," or "I pledge the valuation of So-and-so," he must pay neither more nor less than the valuation prescribed by Scripture, which is a sum that varies with the age of the person valued.

1:3. What is the amount of the valuation? An infant thirty days old or less has no valuation. Hence anyone saying with reference to him, "I pledge the valuation of this infant" is like one saying "I pledge the valuation of this article," and is bound to pay nothing at all. Between the ages of thirty-one days and five complete years, a male's valuation is five shekels, and a female's three. Between five years and one day and the completion of the twentieth year, a male's valuation is twenty shekels, and a female's ten shekelines Between twenty years and one day and the completion of the sixtieth year, a male's valuation is fifty shekels and a female's thirty shekelines From sixty years and one day and until the day of his death, even if he should live many years, a male's valuation is fifteen shekels, and a female's ten shekelines

1:9. Vows of worth are not the same as vows of valuation. For example, if anyone says, "I pledge my worth," or "I pledge the worth of that man," or "I pledge the worth of So-and-so," even if the subject is a one-day-old child, or of doubtful sex, or a hermaphrodite, or a Gentile, he must pay his full worth, computed as if he were a slave being sold in the marketplace, whether this be one *denar* or a thousand.

8:12. Although vows of consecration, devotion, and valuation are matters of religious duty, and it is fitting for a person to conduct himself in these things in such a manner as to subdue his inclination and avoid avarice, thus fulfilling the command of the Prophets, *Honor the Lord with thy substance* (Prov. 3:9), nevertheless, if he never makes any such vows, it does not matter at all, and Scripture itself bears witness to this when it says, *But if thou shalt forbear to vow, it shall be no sin in thee* (Deut. 23:23).

8:13. A person should never consecrate or devote all of his possessions. He who does the reverse acts contrary to the intention of Scripture, for it says, OF ALL *that he hath* (Lev. 27:28), not "ALL that he hath," as was made clear by the Sages. Such an act is not piety but folly, since he forfeits all his valuables and makes himself dependent upon other people who may show no pity toward him. Of such, and those like him, the Sages have said, "The pious fool is one of those who cause the world to perish." Rather, whosoever wishes to expend his money in good deeds, should disburse no more than one fifth, in order that he might be, as the Prophets have advised it, *one that ordereth his affairs rightfully* (Ps. 112:5), be it in matters of Torah or in the business of the world. Even in respect to the sacrifices which a person is obligated to offer, Scripture is sparing of his money, for it says that he may bring an offering in accordance with his means. How much more so in respect to those things for which he is not liable except in consequence of his own vow, should he vow only what is within his means, for Scripture says, *Every man shall give as he is able, according to the blessing of the Lord thy God, which He hath given thee* (Deut. 16:17).

Let us now consider the organization of the tractate, which is in four parts of unequal length, two major units, and then two sections which add up to little more than appendices.

I. *Valuations and vows for the benefit of the Temple.* 1:1-6:3

Leviticus 27:1-8: *The Lord said to Moses, "Say to the people of Israel, When a man makes a special vow of persons to the Lord at your valuation, then your valuation of a male from twenty years old up to sixty years old shall be fifty shekels of silver, according to the shekel of the sanctuary. If the person is a female, your valuation shall be thirty shekels. If the person is from five years old up to twenty years old, your valuation shall be for a male twenty shekels, and for a female ten shekels. If the person is from a month old up to five years old, your valuation shall be for a male five shekels of silver, and for a female your valuation shall be three shekels of silver. And if the person is sixty years old and upward, then your valuation for a male shall be fifteen shekels, and for a female ten shekels. And if a man is too poor to pay your valuation, then he shall bring the person before the priest, and the priest shall value him; according to the ability of him who vowed the priest shall value him.*

A. *Basic rules.* 1:1-4

    1:1   All pledge the Valuation of others and are subject to the pledge of Valuation by others, vow the worth of another and are subject to the vow of payment of their worth by another. Exclusions.

    1:2   The gentile is subject to the pledge of Valuation but does not pledge, so Meir. Judah: Pledges but is not subject to the pledge.

    1:3-4   One who is on the point of death is not subject to the vow or to the pledge of Valuation. Completed at M. 1:4.

B. *Two formal constructions.* 2:1-16, 3:1-5

    2:1   There is no amount of money in connection with Valuations less than a *sela* or more than fifty *selas.*

    [2:2-6   Further formally related statements along these lines, not relevant to the topic of the tractate.]

    [3:1-5   There is in respect to Valuations the possibility to rule leniently and to rule stringently + three other statements, not relevant to our tractate, on the same formal pattern.]

            Relevant to Arakhin: A Valuation is at a fixed price, without regard to the value of that which is valuated, but a vow of the worth of something depends upon the value of what is vowed.

C. *Ability to pay in vows.* 4:1-4

    4:1   The estimate of ability to pay is made in accord with the status of the one who vows, and the estimate of the years is in accord with the status of the one whose Valuation is vowed.

    4:2   But in the case of offerings, the rule is not so.

    4:3   Continuation of M. 4:2.

    4:4   Development of M. 4:1.

D. *The difference between pledging a Valuation and vowing the worth, or price, of someone or something.* 5:1-5

5:1   He who says, "My weight is incumbent on me as a pledge to the sanctuary" pays his weight – if he said, "In silver," he pays in silver, "In gold," he pays in gold.

5:2   He who says, "The price of my hand is incumbent on me" – they make an estimate of how much he is worth with, and without, a hand, and then they pay the difference. More strict is the rule in connection with Valuations than in connection with Vows – *re* estates.

5:3   He who says, "Half of my Valuation is incumbent on me" pays it. If he says, "The Valuation of half of me is incumbent" he pays the whole of his Valuation.

5:4   He who says, "The Valuation of So-and-so is incumbent on me" – *re* estates.

5:5   He who says, "This ox is a burnt-offering" – if the ox died, is not liable to pay. If he pledged the price of the ox and it died, he is liable.

E. *Collecting Valuations.* 5:6-6:5

5:6   Those who owe Valuations – they exact pledges from them.

6:1   The goods of orphans that have been valued by the court to meet the father's debt must be proclaimed for sale during thirty days; those of the Temple (e.g., one redeemed a field which had been bought and not inherited and which had been dedicated to the Temple) for sixty days.

6:2   If a man dedicated his goods to the Temple while still liable for his wife's *hetubah.*

6:3   Although they have said, Pledges must be taken from them that are bound by a vow of Valuation, they leave him food for thirty days.

6:4   Continuation of foregoing.

6:5   Whether a man dedicates his goods or vows his own Valuation, he has no claim on his wife's or children's clothing.

II. *The dedication and redemption of a field which is received as an inheritance.* 7:1-8:3

Leviticus 27:16-25: "*If a man dedicates to the Lord part of the land which is his by inheritance, then your valuation shall be according to the seed for it; a sowing of a homer of barley shall be valued at fifty shekels of silver. If he dedicates his field from the year of jubilee, it shall stand at your full valuation; but if he dedicates his field after the jubilee, then the priest shall compute the money-value for it according to the years that remain until the year of jubilee, and a deduction shall be made from your valuation. And if he who dedicates the field wishes to redeem it, then he shall add a fifth of the valuation in money to it, and it shall remain his. But if he does not wish to redeem the field, or if he has sold the field to another man, it shall not be redeemed any more; but the field, when it is released in the jubilee, shall be holy to the Lord, as a field that has been devoted; the priest shall be in possession of it. If he dedicates to the Lord a field which he has bought, which is not a part of his possession by inheritance, then the priest shall compute the valuation for it up to the year of jubilee, and the man shall give the amount of the valuation on that day as a holy thing to the Lord. In the year of jubilee the field shall return to him from whom it was bought, to whom the land belongs as a possession by inheritance. Every valuation shall be according to the shekel of the sanctuary: twenty gerabs shall make a shekel.*

7:1	They do not dedicate the Field of Possession less than two years before the Jubilee or redeem it less than one year afterward.
7:2	It is all the same whoever redeems the field. But the owner pays the added fifth, and others do not.
7:3	If a man dedicated a field and redeemed it, it does not leave his possession in the Jubilee.
7:4	If a field is not yet redeemed in the Jubilee, then the priests take possession and pay for it.
7:5	If a man bought a field from his father and his father died and he afterward dedicated it, it is regarded as a Field of Possession.
8:1	If a man dedicated his field when the Jubilee is not binding, they say, "You begin," for the owner pays the Added Fifth but others do not.
8:2-3	If a man said, "I bid ten," and another said, "Twenty," and so on, and he recanted....

III. *The devoted thing* (herem). 8:4-7

Leviticus 27:28-29: *"But no devoted thing that a man devotes to the Lord, of anything that he has, whether of man or beast, or of his inherited field, shall be sold or redeemed; every devoted thing is most holy to the Lord. No one devoted, who is to be utterly destroyed from among men, shall be ransomed; he shall be put to death.*

8:4	One may devote part of his flock or herd, but not the whole.
8:5	If one devoted his son or daughter or a field which is purchased, they are not deemed devoted, for one cannot devote what is not his.
8:6	What is devoted for use of the priests cannot be redeemed.
8:7	A man may devote what already has been set apart for animal offerings. How this is evaluated.

IV. *The sale and redemption of a field received as an inheritance and of a dwelling house in a walled city.* 9:1-8

Leviticus 25:25-34: *"If your brother becomes poor, and sells part of his property, then his next of kin shall come and redeem what his brother has sold. If a man has no one to redeem it, and then himself becomes prosperous and finds sufficient means to redeem it, let him reckon the years since he sold it and pay back the overpayment to the man to whom he sold it; and he shall return to his property. But if he has not sufficient means to get it back for himself, then what he sold shall remain in the hand of him who bought it until the year of jubilee; in the jubilee it shall be released, and he shall return to his property.*

"If a man sells a dwelling house in a walled city, he may redeem it within a whole year after its sale; for a full year he shall have the right of redemption. If it is not redeemed within a full year, then the house that is in the walled city shall be made sure in perpetuity to him who bought it, throughout his generations; it shall not be released in the jubilee. But the houses of the villages which have no wall around them shall be reckoned with the fields of the country; they may be redeemed, and they shall be released in the jubilee. Nevertheless the cities of the Levites, the houses in the cities of their possession, the Levites may redeem at any time. And if one of the Levites does not exercise his right of redemption, then the house that was sold in a city of their possession shall be released in the jubilee; for the houses in the cities of the Levites are their possession among the people of Israel. But the fields of common land belonging to their cities may not be sold; for that is their perpetual possession.

9:1   If a man sold his field by inheritance when the law of the Jubilee
          was binding, he may not redeem it for two years [= M. 7:1].
9:2   If it was sold to one for 100 *denars* and to another for 200, he takes
          account only of the first buyer.
9:3   If a man sold a house in a walled city, he may redeem it any time
          in the next twelve months.
9:4   If it is not redeemed in that period.
9:5   Whatever is in a city wall is regarded as a house in a walled city.
9:6   A house in a city whose roofs form the wall, and so on, is not
          regarded as in a walled city.
9:7   Houses in courtyards are given the rights of a house in a walled
          city.
9:8   If an Israelite inherited a house in a city of the Levites, he cannot
          redeem it in line with Lev. 25:32.

The tractate is in four parts of unequal length. We deal first with the most important, which is the matter of Valuations to the Temple as well as vows of one's worth, then with the dedication and redemption of a field which is received as an inheritance and which one has given to the Temple. There are then two brief appendixes, a unit (III) on the devoted thing, and another on the sale and redemption of a dwelling house in a walled city. The organization of the large unit is not especially impressive, since several of the chapters consist of formal constructions only tangentially relevant to the topic under discussion.

The later units are too brief to permit much ambitious work of organization and development.

iii. Mishnah and Tosefta Arakhin to Mishnah-Tractate Arakhin Chapter One

The tractate opens in a way somewhat reminiscent of M. Hul. 1:1, stating that all may pledge the Valuation of themselves or someone else; all are subject to the valuation of others; all vow, or are subject to the vow, that their worth will be paid. This is made specific, which of course limits the force of the opening rule. Limitations then have to do with those whose Valuation is unclear, for example, because their sexual traits are not certain; those who may be evaluated but may not pledge the Valuation of another, because they are not deemed to possess the power of intention. M. 1:2 presents a dispute on the status of the gentile. M. 1:3-4 – the latter joined to the former but irrelevant to the chapter – deal with the status of one who is about to die. The anonymous rule maintains that such a person is not subject to a vow that someone will pay his worth and is not subject to the pledge that someone will pay his Valuation. Hananiah allows the latter, because there is a fixed value, but concedes that in the former case, a person about to die has no worth and therefore is not subject to the stated vow.

1:1

A. All pledge the Valuation [of others] and are subject to the pledge of Valuation [by others],
B. vow [the worth of another] and are subject to the vow [of payment of their worth by another]:
C. priests and Levites and Israelites, women and slaves.
D. A person of doubtful sexual traits and a person who exhibits traits of both sexes vow [the worth of another] and are subject to the vow [of payment of their worth by another], pledge the Valuation [of others], but are not subject to the pledge of Valuation by others,
E. for evaluated is only one who is certainly a male or certainly a female.
F. A deaf-mute, an imbecile, and a minor are subject to the vow [of payment of their worth by another], and are subject to the pledge of Valuation by others, but do not vow the worth, and do not pledge the Valuation, of others.
G. for they do not possess understanding.
H. One who is less than a month old is subject to the vow [of payment of worth by another], but is not subject to the pledge of Valuation.

M. 1:1

The pericope is in four parts, an introduction, A-B, which is limited at C, then three special cases, D explained by E, F explained by G, and H. It is difficult to see the whole as other than a unitary construction. A speaks of paying the fixed Valuation specified at Lev. 27:1-8, and B, of vowing the estimated worth of another, not under the rule of the fixed Valuation. C completes the opening rule but, of course, also reverses the sense of A's blanket statement that *all* effect and are subject to both forms of donation. D then flows from C, also limiting the force of A, and its reason is clear at E. One cannot ascertain the Valuation of one who may be either male or female, since Scripture specifies a different Valuation for each. F then excludes those who, for one reason or another, are not deemed to exercise effective judgment. H simply restates the scriptural specification that Valuations apply to one more than a month old. It links M. 1:1 to M. 1:2, building upon the distinction between M. 1:1A and B, the pledge of a Valuation as against the vow of one's worth.

A.   R. Meir says, "Greater is the applicability of the rule of being subject to the pledge of Valuation than the applicability of the rule of pledging the Valuation of others.

B.   "For: *A deaf-mute, an imbecile, and a minor are subject to the pledge of Valuation by others, but do not pledge the Valuation of others* [M. Ar. 1:1F]."

C.   R. Judah says, "Greater is the applicability of the rule of pledging the Valuation of others than the applicability of being subject to the pledge of Valuation [by others].

D.   "For: *A person of doubtful sexual traits and a person who exhibits traits of both sexes pledge the Valuation [of others] but are not subjected to the pledge of Valuation [to be paid by others]* [M. Ar. 1:1D].

E.   "Also: The Samaritan [MS Vienna, editio princeps: Gentile] should be subject to the rule of pledging the Valuation of others but should not be under the rule of being subject to the pledge of Valuation [by others]" [M. Ar. 1:2A, C].

T. 1:1 Z p. 543, lines 11-13

A.   Women and slaves vow [the worth of others] and are subject to vow [of payment of their worth by others], are subject to the pledge of Valuation [by others] and pledge the Valuation [of others] [M. Ar. 1:1A-C].

B.   If at this time they have [sufficient property], they collect from them. If not, they write a writ of indebtedness and collect it from them after some time.

C.   Gentiles vow [to give the worth of others] and are subject to vow [that others will give their worth] [M. Ar. 1:2D].

D.   Those missing limbs and afflicted by sores, even though they are not of worth, are subject to the pledge of Valuation.

T. 1:2 Z p. 543, lines 13-16

T. 1:1 cites Meir and Judah, then links M. 1:1D to Judah's position at M. 1:2A, C. T. 1:2D's point is that where there is a fixed value, it does not rest on the condition of the one who is evaluated.

1:2

A.   The gentile –
B.   R. Meir says, "He is subject to the pledge of Valuation [by others],
       but he does not pledge the Valuation [of others]."
C.   R. Judah says, "He pledges the Valuation [of others] but is not
       subject to the pledge of Valuation [by others]."
D.   And this one and that one agree that they vow and are subject to
       the vow [of payment of worth].

M. 1:2

The dispute is perfectly balanced, with the point at issue expressed
in the reversal of word order, B/C. Meir's position is that an Israelite
may pledge the Valuation of a gentile, but a gentile may not pledge the
Valuation either of himself or of anyone else. Judah's view is the
opposite. Both parties have to figure out how the gentile is excluded
from the law of Valuations (Lev. 17:1: *speak to the children of Israel).*
In Meir's view, the matter rests upon the action of the person who takes
upon himself to pay the Valuation; hence others may pledge the
Valuation of the gentile, but the gentile may not pledge the Valuation
of others. In Judah's view, the matter rests upon the status of that
which is subject to Valuation. Hence the gentile may pledge the
Valuation of an Israelite, but not of himself. Both parties agree that
vows are permitted in all cases.

1:3-4

A.   He who is on the point of death or he who goes forth to be put to
       death
B.   is not subject to the vow [of payment of his worth by others] nor
       subject to the pledge of Valuation [by others].
C.   R. Hananiah b. Aqabya says, "He is subject to the pledge of
       Valuation,
D.   "because its [a Valuation's] price is fixed.
E.   "But he is not subject to the vow [of payment of his worth by
       others],
F.   "because its [a vow's] price is not fixed."
G.   R. Yosé says, "he vows [the value of another] and declares
       something sanctified.
H.   "And if he caused damage, he is liable to make restitution."

M. 1:3

A.   The woman who goes forth to be put to death –
B.   they do not postpone [the execution] for her until she will give
       birth.
C.   [If] she sat on the travailing stool, they postpone [the execution]
       for her until she will give birth.
D.   The woman who is executed – they derive benefit from her hair.
E.   A beast which is executed – it [the hair] is prohibited from benefit.

M. 1:4

The pericope consists of a dispute, A-B versus. C-F; the form of the second opinion, C-F, follows that of M. 1:1D-E, F-G, that is, the specification of a reason for a rule. One who is about to die is worth nothing, so, too, the one about to be executed. Therefore he is not subject to the vow that others will pay his worth or to the pledge of Valuation. Hananiah rejects this view for the stated reason. The pledge of Valuation certainly is fixed and payable; the worth to be paid by a vow is null. Yosé's saying is separate from the foregoing. The man's estate can be encumbered by these vows or other obligations.

At M. 1:4 we have a pair of balanced rules, A-B (apocopated), then C; and D-E. The rules are attached for obvious reasons, but do not belong to our tractate.

A.   *"He who is on the point of death and one who is eight days old is not subject to the vow [of payment of his worth by others] nor subject to the pledge of Valuation [by others].*

B.   *"And he who goes forth to be put to death is not subject to the vow [of payment of his worth by others] nor subject to the pledge of Valuation [by others],"* the words of R. Meir [M. Ar. 1:3A-B].

C.   R. Hanina b. Aqiba says, *"He is subject to the pledge of Valuation, because its price is fixed. But he is not subject to the vow [of payment of his worth by others], because its price is not fixed"* [M. Ar. 1:3C-F].

D.   R. Yosé says, *"He vows [the value of another] and pledges a Valuation [of another] and declares something sanctified. And if he caused damage, he is liable to make restitution"* [M. Ar. 1:3G-H].

T. 1:3 Z p. 543, lines 16-19

A.   *A woman who goes forth to be put to death* [M. Ar. 1:4A] –

B.   [If] the offspring put forth its hand, they postpone [the execution] for her until she will give birth.

C.   For if she had given birth, her offspring would have been stoned [see *TR II*, p. 275].

D.   The woman who goes forth to be put to death –

E.   [If] she said, "Give my hair to my daughter," they give it to her.

F.   If she died without specifying [to whom the hair should be given], they do not give it to her [the daughter].

G.   For those that are dead are prohibited from the benefit [of any possessions, hence cannot after death be supposed to have disposed of property in this wise].

T. 1:4 Z p. 543, lines 19-21

T. 1:3 cites M. 1:3. T. 1:4A-B then restate M. 1:4C. D-G augment M. 1:4D.

iv. Mishnah and Tosefta Arakhin to Mishnah-Tractate Arakhin
Chapter Four

The present chapter elucidates some fairly obvious principles in regard to the definition of what is to be paid in consequence of a pledge of Valuation. Scripture specifies that a male's valuation, from twenty to sixty years of age, is fifty *sheqels* of silver; the female's is thirty; that of a person five to twenty years of age is, for a male, twenty, and for a female, ten; and that of a person from a month to five years of age is, for a male, five, and for a female, three; and that of one sixty years and older, for a male is fifteen, and for a female, ten. Further, if one is too poor to pay the Valuation, then he brings the person whose Valuation has been pledged before the priest, and the priest values him. "According to the ability of him who vowed, the priest shall value him" (Lev. 27:8). We have the expected construction, a set of four rules, each of them systematically expounded in order, and with a small supplement appended to the final rule. That is, M. 4:1A, B, C, and D, are worked out by M. 4:1D-G, and M. 4:4A-J, with an appendix at M. 4:4K-R. M.4:2-3 are a sizable interpolation, which hardly belongs.

4:1

I	A.	[The estimate of] ability to pay [is made in accord with the status of] the *one who vows* [Lev. 27:8].
II	B.	And [the estimates of] the years [of age is made in accord with the status of] the one [whose Valuation] is vowed.
III	C.	And [when this is according to] the Valuations [spelled out in the Torah], it is in accord with the status [age, sex] of the one whose Valuation is pledged.
IV	D.	And the Valuation [is paid in accordance with the rate prescribed] at the time of the pledge of Valuation.
I	E.	*[The estimate of] ability to pay [is made in accord with the status of] the one who vows: How so?*
	F.	A poor man who pledged the Valuation of a rich man gives the Valuation required of a poor man.
	G.	And a rich man who pledged the Valuation of a poor man gives the Valuation of a rich man.

M. 4:1

The four matched stichs, A-D, state a fairly obvious set of rules. When Scripture speaks of ability to pay, it refers to the person who has to make the payment, the one who vows. When Scripture speaks of the pledge, it refers to the age of the one concerning whom the vow is made A-B, or the age or sex of the one whose Valuation is pledged, C. When a Valuation is pledged and the person to be valuated passes into another age category, D, the Valuation is owed as of the time of the pledge. Since B and C repeat one another (as M. 4:4 will show), the purpose clearly is to give us four remarkably succinct rules, built on the roots NDR and 'RK, respectively. The explanation, E-G, poses no problem of interpretation.

4:2-3

A.   But in the case of offerings, [the rule] is not so.

B.   Lo, [if] one said, "The [obligation to bring] the offering of this mesora' is incumbent on me," if the mesora' was poor, he brings the offering of a poor man. [If the mesora' was] rich, he brings the offering of a rich one.

C.   Rabbi says, "I say, 'Also in the case of Valuations the rule is so.

D.   "And on what account does the poor man who pledged the Valuation of the rich man give the Valuation of a poor man? Because the rich man [under such circumstances, in any case] owes nothing.

E.   "But a rich man who said, 'My Valuation is incumbent on me,' and a poor man heard and said, 'What this one has said is incumbent on me [too],' he [the poor man] gives the Valuation of the rich one."

F.   [If] he was poor and got rich, or rich and grew poor, he gives the Valuation of a rich man.

G.   R. Judah says, "Even if he was poor and got rich and then became poor again, he gives the Valuation of a rich man."

M. 4:2

A.   But in the case of offerings, the rule is not so.

B.   Even if his father is about to die [*Nusah*, p. 574] and leave him ten thousand,

C.   [even if] his ship was at sea and [about to] arrive with ten thousand,

D.   the sanctuary has no claim whatsoever on them.

M. 4:3

M. 4:2-3 present a curious structure, since A explicitly links M. 4:2 to M. 4:1E-G; then M. 4:2F-G – M. 4:3 provide their own expansion of M. 4:1E-G, followed by their expected secondary development in terms of Temple offerings. Accordingly, we have a rather elaborate double expansion of M. 4:1E-G. The point of A-B is that while, in the case of Valuations, the estimate of the ability to pay is made in accord with the status of the one who makes the vow, in the case of offerings, it is made in accord with the status of the one who owes the offering, not the one who vows to pay it. This is spelled out at B. Rabbi then wishes to reject M. 4:1A and to impose the same rule as applies for offerings. His reasoning is spelled out at D-E. When the matter of Valuations is similar to that of offerings, there is no difference in the applicable rule.

F develops M. 4:1F-G. If a man was poor and got rich (M. 2:1), or rich and grew poor, we impose the more stringent status. Judah does not differ; he simply extends the rule. Then M. 4:3 again differentiates Valuations from offerings. If a man was poor and he got rich (B, C), he fulfills his obligation with the original offering required of him at the moment at which he presented it.

A. A poor man and a rich man who pledged the Valuation of a poor man and a rich man –

B. This one gives in accord with his status, and that one gives in accord with his status.

T. 2:12 Z p. 545, lines 8-9

A. [He who says] without further specification, "Lo, I pledge myself to give a Valuation," brings the least of Valuations.

B. And how much is the least of Valuations? Five *selas*.

T. 2:13 Z p. 545, lines 9-10

A. He who says, "The Valuations of ten people are incumbent on me," if he was a poor man, he gives for all of them the Valuation of a poor man.

B. If he was a rich man, he gives for all of them the Valuation of a rich man.

C. [If] he was a poor man and got rich, he gives for all of them the Valuation of a rich man.

D. [If] he was a rich man and grew poor, he gives for all of them the Valuation of a poor man.

E. R. Judah says, "[He gives] the Valuation of a rich man, since for one moment he has entered the category of wealth" [M. Ar. 4:2G].

T. 2:14 Z p. 545, lines 10-13

A. "He who says, 'The Valuation of such and so is incumbent on me,' lo, this one gives a *sela*," the words of E. Meir.

B. For it is said, *Every Valuation shall be according to the* sheqel *of the sanctuary* (Lev. 27:25).

C. And sages say, "He gives only in accord with his capacity, as it is said, *According to the ability of him who vowed the priest shall value him*" (Lev. 27:8).

T. 2:15 Z p. 545, lines 13-16

A. A poor man who pledged his own Valuation – they do not say to him, "Go, borrow money for yourself. Do work. Then bring the Valuation of a rich man."

B. But it is best that he bring the Valuation of a poor man now.

C. And let him not bring the Valuation of a rich man after a while.

T. 2:16 Z p. 545, lines 16-17

A. R. Judah says, "[If] his father was sick or dying,

B. "or his ship was out at sea, so that he may [shortly] bring the Valuation of a rich man,

C. "it is better that he bring the Valuation of a poor man now. And let him not bring the Valuation of a rich man after a while."

T. 2:17 Z p. 545, lines 18-19

A.   R. Eleazar says, "[If] he owed a rising-and-falling offering, they do
         not say to him, 'Go, borrow money for yourself. Do work, and bring
         the offering of a rich man.'
B.   "But it is better that he bring the offering of a poor man now. And
         let him not bring the offering of a rich man after a while."

                                                  T. 2:18 Z p. 545, lines 19-21

A.   R. Simeon says, "The burning of the fats is valid at the end of the
         Sabbath.
B.   "The Torah has said, 'Let them override the Sabbath in the proper
         time. But let them not be offered up at the end of the Sabbath, not
         in the proper time.'
C.   "And so it says, *A wise-hearted man will heed the
         commandments* (Prov. 10:8) – he who makes His commandment
         a commandment [a true imperative]."

                                                  T. 2:19 Z p. 545, lines 22-24

T. 2:12 extends the rule of M. 4:1A/E to a case secondary to M. 4:1F-
G. T. 2:13-15 provide complementary information for M. 4:1A. T. 2:14
then brings us to M. 4:2, as indicated. T. 2:15 shows that sages, not Meir,
stand behind M. 4:1A. What is important to T. 2:16 is that the man give
the Valuation forthwith, whatever he is liable to give at that time (in
line with M. 4:1B, C), rather than postponing it in order to collect
sufficient funds for the full sum of the Valuation of the rich man. T.
2:17, 18 go over this same ground. T. 2:19 then makes the same point,
now with reference to another matter: under all circumstances it is
important to do the commandments right away.

4:4

II   A.   *[The estimate of] the years [of his age is made in accord with the*
              status of] the one [whose Valuation] is vowed: How so?
     B.   A child who pledged the Valuation of an elder gives the Valuation
              of an elder.
     C.   And an elder who pledged the Valuation of a child gives the
              Valuation of a child.
III D.   *And [when this is according to] the Valuations [spelled out in the*
              Torah], it is in accord with the status of the one whose Valuation is
              pledged: How so?
     E.   A man who pledged the Valuation of a woman gives the Valuation
              of a woman.
     F.   And a woman who pledged the Valuation of a man gives the
              Valuation of a man.
IV   G.   *And the Valuation [is paid in accordance with the rate prescribed]*
              at the time of the pledge of Valuation: How so?
     H.   [If] one pledged the Valuation of another when the latter was less
              than five years old, and [that one] passed five,
     I.   less than twenty years old and he passed twenty,
     J.   he pays in accord with what is required at the time of the pledged
              of Valuation.

K.   Thirty days is deemed less than that. The fifth year or the twentieth year is deemed less than that [Danby: Thirty days is accounted under this age; five years or twenty years is accounted under this age],

L.   since it says, *And if it be from sixty years old and upward, if it be a male* (Lev. 27:7),

M.   lo, we derive the rule for all cases from that applicable to the sixtieth year.

N.   Just as the sixtieth year is deemed equivalent to less than that age, so the fifth year or the twentieth year is deemed equivalent to less than that age.

O.   Is this so? If Scripture has treated the sixtieth year as less than it, it is to impose a more stringent rule. Shall we then treat the fifth year and the twentieth year as less than they, to impose a more lenient rule?

P.   Scripture says, *Year...year...*, for the purposes of establishing an analogy.

Q.   Just as *year* stated in connection with the sixtieth year is deemed equivalent to less than it, so *year* stated in connection with the fifth year and the twentieth year are deemed equivalent to less than they, whether this imposes a lenient or a stringent ruling.

R.   R. Eleazar says, "The foregoing applies so long as they are a month and a day more than the years [which are prescribed]."

M. 4:4

The exposition of M. 4:1 is taken up and concluded at M. 4:4A-J. Neither formal nor substantive matters require comment. K + L-N form an appendix to G-J, and O-Q challenge the reasoning but not the conclusion of L-N. Then R forms a further gloss of K. K therefore is the principal addition. A child five years old is deemed less than five; only when the sixth year begins (versus R) do we charge the Valuation specified in Scripture, and so with twenty. The proof is at N. Scripture is explicit that one must be more than sixty years of age. O-Q indicate that the proposed analogy may not hold and provide a formal proof. Eleazar then states that the fifth, twentieth, and sixtieth years are deemed as equivalent to the preceding ones only for thirty-one days. From that point on, the fifth year is deemed equivalent to the following ones, down through the twentieth, and so for the twentieth and the sixtieth. His qualification, as is clear, goes right back to K and bears no relationship to the intervening materialines

v. Mishnah and Tosefta Arakhin to Mishnah-Tractate Arakhin Chapter Five

The present chapter contains law of both substantive and relevant interest; it even bears Tosefta worthy of the name, unlike the foregoing chapters. The problem is the difference between pledging a Valuation and vowing the worth, or price, of someone or something. M. 5:1 deals with the vow to give one's weight to the sanctuary. If a person specifies that he will give silver, then that is what he gives, and so too with gold. If the person offers the weight of his hand, Judah and Yosé discuss how that weight is ascertained. The principal interest of the chapter begins at 5:2 and runs through 5:5. In the case of Valuations, if a person pledges his own Valuation and then dies, his estate pays. If he vows his price or worth and dies, the estate does not pay. If a person pledges the Valuation of his hand or leg, he has said nothing; if he pledges the Valuation of his head or liver, he pays his whole Valuation. M. 5:3 carries forward this same theme. M. 5:4, familiar from M. 4:1, deals with the death of a person who pledges the Valuation of someone else and also the death of the person whose Valuation has been pledged. The estate, as we know, must pay. If a person vows the price of another and dies, the estate pays; if the person concerning whom the vow is made should die, the estate of the person who made the vow pays nothing. M. 5:5 completes the unit. M. 5:6 then makes a quite separate point. It is necessary to exact a pledge from someone who owes a Valuation because he may be dilatory about paying it. But we need not exact a pledge from someone who owes a sin-offering or a guilt-offering, for such a one will be zealous about bringing it. This starts a fresh unit of thought.

5:1

A.   He who says, "My weight is incumbent on me [as a pledge to the sanctuary]" pays his weight –

B.   If [he said], "Silver," [then he pays] in silver;

C.   If [he said], Gold," [then he pays] in gold.

D.   M'SH B: The mother of Yirmatyah said, "The weight of my daughter is incumbent on me." And she went up to Jerusalem, and weighed her [Yirmatyah], and paid her weight in gold.

E.   [He who says], "The weight of my hand is incumbent on me [as a pledge to the sanctuary]" –

F.   R. Judah says, "He fills a jar with water and pokes it [his hand] in up to the elbow. And he weighs out the meat of an ass, with the sinews and bones. And he puts it [the ass meat] into it [the jar] until it [the jar] is filled up [with water]."

G.   Said R. Yosé, "and how is it possible to treat as equivalent one kind of flesh and another, and one kind of bones and another? But:

H.   "They estimate the hand: how much is it likely to weigh?"

M. 5:1

The fundamental sentence pattern is to construct simple declarative sentences, in which the predicate is closely tied to the subject, for example, *he who says...pays*, or *he who says...fills....* We have two distinct but related units, A-C + D, and E + F, with G-H formulated as a gloss, though, of course, in fact, E-H are a dispute. M. 5:2A will continue this matter, but from a fresh perspective. The point of A-C + D requires no comment. (Since, D, the mother was rich, it was assumed she meant gold.) E-H's problem is how to estimate the weight of the hand, in line with A-C. Judah proposes to figure out the volume and to weigh out an equivalent volume of ass meat. Yosé's objection is valid, but his solution is not impressive.

A. He who says, "Lo, incumbent on me is a staff the full measure of my height" brings a staff the full measure of his height, which is not bent.

B. M'SH B: The mother of Yirmatyah, whose daughter was sick, said, "If my daughter will recover from her illness, I shall give her weight in gold."

C. She recovered from her illness. She [the mother] went to Jerusalem and weighed her in gold [M. Ar. 5:1D].

T. 3:1 Z p. 545, lines 25-27

A. [He who says], "The weight of my hand is incumbent on me" gives [the equivalent of the weight] up to the elbow [M. Ar. 5:1E].

B. [He who says], "The weight of my foot is incumbent on me" gives [the equivalent of the weight] up to the ankle.

C. "How does he carry out [the measure]?

D. "He brings a jar full of water and puts his hand in it up to the elbow. He puts in his foot up to the ankle.

E. "And he brings ass meat, sinews, and bones. He weighs it out and puts into it [the water] meat equivalent in volume to his meat and bones equivalent in volume to his bones [M. Ar. 5:1F].

G. "Even though there is no proof for such a procedure, there is an allusion to it: *Whose flesh is the flesh of asses* (Ex. 25:20)," the words of R. Judah.

H. *Said to him R. Yosé, "How is it possible to treat as equivalent one kind of flesh and another, and one kind of bones and another?"* [M. Ar. 5:1G].

I. Said to him R. Judah, "They make a rough estimate of it."

J. Said to him R. Yosé, "While they are making a rough estimate of it, let them make a rough estimate of the hand – how much it weighs, and of the foot – how much it weighs!" [M. Ar. 5:1G-H].

T. 3:2 Z p. 545, lines 27-34

T. 3:1 augments M. 5:1A-D. It now includes the detail that the mother promises gold, in which case the story bears no important point for M. at all.[2] Omitting the detail about giving gold allows the story to contribute to M.'s unfolding. T. 5:2 then goes over the ground of M. 5:1E-H.

---

[2]"T. 3:1 rather illustrates M. 5:1C; if the person pledges gold, he must pay in gold." – Richard S. Sarason.

5:2-3

A.   [He who says], "The price of my hand is incumbent on me" – they make an estimate of him: how much is he worth with a hand, and how much is he worth without a hand?

B.   This rule is more strict in connection with vows than in connection with Valuations.

C.   More strict is the rule in connection with Valuations than in connection with Vows.

D.   How so?

E.   He who says, "My Valuation is incumbent on me" and who dies – the heirs must pay [the Valuation].

F.   [He who says], "My price is incumbent on me" and who dies – the heirs do not pay [the vow].

G.   For corpses have no price [worth].

H.   [He who says], "The Valuation of my hand, or the Valuation of my foot is incumbent on me" has not said a thing.

I.   [He who says], "The Valuation of my head," or "the Valuation of my liver is incumbent on me" pays the Valuation of his whole person.

J.   This is the general principle: [If he refers to] something on which life depends, he pays the Valuation of his whole person.

M. 5:2

A.   [He who says], "Half of my Valuation is incumbent on me" pays half his Valuation.

B.   [He who says], "The Valuation of half of me is incumbent on me" pays the whole of his Valuation.

C.   [He who says], "Half of my price is incumbent on me" pays half of his price.

D.   [He who says], "The price of half of me is incumbent on me" pays the whole of his price.

E.   This is the general principle: [If he refers to] something on which life depends, he pays the Valuation of his whole person.

M. 5:3

M. 5:1E has attended to the pledge of the weight of the hand. Now we turn to a pledge of the price of the hand. A fully explains how this is defined. B-C form a bridge to what will follow, the differing rules for pledges of Valuations as against those for vows of price, M. 5:2E-J, M. 5:3, M. 5:4 (+ M. 5:5). The main point is that in the case of a Valuation, we have a fixed amount, which, once pledged, must be paid. In the case of a vow – for instance, the pledge of one's price or value – the result is variable. E-F + G are clear as stated. The Valuation has a fixed definition and must be paid. But the price of the man depends upon the situation at the point at which the estimate is to be made, G. H of course contrasts to A, since someone can pledge the price of his hand, but not the Valuation of his hand. It is difficult, however, to claim that in the beginning were A and H, which then were separated and augmented. In fact, H goes together with I, and both are explained at J. If the man pledges the Valuation of his head, he has spoken of something essential to his life and therefore pays his whole Valuation. But there is no such thing as a Valuation of the hand. M. 5:3 goes over the ground of M. 5:2H-J. A person can pledge half his Valuation. But if he pledges the Valuation of half of himself, he must pay the whole, in line with M. 5:3E. Now the same rule applies to vows of one's price. The whole assuredly is a unitary construction. Compare M. Tem. 1:3.

A.   *[He who says], "half of my Valuation is incumbent on me" pays half his Valuation* [M. Ar. 5:3A].

B.   R. Judah says, "They impose a fine on him and he pays his entire Valuation."

C.   *[He who says], "Half of my price is incumbent on me" pays half his price* [M. Ar. 5:3D].

D.   R. Yosé bar Judah says, "They impose a fine upon him and he pays his entire price."

T. 3:3 Z p. 545, lines 34-36

T. 3:3 supplies a firm attestation for M., which clearly takes up the position of Judah's opposition.

5:4

A.   He who says, "The Valuation of so-and-so is incumbent on me" –

B.   [If] the one who makes the vow and the one concerning whom the vow is made die –

C.   the heirs [of the former] pay the pledge.

D.   [If he said], "The price of so-and-so is incumbent on me" [and] the one who makes the vow dies, the heirs must pay the vow.

E.   [If] the one concerning whom the vow is made dies, the heirs do not have to pay.

F.   For corpses have no price [value].

M. 5:4

The obligation to pay the Valuation rests on the estate of the man who makes the pledge, A-C. The obligation to pay the vow, D, likewise is incumbent on the estate of the one who makes the vow. But if the one concerning whom the vow is made dies, then we invoke the conception of M. 5:2F-G, which make essentially the same point.

A.   *He who says, "The Valuation of so-and-so is incumbent on me"* –

B.   [if] the one whose Valuation has been pledged dies, the one who has pledged the Valuation is [nonetheless] liable [= M. 4:1D].

T. 3:4 Z p. 545, line 36

A.   A strict rule applies to [vows to pay] the price which does not apply to Valuations, and to Valuations which do not apply to [vows to pay] the price.

B.   [For vows to pay] the price apply to man and beast, to live and
        slaughtered [beasts], to whole ones and to limbs,
C.   and they apply without regard to ability to pay,
D.   which is not the case for Valuations.

                                                    T. 3:4 Z p. 545, lines 36-38

A.   A more strict rule applies to Valuations:
B.   For Valuations are subject to a fixed sum deriving from the Torah,
C.   which is not the case of [vows to pay] the price.
D.   He who says, "The Valuation of so-and-so is incumbent on me,"
        and who dies, is liable [through his estate to pay the pledged
        Valuation] [M. Ar. 5:4A-C].
E.   [He who says], "The price of this beast is incumbent on me" and
        who dies is liable.
F.   [He who says], "The price of this beast is incumbent on me," and
        the beast dies – the one who vows is liable.

                                                    T. 3:6 Z p. 545, lines 38-39,
                                                              p. 546, line 1

A.   A strict rule applies to man which does not apply to beasts, and [a
        strict rule applies to] a beast which does not apply to man.
B.   For he who says, "The price of this beast is incumbent on me," if it
        died, is [still] liable.
C.   [He who says], "The price of so-and-so is incumbent on me," if he
        dies, is exempt [M. Ar. 5:4E].
D.   A more strict rule applies to Valuations, for Valuations apply to
        man and do not apply to beasts.

                                                    T. 3:7 Z p. 546, lines 1-3

T. 3:4 accords with M. 5:4 A-C. Then T.'s construction goes over
points familiar from M. T. 3:5 is wholly fresh. T. 3:6 is familiar, as
indicated, so too T. 3:7.

5:5

A.   [He who says], "This ox is a burnt-offering," "This house is
        qorban,"
B.   [if] the ox died or the house fell down,
C.   is not liable to pay.
D.   [If he said], "The price of this ox is incumbent on me for a burnt-
        offering," or "the price of this house is incumbent on me as
        qorban,"
E.   [if] the ox died or the house fell down,
F.   he is liable to pay.

                                                              M. 5:5

The point of this neatly constructed pericope is obvious. If the man
specifies a particular ox, then he is liable only to hand over that ox. If
he specifies the value of the ox, then he has to pay that value,
whatever happens to the ox. (B. Ar. 20B supplies D's *the price*; without
it, the stress will fall on *on me*, by which words the man undertakes a

heightened responsibility [Albeck]. But the meaning is clear one way or
the other.)

A.   He who sanctifies the produce of his wife's hands, lo, this one
provides for her maintenance therefrom. But the remainder is
deemed sanctified.

B.   He who sanctifies the produce of his servant's hands, lo, this one
provides him with maintenance therefrom. But the remainder is
deemed sanctified.

C.   He who sanctifies himself, lo, this one labors and benefits from
the fruit of his labor. He has sanctified only his value.

T. 3:8 Z p. 546, lines 3-6

A.   [He who says], "the head of this servant is sanctified" – he and the
sanctuary are partners in him.

B.   [He who says], "The head of this ass is sanctified," he and the
sanctuary are partners in him.

C.   [He who says], "The head of this servant is sold to you" – they work
the matter out between them.

D.   [He who says], "The head of this ass is sold to you" – they work the
matter out between them.

T 3:9 Z p. 546, lines 6-8

A.   [He who says], "The head of this cow is sold to you" has sold only
its head.

B.   And not only so, but even if he had said, "The head of this cow is
sanctified," he has sanctified only its head.

T. 3:10 Z p. 546, lines 8-10

A.   [He who says], "This ox is a burnt-offering" – the ox is deemed a
burnt-offering. And it is subject to the laws of sacrilege. And they
are not responsible for [replacing] it [if it should be lost] [M. 5:5A-
C].

B.   [He who says], "This ox is incumbent on me as a burnt-offering" –
the ox is deemed a burnt-offering. And it is subject to the laws of
sacrilege. And they are responsible for [replacing] it [if it should
be lost] [M. 5:5D-F].

T 3:11 Z p. 546, lines 10-11

A.   [He who says], "The price of his ox is a burnt-offering" – the ox is
deemed unconsecrated. And the laws of sacrilege do not apply to
it. And they are not responsible [to replace] it [if it is lost].

B.   [He who says], "The price of this ox is incumbent on me as a
burnt-offering," the ox is unconsecrated. And the laws of sacrilege
do not apply to it. But they are responsible [to replace] it [if it
should be lost].

T. 3:12 Z p. 546, lines 11-13

A.   [He who says], "This house is sanctified" – the house is sanctified.
And the laws of sacrilege apply to it. But he is not responsible for
it.

B.   "This house is incumbent on me as sanctified" – the house is sanctified. And the laws of sacrilege apply to it. And they are responsible for it.

C.   "The price of this house is sanctified" – the house is unconsecrated. The laws of sacrilege do not apply to it. And they are not responsible for it.

D.   "The price of this house is incumbent on me as sanctified" – the house is unconsecrated. And the laws of sacrilege do not apply to it. But they are liable to be responsible [for giving the funds].

T. 3:13 Z p. 546, lines 13-16

T. is formally autonomous of M. But the issue of responsibility does enter. M. 5:5 has made the point that if a person sets aside a particular house or ox, and the house or ox is not available, he has no further responsibility to make it up. But if he sets aside the value or price, he remains liable, no matter what happens to the ox or house. This same point is made at T. 3:11, 3:12, 3:13. Still, it is difficult to see that T. has been constructed in response to M. or in amplification of M.

5:6

A.   Those who owe Valuations [to the Temple] – they exact pledges from them.

B.   Those who owe sin-offerings or guilt-offerings – they do not exact pledges from them.

C.   Those who owe burnt-offerings or peace-offerings – they exact pledges from them.

D.   Even though he does not make atonement [that is, atonement is not effected for him] unless he acts of his own will, as it is said, *At his good will* (Lev. 1:3), [nonetheless], they compel him until he says, "I will it."

E.   And so do you rule in the case of writs of divorce for women:

F.   They compel him until he says, "I will it."

M. 5:6

The point of A-B is that, in the latter case, a person will surely want to expiate his sin and bring the necessary offerings, so we do not exact a surety. But in the matter of merely fulfilling a pledge (A), a person may be less zealous, so he must lay down a surety that he will pay the Valuation. C carries the matter forward, with its augmentation at D (+E-F). Burnt-offerings and peace-offerings fall into the category of A, since people may be slothful about bringing them. D then raises the question of forcing someone to bring an offering. The man does not carry out his obligation to bring a burnt-offering or a peace-offering if he is forced to do so against his will, so, D explains, there is a procedure to compel him to *want* to do so.

A. Those who are liable for vows, freewill-offerings, Valuations, things which have been declared *herem,* things which have been declared sanctified –
B. The court exacts a surety from them [M. Ar. 5:6A].
C. And if they die, the heirs are liable to provide [what has been pledged].

T. 3:14 Z p. 546, lines 16-17

A. Those who owe sin-offerings and guilt-offerings or the price [thereof] –
B. The court does not exact a surety from them [M. Ar. 5:6B].
C. And if they die, the heirs are not liable to provide [what is owed].
D. And as to the price which has been laid on them, lo, it is deemed the equivalent of Valuations.

T. 3:15 Z p. 546, lines 18-19

A. Burnt-offerings which are brought with sin-offerings –
B. The court exacts a surety for them.
C. And if they died, the heirs are liable to provide [what is owed].
D. [If] one brought his sin-offering and did not bring his burnt-offering,
E. the court exacts a surety on its account.
F. And if they died, the heirs are liable to provide [what is owed].
G. [If] he brought his burnt-offering and did not bring his sin-offering, the court does [*TR* II, p. 278 deletes: *not*] exact a surety on its account.[3]
H. And if they died, the heirs are not liable to provide [a sin-offering].

T. 3:16 Z p. 546, lines 19-22

A. Those who owe burnt-offerings and the price [thereof] , peace-offerings, Valuations, things which have been declared *herem,* things which have been declared sanctified, vows, freewill-offerings, sin-offerings, guilt-offerings, gifts of charity, tithes, gleanings, the forgotten sheaf, the corner of the field, firstlings, tithe of cattle, and the Passover –
B. Once three festivals have gone by, they transgress on their account the rule against postponing [and not doing the matter in proper time].

T. 3:17 Z p. 546, lines 22-25

A. R. Simeon says, "Three festivals in proper order, and the festival of unleavened bread comes first."
B. R. Eleazar bar Simeon says, "Once the festival of Sukkot passes by, one transgresses on their account against not postponing."
C. And all the same are the firstling and the tithe, and all the same are all Holy Things which one has sanctified –
D. A year of festivals and the festivals of a year [having gone by].

---

[3]"Lieberman bases his emendation on B. Arakh, 21a, Rav Papa's opinion. But the pericopae in T. and B. are totally independent of each other. Zuckermandel's reading therefore is to be preferred." – Richard S. Sarason.

E.   one transgresses on their account the rule against postponing [T.
Bekh. 3:5 Z p. 537, lines 14-15].

T. 3:18 Z p. 546, lines 25-28

T. 3:14-15 concur with M. and augment its rule, as indicated. T. 3:16
then raises an interesting problem. We do not exact a surety for sin-
offerings, and we do for burnt-offerings. When the two are brought
together, how do we proceed? T. 3:16A-C introduce the real question, at
D, then at G. If one has brought the sin-offering and not the burnt-
offering, the latter is subject to surety. If he brought the burnt-offering
and not the sin-offering, the latter is not subject to surety. T. 3:17-18 are
autonomous of M., T. 3:18C-E are familiar from T. Bekh. 3:5, as
indicated.

vi. Mishnah and Tosefta Arakhin to Mishnah-Tractate Arakhin Chapter Seven

The tractate now shifts its interest from the first fifteen verses of
Leviticus Twenty-seven to the next ten, Lev. 27:16-25. Scripture
distinguishes between a field which one purchases and one which is
inherited ("a field of possession"). When the latter is dedicated to the
Lord ("sanctified"), it is redeemed at a fixed valuation in relationship
to the Jubilee year. If it is not redeemed, when the Jubilee releases it, it
is possessed by the priests. Let us review the relevant verses:

> If a man dedicates to the Lord part of the land which is his by
> inheritance, then your valuation shall be according to the seed for it; a
> sowing of a *homer* of barley shall be valued at fifty *shekels* of silver.
>
> If he dedicates his field from the year of jubilee, it shall stand at
> your full valuation. But if he dedicates his field after the jubilee, then
> the priest shall compute the money-value for it according to the years
> that remain until the year of jubilee, and a deduction shall be made
> from your valuation.
>
> And if he who dedicates the field wishes to redeem it, then he
> shall add a fifth of the valuation in money to it, and it shall remain his.
>
> But if he does not wish to redeem the field, or if he has sold the
> field to another man, it shall not be redeemed any more. But the field,
> when it is released in the jubilee, shall be holy to the Lord, as a field
> that has been devoted; the priest shall be in possession of it.
>
> If he dedicates to the Lord a field which he has bought, which is
> not part of his possession by inheritance, then the priest shall
> compute the valuation for it up to the year of jubilee, and the man
> shall give the amount of the valuation on that day as a holy thing to
> the Lord. In the year of jubilee the field shall return to him from whom
> it was bought, to whom the land belongs as a possession by
> inheritance.

> Every valuation shall be made according to the *shekel* of the sanctuary: twenty *gerabs* shall make a *shekel*.

This brings us to the present chapter.

The chapter itself is in three parts, M. 7:1-12 + M. 7:3, M. 7:4, and M. 7:5. The first unit specifies when a field may be dedicated to the sanctuary in the cycle of the Jubilee and how it is to be redeemed. One pays the sanctuary a *sheqel* (= a *sela*) and a *pondion* for each year remaining in the Jubilee. If one buys it four years before the Jubilee, one pays four *selas* and four *pondions*. M. 7:2 specifies what Scripture has told us, which is that the owner pays an additional fifth, for example, four *selas* and four *pondions* plus one of each, five in all, in the just-mentioned case. M. 7:3 presents three more rules on redeeming the property. A field which is sanctified and redeemed remains in one's domain on the Jubilee. If one's son redeems the field, the field reverts to the father. If someone else redeems it and one then redeems the property from the purchaser's domain, the field likewise remains in one's own domain in the Jubilee. Priests who redeem the property cannot keep it in the Jubilee, just as if they were laymen. M. 7:4 has a dispute on the disposition of a field which is not redeemed by the Jubilee. Judah holds the priests take it over but pay for it. Simeon has them taking it over but not paying for it. Eliezer says the field does not pass to the priests at all, but is kept until a second, then a third Jubilee. M. 7:5, on the subject of dedicating a field, raises an interesting question. If a person purchases a field from his father, is this deemed a field of possession, that is, received by inheritance, when the father dies? Yes, it is. Therefore all parties agree that if the father died and the man then sanctified the field, it falls under the rule of the field of possession. But if the man purchased the field and sanctified it, and only afterward the father died, is it a field of possession or a field which has been bought? Meir takes the position that it is a field which has been bought. Judah and Simeon hold that what is going to happen is deemed already to have happened. Therefore the field is deemed a field of possession. The closing rule, augmented in T., tells us that priests' and Levites' inherited fields are not subject to the rules governing Israelites' property by inheritance.

7:1

A. They do not declare [the field of possession] sanctified less than two years before the year of Jubilee.

B. And they do not redeem it less than a year after the year of Jubilee.

C. [In redeeming the field] they do not reckon the months against the sanctuary.

D. But the sanctuary reckons the months [to its own advantage].

E.　　　He who sanctifies his field at the time of the Jubilee's [being in effect] [compare M. 8:1]

F.　　　pays the *fifty sheqels of silver [for every part of a field that suffices for] the sowing of a homer of barley.*

G.　　　[If] there were there crevices ten handbreadths deep or rocks ten handbreadths high, they are not measured with it.

H.　　　[If they were in height] less than this, they are measured with it.

I.　　　[If] one sanctified it two or three years before the Jubilee, he gives a *sela* and a *pondion* for each year.

J.　　　If he said, "Lo, I shall pay for each year as it comes," they do not pay attention to him.

K.　　　But: He pays the whole at once.

M. 7:1

The pericope encompasses two distinct units, A-D and E-K. The former consists of a unitary pair, A-B, C-D. The latter presents two separate items, E-F + D-H and I + J-K. But the whole flows smoothly from one item to the next, since information essential in the understanding of A-B is presented at I. E-F, for their part, simply repeat what Scripture says, and are inserted for the sake of G-H. If we were to omit G-H, on the other hand, then E-F provide a fine introduction for I (+ J-K). In all, it seems to me a good piece of tradental work.

The field of possession cannot be sanctified in the forty-eighth and forty-ninth year of the cycle, nor redeemed with a deduction in the first. Scripture speaks of years (Lev. 27:18), which must be at least two. If a person wants to redeem his field after the Jubilee, the reckoning in accord with the years remaining up to the Jubilee is made only at the end of a complete year. If he wants to redeem the field immediately following the Jubilee, he pays the full fifty *sheqels* (Lev. 27:17). The payment required for redeeming the field of possession at the outset of the Jubilee-cycle thus is fifty *shekels* for the specified area, that is, one *sheqel* per year (I). This sum then is diminished by one forty-ninth of the fifty *sheqels* as each year passes, one *sheqel* by one forty-ninth of the fifty *sheqels* as each year passes, one *sheqel* and one *pondion* (= 1/48th of a *sheqel*). The amount of money to be paid for redemption consists, therefore, of as many *sheqels* and *pondions* as the number of years up to the next Jubilee.

The point of C-D is that two years and three months, for example, are not deemed as two years to the disadvantage of the Temple. One year and eleven months are reckoned as one year, not two full years.

E-F brings us to the measurement of the field sufficient for the sowing of a *homer* of barley. When the Jubilee law is in force, the redemption price is paid as just now specified. (When it is not in force it is paid in accord with the value of the field.) All E-F say is what is stated by Lev. 27:16-17. G-H's point is that ridges or crevices do not go into the measurement of the specified area.

I goes over familiar ground. The fifty *selas* are paid for forty-nine years from one Jubilee to the next, a *sela* per year. The fiftieth *sela* is added, by having the forty-eight *pondions* of which it is made up divided among the forty-eight years. Thus the man pays a *sela* and a *pondion* per year, just as we have seen. J-K add the further qualification that the full sum must be paid at one time.

A. *They do not declare [the field of possession] sanctified less than two years before the year of Jubilee* [M. Ar. 7:1A] – [two years] of harvest crops [M. Ar. 9:1A].

B. As it is said, *Then the priest shall compute the money-value for it according to the years [that remain until the year of jubilee]* (Lev. 27:18).

C. Behold, if one sanctified it in the Jubilee year itself, lo, this is deemed sanctified.

T 4:8 Z p. 547, lines 21-23

A. *Years* (Lev. 27:18) – There are no fewer than two.

B. Or [may one hold: Just as they do not sanctify [a field of possession] less than two years [before the Jubilee], so they do not redeem [a field of possession which has been sanctified] less than two years [thereafter]?

C. Scripture states, *And a deduction shall be made from your Valuation* (Lev. 27:18) –

D. even [a single] year [M. Ar. 7:1B].

T. 4:9 Z p. 547, lines 23-24

A. You turn out to rule:

B. A Jubilee of forty-nine years requires forty-nine *selas* and forty-nine *pondions.*

C. [If] the sanctuary had the usufruct for ten or fifteen years, the owner deducts from it[s redemption price] a *sela* and a *pondion* per year.

D. [If] it [the sanctuary] enjoyed the usufruct for ten or fifteen years, he pays a *sela* and a *pondion* per year.

T. 4:10 Z p. 547, lines 24-27

A. *He who sanctifies his field at the time of the Jubilee's* [being in effect] *pays fifty sheqels of silver [for every part of a field that suffices for] the sowing of a homer of barley* [M. Ar. 7:1F].

B. [For every part of a field that suffices for] the sowing of a homer of barley – and not by measure.

C. All the same are a field in which one may sow a *kor* of seed, a field of trees, and a field of reeds – all are subject to this measure.

D. [If] they are less than this or more than this, one pays by reckoning.

T. 4:11 Z p. 547, lines 27-30

A.   *[If] there were these crevices ten handbreadths deep or rocks ten handbreadths high* [M. Ar. 7:1G],

B.   lo, *they are not* deemed sanctified and *measured with it.*

C.   *[If they were] less than this, they are measured with it* and are deemed sanctified [M. Ar. 7:1H-I].

T. 4:12 Z p. 547, lines 30-32

A.   The house and the hut and the tower and the dovecot which are in it, lo, they are measured with it.

B.   When they are redeemed, they are redeemed in the status of houses which are in courtyards.

C.   [If] one sanctified the field and then went and sanctified the tree, when he redeems, he redeems the tree by itself and the field by itself.

T. 4:13 Z p. 547, lines 32-33

T. 4:8 goes over the ground of M. 7:1A, linking it to M. 9:1A. At C, however, it derives form the cited proof a further rule, not pertinent to A. T. 4:9 gives the scriptural basis for the rules of M. 7:1A-B. T. 4:10 states the same proposition as M. 7:1I. T. 4:11-13 go over the ground of M., citing and glossing as indicated.

7:2

A.   All the same are the owner [of the field] and every [other] man [in regard to what is paid (M. 7:1I-K) for the redemption of the field].

B.   What is the difference between the owner and every other man?

C.   But: The owner pays the added fifth. And every other person does not pay the added fifth [M. 8:1].

M. 7:2

This unitary pericope restates the rule of Lev. 27:19: *If he who dedicates the field wishes to redeem it, then he shall add a fifth of the valuation in money to it.* If, therefore, there are twenty years remaining in the Jubilee cycle, the man pays twenty *selas* and twenty *pondions*, plus five more of each, twenty-five *selas* and twenty-five *pondions* in all. M. thus reads the verse to exclude the person who has not dedicated his own field but who wishes to redeem a field dedicated by someone else; he does not pay the added fifth.

7:3

A.   [If] he sanctified it and redeemed it, it does not go forth from his domain on the Jubilee.

B.   [If] his son redeemed it, it goes forth to his father on the Jubilee.

C.   [If] someone else redeemed it, or one of the relatives, and he redeemed it from his domain, it does not go forth from his domain in the Jubilee.

D.   [If] one of the priests redeemed it, and lo, it is in his [the priest's] domain, he may not say, "Since it goes forth to the priests in the Jubilee, and since, lo, it is in my domain, lo, it is mine."

E.   But: It goes forth to all his brethren, the priests.

M. 7:3

The pericope is deceptively smooth, since A-C are not continued as to problem or principle by D-E. The first three rules do belong together. A is obvious, setting the stage for the others. The point is that if the original owner of the field redeems the field, he retains possession at the Jubilee. If the son redeems it, the father repossesses it. If the original owner, C, redeemed it from the person who redeemed it from the sanctuary, we invoke once more the rule of A.

D's problem is separate. Scripture is clear that a field which has not been redeemed by the Jubilee year remains in the possession of the priesthood. D excludes the claim of a particular priest to acquire the field. What has happened is that the man has not redeemed the field. A priest has done so. The priest cannot claim the right to keep the field, D. That is, if an Israelite, not the owner, had redeemed the field, the priests would have received it in the Jubilee year; this particular priest – so it is claimed – possesses it and has the right to keep it. That is not acceptable.

D.   [A field of possession:] *[If] one sanctified it and redeemed it, it does not go forth from his domain on the Jubilee* [M. Ar. 7:3A].

T. Ar. 4:13 Z p. 547, line 35

A.   *[If] his son redeemed it, it goes forth to his father on the Jubilee.*

B.   *[If] another person or one of his relatives redeemed it, [and] he redeemed it from his domain, it does not go forth from his domain on the jubilee* [M. Ar. 7:3B-C].

C.   You have nothing which leaves one's domain for that of the father in the case of provision [for the female slave] and of that for the Hebrew slave and of field of possession except in the case of the son alone.

T. 4:14 Z p. 547, lines 35-37

T. glosses M. as indicated.

7:4

A.   [If] the Jubilee arrived and it was not redeemed,

B.   "The priests enter into [possession of] it but pay its price," the words of R. Judah.

C.   R. Simeon says, "They enter, and they do not pay."

D.   R. Eliezer says, "They neither enter nor pay.

F.   "But: It is called an abandoned field until the second Jubilee.

F.   "[If] the second year of the Jubilee came and it was not redeemed, it is called a twice-abandoned field,

G.   "up to the third Jubilee.

H.   "The priests under no circumstances enter into possession until
          another has redeemed it."

                                    M. 7:4

The topic sentence, A, sets the stage for a tripartite apodosis, B, C,
and D. E-H flow from D. The issue is a field which has been dedicated,
but not redeemed either by the original owner or by someone else. Judah
assigns the field to the priests; but they pay the fifty *sheqels* for the
specified area. Simeon says the priests take possession without paying.
Eliezer's position is out of phase. He holds that the priests take
possession of a field at the Jubilee *only* if someone already has
redeemed it, H. Therefore, in the present case, A, the priests do not
take possession and of course do not pay the price, D. E, F, and G simply
spell out the status of the field for the next hundred years:

A.   *[If] the Jubilee arrived and it was not redeemed,*
B.   *"The priests enter into [possession of] it but pay its price," the*
          words of R. Judah.
C.   *R. Simeon says, "They enter and do not pay."*
D.   *R. Eleazer says: "They do not enter and do not pay.*
E.   *"But: It is called an abandoned field, until the second Jubilee.*
F.   *"If the second Jubilee came and it was not redeemed, it is called a*
          twice-abandoned field,
G.   *"up to the third Jubilee.*
H.   *"The priests under no circumstances enter into possession until*
          another will redeem it" [M. Ar. 7:4A-H].
I.   Under what circumstances?
J.   In the case of a field of possession of an Israelite.
K.   But in the case of a field which is purchased of an Israelite,
L.   they sanctify it any time that they want, and they redeem it any
          time that they want.
M.   [If] another person redeemed it, it goes forth to the [original]
          owner at the Jubilee.

                              T. 4:15 Z p. 547, lines 37-39,
                              p. 548, lines 1-4

T. distinguishes the field of possession from the field which is
purchased, K-M. On the reading, see *TR* II, p. 280.

                                    7:5

A.   He who purchases a field from his father, [if] his father died, and
          afterward he sanctified it, lo, it is deemed a field of possession
          (Lev. 27:16).
B.   [If] he sanctified it and afterward his father died,
C.   "lo, it is deemed a field which has been bought," the words of R.
          Meir.
D.   R. Judah and R. Simeon says, "It is deemed a field of possession.
          "Since it is said, *And if a field which he has bought which is not a*
          field of his possession (Lev. 27:22) –

E. "a field which is not destined to be a field of possession,

F. "which excludes this, which is destined to be a field of possession."

G. A field which has been bought does not go forth to the priests in the Jubilee,

H. for a man does not declare sanctified something which is not his own.

I. Priests and Levites sanctify (their fields) at any time and redeem them at any time, whether before the Jubilee or after the Jubilee.

M. 7:5

We recall (M. 3:2) that a field of possession differs from a field which has been purchased. The former is acquired by inheritance, the latter is bought. The former is subject to the fixed valuation of Lev. 27:16ff., the latter is evaluated in accord with its actual worth. The former if not redeemed by the Jubilee falls to the priests; the latter does not. Now we ask some secondary questions on the disposition of fields which may fall to one by inheritance but which also are purchased by the potential heir. A makes the basic point that if one purchases a field from his father but afterward will have inherited it in any case, then the field is deemed a field of possession. If after the father's death the man sanctifies the field, it falls into the category of a field he has acquired through inheritance, not purchase. B then asks the more interesting question: What if the man purchased it from the father and sanctified it. He has not then inherited the field. But he is *going* to acquire by inheritance what he already has acquired through purchase. Meir does not treat that which is going to happen as if it already has happened. Therefore if the man purchased the field and sanctified it before the death of the father, then at the time the field was sanctified, it is in the status only of a field which has been bought. Judah and Simeon take up the contrary position, for reasons which are specified nicely at E-F. G-H then tell us what difference is made between the field of possession and the one of purchase. Scripture, of course, states this same rule.

I (= Lev. 25:32) is distinct from the foregoing construction. It excludes priests and Levites from the Jubilee rule. They may redeem a field even after the Jubilee year. I do not understand why it has been placed here.

A. A field which has gone forth from the domain of the sanctuary to the priests in the Jubilee year, lo, it is in the status of a field of possession of an Israelite.

B. The priests and Levites in a field in a city of their dwelling sanctify [property] any time they like.

C. And they redeem property at any time [that they like].

D.   [If] another person redeemed it, it returns to the owner at the Jubilee.

T. 4:16 Z p. 548, lines 4-6

A.   A field which has gone forth from the domain of the sanctuary to the priests, lo, it is deemed equivalent to the field of possession of an Israelite.

B.   The priests and Levites in the field of their possession in the cities of their dwelling sanctify [property] at any time that they like and redeem it at any time that they like.

C.   [If]] another person redeemed it, it goes forth to the [original] owner at the Jubilee.

T. 4:17 Z p. 548, lines 6-8

A.   A priest who inherited the estate of the father of his mother who was a Levite [*TR* II, p. 282],

B.   and so the son of a Levite, a Netin, a Mamzer who inherited a field of his fathers,

C.   lo, it is deemed to be equivalent to a field of possession of an Israelite.

T. 4:18 Z p. 548, lines 8-10

T. 4:16 clarifies M. 7:5I. T. 4:17 duplicates 4:16, correcting the scribal error at T. 4:16A. Property which comes to a priest in the specified way is not equivalent to fields of possession (inheritance) and is subject to the rules governing property of Israelites. This is in contrast to T. 4:16B-D.

Part Two

"ITS CONTOURS ARE A REFLECTION OF LIFE ITSELF"
Steinsaltz

"...THE TALMUD IS, IN TRUTH, ABOUT ALL THINGS"
Wieseltier

FALSE FOR BABYLONIAN TALMUD TRACTATE
ARAKHIN CHAPTERS ONE, FOUR, AND FIVE

3

Bavli Arakhin
Chapter One

Unit by unit, we ask these questions for the chapter at hand, in the language of Steinsaltz and Wieseltier:

1. Is it true that "The Talmud...deals with an overwhelmingly broad subject – the nature of all things according to the Torah. Therefore its contours are a reflection of life itself. It has no formal external order, but is bound by a strong inner connection between [sic!] its many diverse subjects."

2. Is it true that "...the Talmud is, in truth, about all things. There is no corner of human life and no corner of Jewish life into which the fastidious rabbis did not peer."

Accordingly, at the end of my descriptive-analytical comments, I shall simply register this question and answer it: Does this unit talk about "everything" or some few things? Can we explain why the Talmud includes everything that is before us – and therefore can we postulate that the authorship of the Bavli has excluded what it found irrelevant and included only what served its purpose?

1:1 A-G

A   [2A] All pledge the Valuation [of others] and are subject to the pledge of Valuation [by others],

B.   vow [the worth of another] and are subject to the vow [of payment of their worth by another]:

C.   priests and Levites and Israelites, women and slaves.

D.   A person of doubtful sexual traits and a person who exhibits traits of both sexes vow [the worth of another] and are subject to the vow [of payment of their worth by another], pledge the Valuation [of others], but are not subject to the pledge of Valuation by others,

E.   for evaluated is only one who is certainly a male or certainly a female.

F. A deaf-mute, an imbecile, and a minor are subject to the
    vow [of payment of their worth by another], and are subject
    to the pledge of Valuation by others, but do not vow the
    worth, and do not pledge the Valuation, of others,

G. for they do not possess understanding.

I.

A. [When the framer explicitly refers to] *all*, [in framing the Mishnah
    paragraph at hand, saying *All pledge....*,] what [classification of
    persons does he intend] to include, [seeing that in what follows, C,
    he lists the available classifications of persons in any event, and,
    further, at D-G specifies categories of persons that are excluded.
    Accordingly, to what purpose does he add the encompassing
    language, *all*, at the outset?]

B. It serves to encompass a male nearing puberty [who has not yet
    passed puberty. Such a one is subject to examination to
    determine whether he grasps the meaning of a vow, such as is
    under discussion. A child younger than the specified age, twelve
    years to thirteen, is assumed not to have such understanding, and
    one older is taken for granted to have it.]

C. [When the framer explicitly frames matters as *all*] *are subject to
    the pledge of Valuation*, what [classification of persons does he
    intend] to include?

D. It is to include a person who is disfigured or afflicted with a skin
    ailment.

E. [Why in any event should one imagine that persons of that
    classification would be omitted?] I might have supposed that,
    since it is written, "A vow...according to your Valuation" (Lev. 27:2),
    [with Scripture using as equivalent terms "vow" and "Valuation,"]
    the rule is that [only] those who possess an [intrinsic] worth [e.g.,
    whoever would be purchased for a sum of money in the
    marketplace, hence excluding the disfigured persons under
    discussion, who are worthless] also would be subject to a vow of
    Valution [at a fixed price, such as Scripture specified]. On the
    other hand, [I might have supposed that] whoever does not
    possess an [intrinsic] worth also would not be subject to a vow of
    Valuation. [Thus, according to this line of reasoning, I might think
    a person disfigured or afflicted with a skin ailment is not subject
    to the pledge of Valuation.]

F. Accordingly, [the formulation of the Mishnah passage at hand]
    tells us, [to the contrary, that a pledge of Valuation is not
    dependent upon the market value of the person subject to that
    pledge. The Valuation represents an absolute charge and is not
    relative to the subject's market value.]

G. [How does Scripture so signify? When the framer of Scripture
    refers at Lev. 27:2 to] "persons," [the meaning is that a pledge of
    Valuation applies] to anyone at all.

H. [When the framer of the Mishnah, further, states that *all*] *vow* [the
    worth of another], what [classification of persons does he thereby
    intend] to include [seeing that at C we go over the same matter,
    specifying those who may make such a vow]?

I. It is necessary for him [to specify *all* to indicate that *all* also applies to] those concerning whom such a vow is taken.

J. [Therefore, when the framer specifies that all] are subject to a vow, what [classification of persons does he thereby intend] to include?

K. [Here matters are not so self-evident, for] if the intention is to include a person of doubtful sexual traits and a person who exhibits the traits of both sexes, both of these classifications are explicitly stated [in the formulation of the Mishnah passage itself].

L. And if the intention is to include a deaf-mute, an imbecile, and a minor, these classifications also are explicitly stated. [So what can have been omitted in the explicit specification of the pertinent classification, that the framer of the Mishnah passage found it necessary to make use of such amplificatory language as *all*?]

M. If, furthermore, the intent was to include an infant less than a month old, that classification also is explicitly included [below].

N. If, furthermore, the intent was to include an idolator, that classification furthermore is explicitly included as well. [Accordingly, what classification of persons can possibly have been omitted in the framing of the Mishnah passage at hand, that the author found it necessary to add the emphatic inclusionary language to imply that further categories, beyond those made explicit, are in mind?]

O. In point of fact, [the purpose of adding the emphatic language of inclusion] was to encompass an infant less than a month in age.

P. [The framer of the passage] taught [that such a category is included by use of the word all] and then he went and stated the matter explicitly [to clearly indicate the inclusion of that category].

II.

A. [When, at M. Men. 9:8, we find the formulation], *All lay hands [on a beast to be slaughtered, that is, including not only the owner of the beast, who set it aside and consecrated it for the present sacrificial purpose, but also some other party]*, whom do we find included [by the inclusionary language, *all* of M. Men. 9:8]?

B. [It is used to indicate] the inclusion of the heir [of the owner of the beast who consecrated it and subsequently died. The heir of the deceased owner may take his place *vis-à-vis* his beast, and lay his hands on the beast, and so derive benefit from the sacrifice of that beast, even though he did not originally designate it as holy].

C. And that inclusion does not accord with the position of R. Judah [who maintains that, since Scripture specifies at Lev. 1:3 that the person who has designated the beast as a holy sacrifice "shall lay hands on it," excluded are all other parties, who did not designate the beast as holy. Only the owner of the beast may lay hands, and no one else. In so formulating the rule by using the inclusionary language, *all*, the framer of the passage has indicated that he rejects the position of Judah].

D. [And when, at M. Tem. 1:1, we find the formulation,] *All effect an act of substitution* [so consecrating the beast that is supposed to take the place of the originally consecrated beast, in line with Lev. 27:10, but leaving that originally consecrated beast in the status of consecration nonetheless], what category [of person] do we find included [by the use of such language]?

E.   [Once more], the use of such language indicates the inclusion of the heir [of the owner of the beast, who originally consecrated it and died before sacrificing it, just as at B, above].

F.   And that inclusion once more does not accord with the position of R. Judah [for Lev. 27:10 states, "*He* shall not alter it...," thus referring solely to the owner of the beast, and not to an heir or any other third party].

G.   [Now the statements just given accord with] that which has been taught [in a tradition external to the Mishnah but deriving from authorities named in the Mishnah], as follows:

H.   An heir lays hands [on a beast originally consecrated by the deceased], an heir effects an act of substitution [in regard to a beast originally consecrated by the deceased].

I.   R. Judah says, "An heir does not lay on hands, an heir does not effect an act of substitution."

J.   What is the scriptural basis for the position of R. Judah?

K.   "His offering..." (Lev. 3:2, 7, 13: "He shall lay his hand upon the head of his offering") – and not the offering that was set aside by his father.

L.   From the rule governing the end of the process of consecrating [the laying on of hands] [R. Judah further] derives the rule governing the beginning of the process of consecrating a beast [e.g., through an act of substitution, which indicates that a given beast is substituted for, therefore shares the status, of another beast that already has been consecrated. In this way the beast put forward as a substitution is itself deemed to be sanctified.] [Accordingly, a single principle governs both stages in the sacrificial process, the designation of the beast as holy and therefore to be sacrificed, e.g., through an act of substitution, and the laying on of hands just prior to the act of sacrificial slaughter itself. Just as the latter action may be performed solely by the owner of the beast, who derives benefit from the act of sacrifice, so the former action likewise is effective only when the owner of the beast carries it out.]

M.   Accordingly, just as, at the end of the process of consecration, the heir does not lay on hands, so at the beginning of the process of consecration, an heir does not carry out an act of substitution.

N.   And as to the position of rabbis [*vis-à-vis* Judah, who maintain that the heir may do so, how do they read Scripture in such wise as to derive their view?]

O.   [Scripture states,] "And if changing, he shall change" (Lev. 27:10) [thus intensively using the same verb twice, with one usage understood to refer to the owner himself, the other usage to some closely related person].

P.   [The use of the verbal intensive therefore is meant] to include the heir, and, as before, we derive the rule governing the conclusion of the sacrificial process [with the laying on of hands] from the rule governing the commencement of the sacrificial process [the designation of the beast as holy, by its substitution for an already consecrated beast].

Q. Accordingly, just as, at the beginning of the process of consecration, the heir does carry out an act of substitution, so at the end of the process of consecration, the heir does lay on hands.

R. Now [given rabbis' reading of the relevant verses], how do these same rabbis deal with Scripture's three references to *"his* offering" [which in Judah's view makes explicit that only the owner of the beast lays hands on his beast, cf. Lev. 3:2, 7, 13]?

S. They require that specification of Scripture to lay down the rule that [an Israelite] lays hands on his sacrifice, but not on the sacrifice of an idolator, on his sacrifice and not on the sacrifice of his fellow:

T. on his sacrifice, further, to include all those who own a share in the sacrificial animal, according to each the right to lay hands upon the beast [of which they are partners].

U. And as to R. Judah? He does not take the view that all those who own a share in the sacrificial animal have a right to lay hands on the beast.

V. Alternatively, [one may propose that] he does maintain the stated position [concerning the partners in a sacrificial animal].

W. [But he derives the rule governing [2B] the idolator['s beast] and that of one's fellow from a single verse of Scripture [among the three verses that make explicit that one lays hands on *his* animal], leaving available for the demonstration of a quite separate proposition two [other] of these same [three] references.

X. [It follows, for Judah's position, that] one of these verses serves to indicate, *"His* offering" and not "the offering of his father," and another of the available verses then serves to include [among those who indeed may lay hands on the sacrificial beast] all shareholders, according to each of them the right to lay hands on the beast held in common partnership.

Y. [Further exploring the thesis of Judah about the scriptural basis for his view, exactly] how does R. Judah interpret the intensive verb used at Lev. 27:10, "And if changing, he shall change?"

Z. He requires that usage to include the participation of the woman [in the process of substitution, so that if a woman makes a statement effecting an act of substitution, that statement is as valid as if a man had made it].

AA. That [view of his reading] is in accord with the following tradition assigned to tannaitic authority:

BB. Since the entire formulation of the passage concerning an act of substitution speaks of the male, how in the end shall we include the female as well [so that an act of substitution of a woman is regarded as valid]?

CC. Scripture states, "And if changing, he shall change..." [The intensive language serves to include the woman.]

DD. And as to rabbis, [how do they prove the same position]?

EE. It is from the use of the inclusionary words, *and, if,* in the phrase, "And if changing..."

FF. And as to the view of R. Judah [in this same regard]?

GG. The usage, "And if...," in his view is not subject to exegesis at all [and yields no additional information about the rule under discussion. Accordingly, in order to prove that a woman is involved in the process of substitution, as much as a man, Judah must refer solely to the intensive verb construction.]

III.

A. All are obligated [to carry out the religious duty of dwelling in] a tabernacle [on the Festival of Tabernacles].

B. [When the framer of the foregoing statement makes explicit use of the inclusionary language, *all*], what [classification of persons is] encompassed, [that otherwise would have been omitted]?

C. It is to include a minor who does not depend upon his mother [but can take care of himself], in line with the following statement found in the Mishnah [M. Suk. 2:8:] *A child who does not depend upon his mother is liable to [carry out the religious duty of dwelling in a] tabernacle.*

D. All are liable [to carry out the religious duty of taking up] the palm branch [enjoined at Lev. 23:40].

E. [When the framer of the foregoing statement makes explicit use of the inclusionary language, *all*,] what [classification of persons is] included, [that otherwise would have been omitted]?

F. It is to include a minor who knows how to shake [the palm branch, so, with proper intention, making appropriate use of the holy object].

G. That is in line with the following statement found in the Mishnah [M. Suk. 3:15:] *A minor who knows how to shake [the palm branch with proper intention] is liable to [the religious duty of taking up] the palm branch.*

H. All are liable [to carry out the religious duty of affixing] fringes [to the corners of garments].

I. [When the framer of the foregoing statement makes explicit use of the inclusionary language, *all*,] what [classification of persons is] included, [that otherwise would have been omitted]?

J. It is to include a minor who knows how to cloak himself [in a garment, and so enters the obligation of affixing to said cloak the required fringes, cf. T. Hag. 1:2].

K. For it has been taught [at T. Hag. 1:2:] **A minor who knows how to cloak himself [in a garment] is liable to [affix to that garment the required show] fringes.**

L. All are liable [to carry out the religious duty of wearing] phylacteries.

M. [When the framer of the foregoing statement makes explicit use of the inclusionary language, *all*,] what [classification of persons is] encompassed, [that otherwise would have been omitted]?

N. It is to include a minor who knows how to take care of phylacteries [and therefore may be entrusted with them].

O. For it has been taught [at T. Hag. 1:2:] **As to a minor who knows how to take care of phylacteries, his father purchases phylacteries for him.**

IV.

A   *All are obligated [on the occasion of a pilgrim festival to bring] an appearance-offering [to the Temple and to sacrifice it there in honor of the festival, cf. M. Hag. 1:1].*

B.   [When the framer of the foregoing statement makes explicit use of the inclusionary language, *all*,] what [classification of persons is] included, [that otherwise would have been omitted]?

C   It is to include a person who is half-slave and half-free. [Such a person is subject to the stated liability of bringing an appearance-offering. But a person who is wholly a slave is exempt from the stated requirement of making the pilgrimage and bringing the offering.]

D.   But in the view of Rabina, who has made the statement that one who is half-slave and half-free [also] is exempt from the obligation of bringing an appearance-offering [in celebration of the pilgrim festival], [in his view] what [classification of persons] is included [by the specification that *all* are subject to the stated obligation]?

E   It is to include a person who is lame on the first day of the festival but is restored [to full activity] on the second day. [A lame person is exempt from the religious obligation of coming up to Jerusalem on the pilgrim festival, since he obviously cannot make the trip. If, however, as of the second day of the festival, the lame person should be healed, then, according to the formulation of the rule at hand, such a person would become obligated, retrospectively, to bring the required appearance-offering as of the first day.]

F.   [The foregoing statement rests on the position that on the successive days of the festival, one has the option of meeting an obligation incurred but not met on the earlier day. Thus if one did not make the required appearance-offering on the first day, he is obligated for it but also may make up for it on the later days of the festival. The obligation for one day pertains to, but then may be made up, on the days following, thus, on day three for day two, on day four for day three, and the like. Accordingly, at E we maintain first, that the person becomes obligated on the second day, and, second, that the obligation then is retroactive to the first. So he can make up what he owes. But the obligation to begin with likewise is retroactive. On day two he became obligated for an appearance-offering to cover day one. Accordingly, what we have just proposed] fully accords with the position of him who said that [offerings made on] all [of the days of the festival] serve as a means of carrying out the obligations incurred on each one of them [as just now explained].

G.   But in the view of him who says that all of the days of the festival [may serve to make up only for an obligation] incurred on the first day [of the festival alone, so that, first, one does not incur an obligation on a later day of the festival affecting what one owes for an earlier day of the festival, and so that, second, if one is not obligated to bring an appearance-offering on the first day of the festival, he is not obligated to do so on any later day of the festival], what [classification of persons] is included [by use of the inclusionary language, *all*]?

H.   It serves to include a person who is blind in one eye. [A person blind in both eyes is exempt from the appearance-offering on the pilgrim festival. One fully sighted, of course, is liable. The intermediate category then is dealt with in the stated formulation].

I.   Now that view would not accord with the following teaching in the authority of sages of the Mishnah, as it has been taught:

J.   Yohanan b. Dahabbai says in the name of R. Judah, "One who is blind in one eye is exempt from the religious duty of bringing an appearance-offering, for it is said, 'He will see...he will see...' (Ex. 23:14) [reading the scriptural language not as 'make an appearance,' but, with a shift in the vowels, 'will see,' cf. T. Hag. 1:1].

K.   "[The proposed mode of reading the verse at hand yields the following consequence:] Just as one comes to see [the face of the Lord], so he comes to be seen. Just as one sees with two eyes, so one is seen with two eyes" [cf. T. Hag. 1:1F-H]. [The exegesis then excludes a person blind in one eye.]

L.   If you prefer, [however, we may revert to the earlier proposal, and] state: Indeed, [the use of the inclusionary language *all* is meant] to include a person who is half slave and half free.

M.   And now as to the question you raised above [D], that that position would not accord with the opinion of Rabina, that indeed poses no problem.

N.   [Why not?] The formulation at hand, [which prohibits the half-slave half-free man from bringing the necessary offering] is in line with the original formulation of the Mishnah law [prior to the debate, cited presently, between the Houses of Shammai and Hillel]. The other formulation [which permits and hence requires the half-slave person, half-free person, in the intermediate status, to bring the appearance-offering] is in line with the posterior formulation of the Mishnah law.

O.   For we have learned [at M. Git. 4:5:]

P.   *"He who is half-slave and half-free works for his master one day and for himself one day," the words of the House of Hillel.*

Q.   *Said to them the House of Shammai, "You have taken good care of his master, but of himself you have not taken care.*

R.   *"To marry a slave-girl is not possible, for half of him after all is free [and free persons may marry only other free persons].*

S.   *"[To marry] a free woman is not possible, for half of him after all is a slave [and slaves may marry only slaves].*

T.   *"Shall he refrain?*

U.   *"But was not the world made only for procreation, as it is said, 'He created it not a waste, he formed it to be inhabited' (Isa. 45:18).*

V.   *"But: For the good order of the world, "they force his master to free him.*

W.   *"And he [the slave] writes him a bond covering half his value."*

X.   *And the House of Hillel reverted to teach in accord with the opinion of the House of Shammai.* [Accordingly, the law prior to the reversion specified at X treated one who is half-slave and half-free as in a fixed category, and such a one would not bring an appearance-offering, since he was partially a slave. But after the reversion, one who was half-slave and half-free could leave that interstitial category easily and so would not be regarded as essentially a slave. Such a one then would be obligated to bring the appearance-offering, there being no permanent lord over him except for the Lord God.]

V.

A. All are obligated [to the religious duty of hearing] the sounding of the ram's horn [on the New Year], [T. R.H. 4:1].

B. [When the framer of the passage makes use of the inclusionary language, *all,*] what [classification of persons does he thereby] include?

C. It is to include a minor who has reached the age [at which he is able to benefit from] instruction.

D. For we have learned [in a teaching attributed to the authority of Mishnah sages:] They do not prevent a minor from sounding the ram's horn on the festival day [cf. B. Yoma 72a].

VI.

A. All are subject to the religious obligation of hearing the reading of the Scroll of Esther, [T. Meg. 2:7A-B]

B. *All are suitable to read the Scroll of Esther aloud [for the community, thereby fulfilling the religious obligation of all those who are present,* M. Meg. 2:4].

C. [When the framer of the passage makes use of the inclusionary language, all,] what [classification of persons does he thereby] include [3A]?

D. It is to include women [who may read the Scroll of Esther aloud for the community and thereby carry out the obligation of all present to do so].

E. This view accords with the position of R. Joshua b. Levi. For R. Joshua b. Levi said, "Women are liable [to the religious duty of] the reading of the Scroll of Esther, for they too were included in the miracle [of redemption from Israel's enemies, celebrated on Purim, cf. B. Meg. 4a]."

VII.

A. All are liable to the religious duty of saying Grace in public quorum [if they have eaten together. They thus may not say Grace after meals by themselves, if a quorum of three persons is present. In that circumstance a public recitation, involving a call to Grace, is required, T. Ber. 5:15.]

B. [When the framer of the rule uses the inclusionary language,] what [classificaton of persons] does he mean to include?

C. He means to include women and slaves.

D. For it has been taught [in a teaching bearing the authority of Mishnah teachers:] Women say Grace in public as a group [unto] themselves, and slaves do likewise. [Accordingly, both

classifications of persons are subject to the liability of saying a
public Grace should a quorum of appropriate persons be
present].

VIII.

A.   All join in the public saying of Grace [responding to the call to say
      Grace].

B.   [When the framer of the ruler uses the cited inclusionary
      language,] what [classification of persons] does he mean to
      include?

C.   It is to include a minor who has knowledge on his own concerning
      Him to whom they say a blessing [in the Grace after meals].

D.   That is in line with what R. Nahman said, "He who knows to
      Whom they say a blessing [in the Grace after meals] – they
      include such a one in the public call to say the Grace after meals."

IX.

A.   *All are subject to becoming unclean by reason of the flux*
      [specified at Lev. 15:1ff., M. Zab. 2:1].

B.   [When the framer of the rule uses the cited inclusionary
      language,] what [classification of persons does he mean to]
      include?

C.   It is to include an infant one day old [who, should he produce a
      flux, would be deemed subject to flux uncleanness under
      appropriate circumstances. This form of genital uncleanness is
      not limited to an adult.]

D.   For it has been taught [in a teaching bearing the authority of
      Mishnah sages:] "[When any] man [produces flux out of his
      flesh]" (Lev. 15:2).

E.   "Now why does the author of Scripture state, "When any man..."
      [so indicating an inclusion of some category beyond man]?

F.   "It is to include even an infant a day old, who thus is subject to the
      uncleanness of flux, "the words of R. Judah.

G.   R. Ishmael, the son of R. Yohanan b. Beroqah, says, "It is hardly
      necessary [to interpret Scripture in such wise]. Lo, [Scripture] says,
      'And any of them who has an issue, whether it is male or female'
      (Lev. 15:33).

H.   "[The sense is], 'Male,' meaning whoever is male, whether minor
      or adult. 'Female' [means], whoever is female, whether minor or
      adult. [Both categories, minor and adult, male and female, fall
      within the classification of those subject to uncleanness through
      flux. Scripture is explicit in this matter, without the necessity of
      interpreting the language important in Judah's view.]

I.   "If that is the case, then on what account does [the author of
      Scripture] use the language, 'If any man...'? [The author of] the
      Torah made use of the language of common speech [and did not
      mean to provide occasions for exegesis of minor details of
      formulation]."

X.

A.   All are subject to being made unclean through corpse
      uncleanness.

B.　[When the framer of the foregoing statement uses the inclusionary word, *all*,] what [classification of persons does he thereby] to include?

C.　It is to include a minor.

D.　[How so?] I might have proposed that [when Scipture states,] "When a man becomes unclean and does not undertake a rite of purification" (Num. 19:20), [the meaning of the author of Scripture is,] "a man indeed [is subject to the law of corpse uncleanness] but a minor is not [subject to that same law]."

E.　Accordingly [by using the inclusive language *all are subject*] [the framer of the passage] informs us [that this is not the case].

F.　[And indeed the same passage continues,] "And upon the persons that were there" (Num. 19:18), [Thus using the language, "persons," which also is inclusive and encompasses a minor, we are able to prove the besought point. Accordingly, we must ask for some other exegetical value to be associated with the language, "When a man...." For we now realize that the minor is included by the language, "persons," and thus we recognize that the further word choice, "man," serves to exclude some classification. So we need to find out – as the passage unfolds – what classification of persons is included by the one, yet excluded by the other, or for what purpose an inclusion and an exclusion are joined. It is to that secondary issue that we now proceed.]

G.　[Accordingly, we ask,] But what [sort of] exclusion [is effected by the language,] "Man" [used at Num. 19:20]?

H.　It serves to exclude a minor from the penalty of extirpation [should he violate the law governing cultic cleanness. Although a minor is expected to observe the laws of flux he would not suffer the penalty specified at Num. 19:20 if he failed to do so, since that verse speaks only of an adult.]

XI.

A.　*All are subject to becoming unclean through the skin ailment* [M. Neg. 3:1A].

B.　[When the author of the foregoing statement uses the inclusionary language, *all*,] what [category of persons does he mean to] include?

C.　[He means] to include a minor.

D.　[How so?] I might have entertained the proposition [that the language of Scripture], "A man afflicted by the skin disease" (Lev. 13:44), [means] that a man indeed [is subject to the uncleanness under discussion], but a minor is not [subject to that same form of uncleanness].

E.　Accordingly, [by using the language *all are subject*, the framer of the passage] informed us [that that is not the case].

F.　Now may I claim [to the contrary] that that indeed *is* the case, [that Scripture intends to exclude a child from the form of uncleanness at hand]?

G.　[No, I may not. For Scripture states,] "As to a person, when there will be on the skin of his flesh..." (Lev. 13:2), [meaning a person], under all circumstances [whether adult or minor].

H.   [If that is the case, then] what need do I have for the explicit reference to a man [at Lev. 13:44]?

I.   It is to accord with the following teaching in the name of authorities of the Mishnah:

J.   "A man [afflicted by] skin disease" (Lev. 13:44).

K.   I know only that a man is subject to the stated skin ailment. How do I know [that the same skin ailment affects] a woman?

L.   When [the author of the Torah] states, "*And* the one afflicted by skin disease," lo, [by using the word, *and*, the Author indicates that] subject to the rule are two [classifications of persons, hence both male and female].

M.   Why then [does the author] specify, "...man"?

N.   It [is to speak to a matter that comes] later [in the same passage, namely, Lev. 13:45, that the one afflicted by the skin disease tears his clothing and messes up his hair. The point, in particular, is that] a man tears his clothing and messes up his hair, and a woman does not tear her clothing and mess up her hair [should she be afflicted by the skin ailment].

XII.

A.   All examine cases of the skin ailment.

B.   *All are suitable to examine cases of the skin ailment* [M. Neg. 3:1B].

C.   [When the framer of the foregoing statement used the inclusionary language, *all*,] what [classification of persons did he mean] to include?

D.   It was to include [among those suitable to examine cases of the skin ailment even] those who are not expert in such matters and in the [various] classifications among which skin ailments are divided [cf. T. Neg. 1:1C].

E.   But has not an authority stated, "[If] one is not expert in them and in the classifications among which skin ailments are divided, he [should] *not* examine [cases of] the skin ailment"?

F.   Said Rabina, "[The contradiction between the statements at D and E] does not pose a problem. The former statement refers to someone who understands the matter when it is explained to him, while the latter speaks of one who, even when people explain to him, still will not understand the matter."

XIII.

A.   *All are suitable to mix [together the ashes of the red cow when it is burned (Num. 19:1ff.) with the requisite water and so to produce the purification water required for purifying one who has become unclean by reason of corpse uncleanness* (M. Par. 5:4).

B.   [When the framer of the passage at hand uses the inclusionary language, *all*,] what [classification of persons does he mean] to include?

C.   In the view of R. Judah [cited below], it is to include a minor, and in the view of rabbis [of the same passage] it is to include a woman.

D.   For we have learned in the Mishnah [at M. Par. 5:4]: *All [classifications of persons] are suitable to mix [the ashes and the* water], except for a deaf-mute, an imbecile, and a minor. [The Talmud assumes this statement reflects the view of rabbis.]

E. *R. Judah declares a minor valid, but invalidates a woman and a person who exhibits the sexual characteristics of both sexes.*

XIV.

A. *All are valid to sprinkle [purification water on one requiring the rite of purification].*

B. [When the framer of the passage at hand uses the inclusionary language, *all,*] what [classification of persons does he mean] to include?

C. It is to include an uncircumcized [person], and that accords with the position of R. Eleazar.

D. For R. Eleazar has stated, "An uncircumcized [person] who sprinkled [purification water] – his act of sprinkling is valid."

XV.

A. *All may carry out a rite of slaughter [of an animal for secular use of the meat.* The Mishnah repeats this statement twice, once at M. Hul. 1:1 and a second time at M. Hul. 1:2.]

B. [When the framer of the passage at hand uses the inclusionary language, *all,*] what [classification of persons does he mean] to include?

C. The first time [at M. Hul 1:1], he means to include a Samaritan, the second time [at M. Hul. 1:2], he means to include an apostate Israelite. [Both of these categories are assumed to fulfill the dietary rules and hence may carry them out.]

XVI.

A. *All may impose the requirement of emigrating [from the Exile to] the Land of Israel* [M. Ket. 13:11].

B. [When the framer of that statement uses the inclusionary language, *all,*] what [classification of persons does he mean] to include?

C. [3B] He means to encompass slaves. [If a person overseas owns a circumcized slave whom he wishes to sell, the slave may impose upon the master the requirement that the sale take place only in the Land of Israel.]

D. But in the view of him who repeats the tradition at hand in such wise as to make explicit reference to slaves [along with others specified, cf. M. Ket. 13:11 in Albeck, all of whom may impose the requirement of emigrating from the Exile to the Land of Israel], what [classification of persons is to be] included [by the formulation using the inclusionary language, *all*]?

E. It is meant to encompass [a move from] a lovely home [in the Exile] to a mean hovel [in the Land of Israel].

F. [And when the framer of the same passage uses the language,] *But all may not remove [a person from the Land of Israel to the Exile,* M. Ket. 13:11], what [classification of persons does he mean] to include?

G. It is to include a slave who fled from overseas to the Land [of Israel].

H.   *All may impose the requirement of going up [to dwell] in Jerusalem* [M. Ket. 13:11].

I.   [When the framer of that statement uses the inclusionary language, *all*, he means] to include [one who wishes to move] from a lovely home [in some town in the Land of Israel other than Jerusalem] to a mean hovel [in Jerusalem].

J.   [When the framer of the same passage uses the passage,] *But all may not remove [a person from Jerusalem to some other town in the Land of Israel*, M. Ket. 13:11], what [classification of cases does he mean] to include?

K.   It would be a case in which one proposed to move from a mean hovel [in Jerusalem] to a lovely home [outside of Jerusalem].

XVII.

A.   [The framer now returns to the statement made at III.A.] All are obligated [to dwell during the days of the Festival of Tabernacles] in a tabernacle, [specifically including] priests, Levites, Israelites.

B.   [The foregoing statement is] self-evident [and hardly requires specification, for] if these classifications of persons are not subject to the stated obligation, then who [in the world] would be subject to it!

C.   [We now proceed to explain why one of the stated categories of person, drawing in its wake the other two, must be explicitly included in the formulation of the rule.] It was necessary to make reference to priests. [Why so?]

D.   It is conceivable that I might have reasoned as follows: We know that it is written, "You will dwell in tabernacles" (Lev. 23:42), and [in that connection] a master has explained that dwelling in the tabernacle for seven days is comparable to an ordinary state of habitation, so that, just as under ordinary conditions of habitation, a man lives with his wife, so in the case of the tabernacle, a man should dwell with his wife.

E.   [What follows from that fact is simple.] Since priests bear the obligation of carrying on the sacred service [in the Temple], [we might suppose that] they should be exempt from the obligation of dwelling in the tabernacle, [for they cannot do so in the accepted manner, with their wives. Since they must go to the Temple to participate in the rite, they also cannot remain with their wives for the entire period at hand. Accordingly, one might have imagined that priests are exempt from the religious requirement of dwelling in the tabernacle.]

F.   [The framer of the passage makes explicit reference to priests] so as to inform us that, while priests are exempt at the time of their service in the Temple from the religious duty of dwelling in the tabernacle, when they are not engaged in the Temple service, they indeed are obligated to do so [since at this time they can fulfill the obligation in the proper manner].

G.   This indeed accords with the rule governing those who are engaged in travel.

H. For a master has stated, those who are engaged in travel by day are exempt by day from the religious requirement of dwelling in a tabernacle but obligated by night.

XVIII.

A. [The framer returns to the statement made at III.H.] All are obligated to carry out the religious duty of [affixing to their garments] show-fringes: priests, Levites, Israelites.

B. [The foregoing statement is] self-evident [and hardly requires specification, for if these classifications of persons are not obligated, then who in the world would be]?

C. It was necessary to make the specification at hand on account of the priests.

D. [How so?] I might have reasoned as follows: Since it is written, "You will not wear hybrid fabrics [e.g., a garment made from both wool and flax which derive from different categories, vegetable and animal, respectively]....You will make twisted cords [that is, show-fringes] for yourself" (Deut. 22:11, 12).

E. [From the juxtaposition of the previous two verses, the framer reasons as follows:] As to one who in no way enjoys remission of the prohibition against wearing hybrid fabrics in his clothing, he is obligated to observe the religious duty of wearing show-fringes.

F. Thus, since priests [under cultic circumstances] enjoy remission of the prohibition against wearing hybrid fabrics in their garments [Ex. 39:29 is understood as specifying that the priest wears linen and wool cloth, one might reason that] they ought not to be subject to the religious duty of wearing show-fringes [on their garments].

G. Accordingly, [by phrasing the matter to make explicit reference to the priesthood, the author] informs us [that that is not the case].

H. Accordingly, while during the time of their service in the cult, they enjoy a remission [of the stated taboo], at other times they do not.

XIX.

A. All are obligated [to carry out the religious duty of wearing] phylacteries: priests, Levites, and Israelites.

B. [The specification of the three categories is hardly required, for the rule affecting them] is self-evident.

C. [No,] it was necessary to make the explicit specification at hand on account of the priests [in the tripartite formula].

D. [How so?] I might have reasoned as follows: Since it is written, "And you shall bind them for a sign upon your hand, and they shall be for frontlets between your eyes," (Deut. 6:8).

E. [I might conclude that] whoever is subject to the religious duty [of putting a phylactery] upon the hand [arm] also is subject to the religious duty of placing a phylactery upon the] head.

F. So, [it would follow], since priests are not subject to the religious duty of placing the phylactery upon the hand,

G. (for it is written, "[His linen garments] he shall place [directly upon] his flesh," (Lev. 6:3), meaning that nothing should interpose between [the linen garment] and his flesh [thus excluding the

possibility of his placing a phylactery upon his arm, for it would
interpose between the garment and his flesh],)

H.   I might therefore conclude that priests likewise should not be
subject to the religious duty of placing a phylactery also upon the
head.

I.   Accordingly, [by framing the passage as he has, the author] has
informed us that that is not the case.

J.   For [the phylactery placed upon one limb] does not form a
necessary precondition [for placing the phylactery upon the other
limb. The two are separate religious duties, and if one cannot do
the one, he remains liable to the other.]

K.   This accords with what we have learned in the Mishnah [at M.
Men. 3:7] *The phylactery of the hand [arm] is not indispensable to
the one of the head, and the one of the head is not indispensable
to the one of the hand.*

L.   Now what [really] differentiates the [priest's obligation with
respect to the two types of phylacteries]? For concerning [the
phylactery] to be placed on the hand it is written, "[His linen
garment] he shall place [directly] upon his flesh [implying that a
priest may not interpose the phylactery between his arm and his
garment]" (Lev. 6:3). Concerning the phylactery of the head, it
likewise is written, "And you will place the mitre upon his head"
(Ex. 29:6). [Would not the phylactery on the head interpose
between the hair of the head and the mitre just as the phylactery
on the hand would interpose between the arm and the linen
garment? Why then is the priest permitted to wear a phylactery
upon his head, while he may not wear one on his arm?]

M.   It has been taught: His hair was visible between the plate and the
mitre, where he placed his phylactery.

XX.

A.   [The framer comments upon the statement made above at V.A.]
**All are liable [to carry out the religious duty of hearing] the
sound of the ram's horn, [inclusive of] priests, Levites, and
Israelites [T. R.H. 4:1].**

B.   [The inclusion of the three castes] is self-evident.

C.   [Nonetheless,] it was necessary [to frame matters in such a way]
on account of the priests [in particular].

D.   [How so?] I might have imagined the following argument: Since it
is written, "You will have a day for sounding [the ram's horn]"
(Num. 29:1), one who is subject [to hear] the sounding [of the
ram's horn] only one day [in the year] is liable [to carry out the
stated religious duty].

E.   But as to the priests, since they are subject [to the religious duty
of] hearing the sounding [of the ram's horn] throughout the year,
its being written, "And you will sound the trumpets over your
burnt-offerings" (Num. 10:10), I might have maintained that they
are not liable [to the hearing of the sounding of the ram's horn on
the New Year in particular].

F.   But are the two statements parallel [that such reasoning is in
order]? For there, "trumpets," while here, "a ram's horn" [is what

is specified. Accordingly, the two matters really are not parallel anyhow, and the proposed reason for the formulation at A does not stand.]

G. [Nonetheless, the inclusion of the priests at A remains] necessary. [How so?] I might have imagined the following argument: Since we have learned [at M. R.H. 3:5], *The day on which the Jubilee year begins is equivalent to the New Year's [day in the liturgy as to] the sounding of the ram's horn and also as to the blessings [said in the prayers of both days],* [I might have imagined that] whoever is subject to the religious duties governing the Jubilee Year also is subject to the religious duties governing the New Year, and whoever is not subject to the religious duties governing the Jubilee Year is not subject to the religious duties governing the New Year.

H. Now, since the priests are not subject to the religious duties governing the Jubilee Year, for we have learned [at M. Ar. 9:8], *"Priests and Levites [but not others] may sell and redeem property at all times [inclusive of the Jubilee Year],"* [4A] I might have maintained that they also should not be held liable for carrying out the religious duties affecting the New Year (inclusive of hearing the sound of the ram's horn].

I. [The cited formulation, A] serves, therefore, to inform us that even while they are not liable to the religious duty of restoring real estate to the original owners [a duty of the Jubilee Year], they nonetheless are liable to the [other obligation in the Jubilee Year] of remitting debts and releasing slaves.

XXI.

A. [The framer now takes up the statement above at VI.A.] **All are subject to carry out the religious obligation of hearing the reading of the Scroll of Esther, [inclusive of] priests, Levites, and Israelites** [T. Meg. 2:7 A-B].

B. [The inclusion of the three castes] is self-evident.

C. [Nonetheless,] it was necessary [to frame matters in such a way on account of the priests in particular].

D. [In so stating matters, the framer wishes to indicate] that they must leave off their [sacred] service [at the altar, in order to hear the public reading of the Scroll of Esther].

E. And that view conforms to what Rab Judah said that Samuel said, for Rab Judah said that Samuel said, "Priests in connection with their sacred service [at the altar], Levites in connection with their [singing on] the platform, and Israelites [attending the Temple service as] the delegation [from their particular village, all must] leave off [the performance of their holy] service in order to listen to the public reading of the Scroll of Esther.

XXII.

A. **All are subject to the religious obligation of saying Grace in public quorum if they have eaten together,** [as expained at VII.A], [inclusive of] **priests, Levites, and Israelites** [T. Ber. 5:15].

B. [The inclusion of the three castes] is self-evident.

C.   [Nonetheless,] it was necessary to frame matters in such a way [on
       account of the priests in particular,] in a case in which the group
       had eaten Holy Things.

D.   [How so?] I might have imagined the following argument: "And
       they shall eat those [Holy] Things with which atonement has been
       effected" (Ex. 29:33), has the All-Merciful stated [in Scripture],
       indicating that [the present act of eating constitutes an act of]
       atonement.

E.   [But in regard to the obligation of saying Grace, the All-Merciful
       said only that "You shall eat and be satisfied and say a blessing"
       (Dt. 8:10) implying that one only need say Grace when eating in
       order to satisfy one's hunger and not when eating as an act of
       atonement. It would seem, therefore, that priests are exempt
       from Grace when eating for atonement purposes.]

F.   [Accordingly, it was necessary] to indicate otherwise [namely that
       with regard to that which the All-Merciful has said, "You shall eat
       and be satisfied [and say a blessing]," even [priests who are eating
       for the purposes of atonement] are included.

XXIII.

A.   **All are liable to join in the public saying of Grace
       [responding to the call to say Grace, as explained at VII.A,
       inclusive of] priests, Levites, and Israelites** [T. Ber. 5:15].

B.   [The inclusion of the three castes] is self-evident.

C.   [Nonetheless,] it was necessary [to frame matters in such a way]
       on account of the case of priests who ate food in the status of
       priestly rations or Holy Things, while [at the same meal] a non-
       priest ate food in secular [not consecrated] status.

D.   I might have imagined the following argument: since, if the non-
       priest had wished to eat along with the priest [out of the food that
       the priest was eating], he could indeed not have done so, the
       [priest] therefore should not join with him [in responding to the
       public call to form a quorum to say Grace] since clearly they did
       not share a meal.

E.   [But that argument is invalid, and thus the framer of A] has
       informed us, [in framing matters as indicated that the priest must
       join him in saying Grace. This is justified on the basis of the
       following consideration:] since if it is the case that the non-priest
       could not have eaten [the food of] the priest, the priest,
       nonetheless, may perfectly well eat [the food of] the non-priest,
       [the consequence is that all parties join together in the common
       quorum].

XXIV.

A.   *All pledge the Valuation [of others] [inclusive of] priests, Levites,
       and Israelites* [M. Ar. 1:1A, C].

B.   [The inclusion of the three castes] is self-evident.

C.   [Nonetheless,] said Raba, "It was necessary [to frame matters in
       such a way] on account of the opinion of Ben Bukhri."

D.   For we have learned [at M. Sheq. 1:4]:

E.   *Said R. Judah, "Testified Ben Bukhri in Yabneh: 'Any priest who
       pays the "sheqel" does not sin.'*

F.   *"Said to him Rabban Yohanan ben Zakkai, 'Not so. But any priest who does not pay the 'sheqel' does sin.*

G.   *"'But the priests expound this scriptural verse for their own benefit: And every meal-offering of the priest shall be wholly burned, it shall not be eaten (Lev. 6:23).*

H.   *"'Since the "omer", two loaves, and show bread are ours, how [if we contribute] are they to be eaten?'"*

I.   [We now spell out the relationship between the opinion of Ben Bukhri, that the priests do not pay the *sheqel*, and the present matter.   Raba resumes discourse,] "Now, in the view of Ben Bukhri, since to begin with [the priests] are not obligated to bring [the *sheqel*-offering to the Temple], if they actually do bring it, the priests commit a sin.   [How so?]   They turn out to bring unconsecrated offerings to the Temple courtyard [and that is a sin.   One may bring only consecrated offerings, designated for the purpose of the cult, to the Temple courtyard.   One can consecrate only something that he is obligated to consecrate in accord with the Temple rules.   Ben Bukhri, however, would permit the priest to] bring [the *sheqel*-tax] by handing over ownership over to the community at large.]

J.   "Now," [Raba continues,] "I might have supposed that the following argument applies: since it is written, 'And all your Valuations will be according to the *sheqel* of the sanctuary' (Lev. 27:25), [it would follow that] whoever is subject to the requirement of bringing the *sheqel*-tax also can pledge the Valuation [of others].   It would then follow that, since the priests are not subject [in Ben Bukrhi's view] to the religious duty of bringing the *sheqel*-tax [in support of the public offerings], they cannot pledge Valuations.

K.   "Thus the framer of the cited passage has informed us [that that, in fact, is not the case.   Priests may also pledge the Valuation of others.]"

L.   [The foregoing explanation of the language used at A is now rejected.]   Abayye said to him, "[The scriptural language,] 'All your Valuations' [cited by Raba at J as part of his proof for the position imputed to Ben Bukhri's principle serves for a quite separate purpose, namely, to indicate that] all the pledges of Valuation that you make should add up to no less than a *sela* [per Valuation]."   [Since a particular verse may bear only one interpretation, the cited verse could not also support the position proposed at J, which, therefore, cannot have been in the mind of the framer of the cited passage, K, when he stated matters as he did.]"

M.   "Rather," said Abayye, "[It still was] necessary [for the framer to make explicit reference to the priesthood at A for another reason].   I might have proposed the following argument:

N.   "Since it is written, 'And their redemption money – from a month old you shall redeem them – shall be according to your valuation' (Num. 18:16).

O.   "[The use of the word Valuation in the cited verse, which deals with the redemption of the firstborn by ordinary Israelites then would indicate that] whoever is subject to the requirement of redeeming the firstborn can pledge the Valuations [of others]. But since priests are not subject to the law of redemption of the first born, they cannot pledge the Valuations [of others]. Accordingly, [by framing matters as he did at A, the author] informed us [that that is not the case]."

P.   Said Raba to him, "[If that is the basis for your position], then how do you deal with the following statement made in connection with the ram that is brought as a guilt-offering: 'And he shall bring as his guilt-offering to the Lord a ram without blemish out of the flock, according to your valuation' (Lev. 5:25).

Q.   "We may then draw the parallel as follows: Whoever can [pledge] Valuations is subject to the law governing the ram brought as a guilt-offering.   Then one of concealed sexual traits and one who has the sexual traits of both genders, classifications of persons who are not subject to the law of Valuations at all, also will not be subject to the requirement of bringing the ram brought as a guilt-offering [– a position that is manifestly impossible!]" [Abayye's proposed interpretation is weak because the same reasoning would lead to an impossible conclusion, if every time we introduce the word "Valuation," we must exclude those classifications of persons that, for reasons particular to Valuations, are not subject to the possibility of having their Valuation pledge.]

R.   "Rather," said Raba – and there are those who maintain that it was stated by R. Ashi, "[The formulation given at A, specifying the obligation of priests] is necessary.

S.   [How so?] "I might have imagined the following argument: since it is written, 'Then he shall be set before the priest' (Lev. 27:8), [I might suppose that only an Israelite would be set before the priest], but not *a priest* before a priest.

T.   "Therefore [the framer of the passage] informs us [that that is not the case]."

XXV.

A.   *[All] are subject to the pledge of Valuation [by others]* [M. 1:1A].

B.   [What classification of persons does the framer of the passage intend] to include [by stressing the word, *all*]?

C.   It is to include a person who is disfigured or afflicted with a skin ailment [=I C-D].

D.   Whence the authority [in Scripture] for that statement?

E.   It is in line with that which our rabbis have taught: "According to your Valuation" (Lev. 27:8) serves to encompass a generalized statement of Valuation [explained at XXVII, below].

F.   Another interpretation of "According to your Valuation:"   the Valuation of the whole of a person one pays, and he does not pay the Valuation of distinct limbs.

G.   Is it possible that I should exclude [from a pledge of Valuation] even some [part of the person's body] on which life depends? [If someone should pledge the Valuation, for example, of the other person's heart, would the foregoing statement excluding limbs from the process of Valuation apply in such a case?]

H. Scripture states, "[When a man makes a special vow of] persons [to the Lord at your Valuation]" (Lev. 27:2).

I. [The meaning, then, is that] persons [are subject to the vow of Valuation,] excluding [therefore] a corpse [who would not be subject to such a vow. Hence if a person vows the Valuation of a part of a person on which life depends, the pledge of Valuation is valid and to be paid.]

J. Thus I shall exclude a [pledge of Valuation] of a corpse. But perhaps I should not exclude a dying person [who then may be subject to a vow of Valuation]?

K. Scripture states, "Then he shall be set [before the priest] and the priest shall value him" (Lev. 27:8).

L. Whoever is subject to the condition of being set before the priest also is subject to Valuation, and whoever is not subject to the condition of being set before the priest [such as a dying man, who cannot be moved] also is not subject to Valuation.

M. Another interpretation [of the reference, at Lev. 27:2, to] "persons:"

N. I know only that the pledge of Valuation applies to a single individual who pledged the Valuation of a single individual. How do I know that the same obligation aplies to a single individual who pledged the Valuation of a hundred persons?

O. Scripture states, "...persons..."

P. Another interpretation [of the reference, at Lev. 27:2, to] "persons:"

Q. [4B] I know only that the law applies in the case of a man who pledged the value of either a man or a woman.

R. How do I know that the law applied to a woman who pledged the value of a man, [or to] a woman who pledged the value of a woman?

S. Scripture states, "...persons..."

T. Another interpretation: "...persons..." serves to include one who is disfigured or afflicted with a skin ailment.

U. For it is possible that I might have reasoned as follows: "When a man makes a special vow of persons to the Lord at your Valuation" (Lev. 27:2) [means that only] whoever possesses a worth [as above, I E-F] would be subject to a vow of Valuation. On the other hand, whoever does not possess a worth would not be subject to a vow of Valuation. [Thus excluding the disfigured person or person with skin ailment who could not be sold in the marketplace.]

V. Now when Scripture states, "Persons...," [it serves to include the categories under discussion here].

XXVI.

A. "And... [then] your valuation [of a male from twenty years old up to sixty years old shall be fifty shekels of silver..." (Lev. 27:3).

B. Does [the use of *and*] serve to include as subject to value one of unclear sexual traits or of dual sexual traits, male and female?

C. For it is possible that one might have reasoned as follows: "When a man makes a special vow of persons to the Lord at your valuation" (Lev. 27:2) means that whoever possesses an [intrinsic] worth also would be subject to a vow of Valuation. On the other hand, whoever does not possess an [intrinsic] worth also would not be subject to a vow of Valuation. [Since the person of unclear sexual traits and the hermaphrodite have value, so we might suppose they should be subject to Valuation.]

D. Accordingly, Scripture says, "...then your valuation of a male," meaning, a male, but not one of unclear sexual traits or dual sexual traits. [These are excluded.]

E. Is it possible to suppose that while such a one should not be subject to the Valuation pertaining to a man, persons in those classifications should be subject to the Valuation of a woman?

F. Scripture says, "...then your valuation of a male...if the person is a female..." (Lev. 27:3-4).

G. [What is required therefore is status as] a male beyond doubt, or as a female beyond doubt, accordingly excluding one of unclear sexual traits or of dual sexual traits.

XXVII.

A. [Reverting to the amplification of XXV E,] a master said, "'According to your Valuation' (Lev. 27:8) serves to include an unspecified statement of Valuation."

B. What is "an unspecified statement of Valuation"?

C. [It is in accord with the following] teaching attributed to the authority of Mishnah teachers:

D. He who says, "An unspecified statement of Valuation is incumbent on me [by vow]" pays [what he has vowed] in accord with the minimum of all Valuations. [Since he did not specify the amount of the Valuation, he pays according to the minimum.]

E. And what is the minimum of all Valuations? It is three sheqels [in line with the Valuation of an infant female, Lev. 27:6].

F. [But why impose the minimum? Why not the maximum Valuation?] May I propose [that the person pay] fifty [in line with Lev. 27:3's Valuation of an adult male]?

G. [If] you lay hold of too much, you hold nothing, [but if] you lay hold of a little, you [indeed] hold [on to it].

H. [In that case,] may I propose [that the person pay] [a single] sheqel, in line with the following verse: "And every valuation shall be according to the *sheqel* of the sanctuary" (Lev. 27:25). [So, it follows, the minimum amount would be a single *sheqel*]?

I. That [passage] alludes to the issue of the minimum assessed in terms of the means of the one who made the pledge. [The least acceptable payment even from a very poor person is a sheqel. But when a specified Valuation comes under discussion, it can be no less than three sheqels.]

J. [If a general vow of Valuation cannot fall below the figure of three sheqels,] then what purpose is stated by the verse of Scripture (Lev. 27:2) [which specifies, "According to your Valuation]?"

K. Said R. Nahman said Rabbah bar Abbuhah, "This verse indicates that a person [who makes an unspecified Valuation] does not fall into the category of payment relative to one's resources [but however poor, he must come up with a minimum of three *sheqels*, no fewer].

L. "What is the reasoning behind such a view? It is that the person who has taken an unspecified vow of Valuation is in the status of one who has made the [minimum] sum explicit. [Since it is commonly the fact that the minimum to be paid for a vow of Valuation is three *sheqels*, if someone takes such a vow, we assume that was his intent, without further specification.]

M. [Providing a different version of the same matter,] there are those who report the matter as follows: Said R. Nahman said Rabbah bar Abbuhah, "[One who takes an unspecified vow of Valuation, not specifying the amount he will pay,] falls into the category of one who is adjudged in terms of his capacity to pay.

N. "[Now is] such an opinion is self-evident? [No.] For you might have said he is in the status of one who makes explicit the [minimum] sum of money he pledges to pay on account of his vow of Valuation. Accordingly, we are informed that that is not the case [by the statement in Scripture, 'According to your Valuation']."

XXVIII.

A. [Continuing the amplification of XXV, now with F:] "Another interpretation of 'According to your Valuation' (Lev. 27:2): the Valuation of the whole of a person one pays, and he does not pay the Valuation of distinct limbs."

B. And lo, you have taken up that same phrase [as a prooftext in the explanation of the meaning of] an unspecified Valuation [as at XXVII.K and a single phrase may bear only one interpretation].

C. [For the purpose of a single exegesis of the word,] one [may have stated it as,] "Valuation." [But since the phrase is given as,] "In accord with your Valuation," [with the suffix, "Your," the possibility of a dual interpretation of the same word is realized].

D. [Moving on to XXV.G-I:] "[Another interpretation of 'According to your Valuation:' the Valuation of the whole of a person one pays, and he does not pay the Valuation of distinct limbs.] Do I therefore exclude the case of a person who vows the Valuation of a part of a person on which life depends? [No.] For Scripture states, '[When a man makes a special vow of] persons' (Lev. 27:2). [Its meaning is that] persons [are subject to the vow of Valuation,] excluding [therefore] a corpse. [Hence if a person vows the Valuation of a part of a person on which life depends, the pledge of Valuation is valid and to be paid.]

E. And lo, you have taken up that phrase [in another connection].

F. [For the purpose of a single exegesis of the word, one might have stated it in the singular, as] "Person." [Since the word is given in the plural, as,] "Persons," [it serves for a dual interpretation].

G. [Moving on to XXV.J-K:] "Thus I shall exclude [a pledge of Valuation] of a corpse. But perhaps I should not exclude a dying person [who then may be subject to a vow of Valuation]? Scripture states, 'Then he shall be set [before the priest] and the priest shall value him' (Lev. 27:8). [XXV.L: Whoever can be set before the priest also is subject to Valuation by another, etc.]"

H. If that is the case, then I [surely should derive from the same exegesis] the exclusion of the corpse [from the process of Valuation], relying on the exegesis of the words, "...shall be set... shall value..." [That is, whoever can be set before the priest is also subject to Valuation by another.]

I. [On the basis of the foregoing, we proved that a corpse is subject to Valuation, thus rendering the exegesis at D-F unnecessary which says that from the plural "persons" we learn that a corpse is not subject to Valuation. In that case, Scripture should have written] "person." Why did it state the plural "persons"?

J. It serves for our exegetical requirements in what is to follow [concerning the disfigured person, below].

K. [Proceeding to XXV.M-T:] "Another interpretation [of the reference, at Lev. 27:8, to] 'Persons:' I know only that the pledge of Valuation applies to a single individual who pledged the Valuation of a single individual. How do I know that the same obligation applies to a single individual who pledged the Valuation of a hundred persons? Scripture states, '...persons...'

L. "Another interpretation [of the reference to 'persons,'] I know only that the law applies in the case of a man who pledged the value of either a man or a woman. How do I know that the law applies to a woman who pledged the value of a man, [or to] a woman who pledged the value of a woman? Scripture states, '...persons...'

M. "Another interpretation: '...persons...' serves to include one who is disfigured or afflicted with a skin ailment."

N. But [referring to the case of the disfigured party], you have already made use [of the formulation, "Persons,"] for these other cases [K-L]!

O. These other cases [involving numerous vows, or the vow of a female for a male] do not require a prooftext [of Scripture at all].

P. Why not? Because each of the categories [listed just now] is equivalent [to the others. Thus if one category is included, all by definition are included. Even if Scripire had merely used the singular "person," indicating that an individual is subject to Valuation, we would know that the other categories are included as well. Accordingly,] all of them derive [from the same reference of Scripture].

Q. Where a verse of Scripture is required [to make explicit what otherwise would not enter the already proved classification of persons and vows,] it is in the case of one who is disfigured or afflicted with a skin ailment.

XXIX.

A. [Proceeding to XXVI.A-B:] "And your valuation [of a male...]" (Lev. 27:3). [The use of *and*] serves to include [in the category of people who possess intrinsic value] one of unclear sexual traits or of dual sexual traits, male and female.

B. Possessing intrinsic value? Why should I need a verse of Scripture to prove that these classifications of persons possess intrinsic value? Let the Valuation of the persons at hand be merely that of the value of a palm tree! If [the person who took the vow] had stated only, "The value of a palm tree [is incumbent on me]," would he not have given it? [So the purpose of the proof-text at hand seems hardly clear.]

C. Said Raba [alt.: Rabbah], "[It is to indicate] that one is assessed in terms of his personal standing [even in the case of the classifications at hand].

D. "It might have entered my mind to maintain that, since it is written, '...makes a special vow of persons...' (Lev. 27:2), the rule is that whoever is subject to Valuations is assessed in accord with his personal standing, and whoever is not subject to Valuations is not assessed in accord with his personal standing. [We note that the classifications of those of unclear sexual standing are excluded at XXVI from being subject to Valuations in general. Therefore, if a person should pledge the Valuation of such a party, whose value is not fixed by Scripture because of the unclarity of his or her (we know not which) sexual category, I might have imagined that such a one is not assessed in terms of his personal standing. That is why it is necessary for the scriptural exegesis to establish what I should not otherwise have known]."

E. Said to him Abayye, "But if one is not subject to a vow of Valuations at all, is he indeed assessed in terms of his personal standing?" [Surely not!]"

XXX.

A. [The framer now raises the following objection to Abayye's position.] And has it not been taught: [If someone said,] "The head of this slave is sanctified," he [the owner] and the sanctuary are partners in [owning] him.

B. "The head of this slave is sold to you" – they divide [the value of the slave] between them [so that the one who purchased the head gets half the value of the slave, and the other party retains half of his value even though the head is obviously worth more than the rest of the body].

C. "The head of this ass is sanctified" – he and the sanctuary are partners in [owning] it.

D. "The head of this ass is sold to you" – they divide between them [the value of the ass].

E. "The head of this cow is sold to you" – the owner has sold only the head of the cow.

F. And not only so, but even if he said, "The head of the cow is sanctified," the sanctuary receives only the head of the cow [and does not enter joint ownership of the cow].

G. [Explaining why the case of the cow differs from the foregoing cases], said R. Pappa, "For lo, butchers sell the head of a cow in butchershops. [Thus when a man says, 'I sell to you the head of the cow,' it is clear he specifically means the head. It is not merely a way of saying I sell you half.]"

H.   [The framer now asks whether the foregoing A-G is consistent with the view of Abbaye, at XXIX. E, that one not assessed under a vow of Valuations also is not assessed in terms of the specific value of the limb that is sold or dedicated,] now, lo, [Abayye's view is consistent with the case of the ass and cow, C-G, for an] ass and a cow are not subject to a vow of Valuations [which applies only to persons], and they are not assessed in terms of the standing [of the limb involved in the sale], but rather, simply in terms of a partnership in which each partner owns half of the beast, without regard to the issue of the value of the limb under discussion. Further, if one has sanctified the head of a slave, he has not sanctified the entire slave, only half.]

I.   Now, in accord with your [Abbaye's] reasoning, you have the problem of the slave, for he indeed is subject to the vow of Valuations, but he is not assessed in terms of his standing [e.g., the individual limb that is sanctified, cf. B above.]

J.   But there is in fact no insuperable difficulty, for one rule applies to things that have been sanctified for use on the altar [i.e., the foregoing rule concerning slave, cow, and ass] [but the rule that an object that is subject to Valuation is assessed in terms of the value of his limb applies only to things that have] been sanctified for the upkeep of the Temple building. [Where one has made a vow of Valuation of the value of someone, it is solely for the upkeep for the Temple building. There the vow is valid and would apply, e.g., to a vital organ. But where a vow covers something to be used on the altar itself, a separate rule pertains. The person of unclear sexual traits falls into the former category.]

K.   How, then, have you disposed of matters? Is it that we speak of things that have been sanctified for use on the altar [at A-H]? How, then, do we account for the latter part of the cited passage: "And not only so, but even if he said, 'The head of the cow is sanctified,' the sanctuary receives only the head of the cow [and does not enter joint ownership of the cow]." Here, the animal is valued in terms of a single limb.]

L.   Now why should this be so?   [I might propose that] the sanctification [imposed by the deciation of the cow] should spread throughout the entire corpus of the cow [and not be limited to its head, for an animal dedicated for the altar as this one is, is not to be valued in terms of a single limb, but in terms of its whole body as at J].

M.   Has it not been taught: [5A] "If someone said, the hoof of this [cow] is for a whole-offering.

N.   "Is it possible that the entire beast shall serve as a whole-offering?

O.   "Scripture states, "All that any man shall give thereof shall be holy (Lev. 27:9).

P.   "'Thereof' [a part thereof] shall be holy, but the whole of it shall not be holy.

Q. "May I then suppose that the rest of the beast [apart from the dedicated limb] may go forth for secular use [since it is not sanctified in its entirety]?

R. "Scripture says, '...shall be...,' meaning, 'will remain in its established state of being,' [which is a condition of sanctification].

S. "How is this to be carried out? Let the beast be sold for use by those who require animals for burnt-offerings, and the proceeds received will be deemed unconsecrated except for that portion of the proceeds which covers the limb [that alone has been declared consecrated,]" the words of R. Meir.

T. R. Judah and R. Yosé and R. Simeon say, "How do we know that in the case of one who says, 'The hoof of this beast shall be a burnt-offering,' the whole of the beast enters the category of burnt-offering?

U. "Scripture states, 'All that any man shall give thereof shall be holy' (Lev. 27:9).

V. "That statement serves to include the whole of the beast [even where only part of it has been declared consecrated]."

W. Now even in accord with the view of him who has stated that the whole of the beast does not fall into the category of a burnt-offering, that ruling applies to the case in which one has sanctified a part of the beast on which life does not depend. But if he consecrated a part of the beast on which life depends, the act of consecration takes effect over the entire beast. [How, then, do we explain the ruling above, E-F, that states that when a man dedicates the head of his cow, only the head is dedicated? Shouldn't the whole cow become holy?]

X. There is no difficulty. The one ruling pertains to the act of sanctification of the body of the beast itself [in which case the whole animal is consecrated], the other to the sanctification of the value [in which case, as above, only the value of the limb is owing to the Temple.]

Y. But the master himself has stated, "He who consecrates a male beast only as to its value – the sanctification covers the body of the beast [and not only the funds received in payment for it. Since the beast can be used on the altar, it is deemed consecrated for use on the altar. So X's distinction does not serve.]

Z. Indeed, there still is no difficulty. The one rule applies to a case in which one has consecrated the whole of the beast, the other to a case in which he has consecrated only one limb.

AA. But even a vow concerning a single limb is a matter of difficulty for us, for Rabbah raised the question, "If one has sanctified the value of a single limb of a beast, what is the rule?"

BB. [No, that is not pertinent, for] when that question was raised, it was raised in the context of an unblemished animal [so that the beast *could* serve on the altar]. But here we deal with a blemished beast, which, like an ass, [cannot serve on the altar in any case].

CC. No, the case of a blemished beast also poses a problem for us, for Rabbah raised the following question: "If one has vowed the value of his head for the altar, what is the law?" [And surely one could not make such into a sacrifice on the altar]."

DD. When we raised the question, it was before this teaching [about the status of the ass was announced, but now that this teaching has been announced, it is no longer a problem for us].

XXXI.
A. Returning to the body of the matter: Rabbah asked, "If someone said, 'Let the value of my head be used for the altar,' what is the law? Is the man assessed in terms of the value [of his head] or not assessed in terms of the value [of his head]?"

B. We do not find a case involving money equivalents in which [a person's limb] is not assessed in terms of its value.

C. Or perhaps, we do not find a case involving what is consecrated for the altar in which [a person's limb] *is* assessed in terms of its value.

D. The question must stand [there being no clear criterion for choosing between the two conflicting principles].

E. Rava asked, "If someone said, 'My Valuation is incumbent on me for use on the altar,' what is the rule? Is he assessed in terms of his resources, or is he not assessed in terms of his resources [but rather according to a set standard supplied by Scripture]?"

F. We do not find a case involving Valuations in which a man is *not* assessed in terms of his resources.

G. Or perhaps the operative principle is that we do not find a case involving the altar in which a person *is* involved solely in terms of his resources.

H. The question must stand.

I. R. Ashi raised the following question: "If one has consecrated an inherited field [ownership of which cannot permanently be alienated] for use for the altar, what is the rule?"

J. Do we maintain that we find no case in which an inherited field can be redeemed except on the basis of *fifty* sheqels *for each part of the field that suffices for the sowing of a homer of barley?*

K. Or do we rule that we find no case of something consecrated for the altar that may be redeemed other than in accord with its actual value [without reference to the price fixed in Scripture]?

L. The question must stand.

The Mishnah pericope is in four parts, an introduction, A-B, which is limited at C, then three special cases, D, explained by E, F, explained by G. A speaks of paying the fixed Valuation specified at Lev. 27: 1-8, and B, of vowing the estimated worth of another, not under the rule of the fixed Valuation. C completes the opening rule but, of course, also reverses the sense of A's blanket statement that *all* effect and are subject to both forms of donation. D then flows from C, also limiting the force of A, and its reason is clear at E. One cannot ascertain the Valuation of one who may be either male or female, since Scripture specifies a different Valuation for each. F then excludes those who, for one reason or another, are not deemed to exercise effective judgment.

The Talmud's opening exercise, units I, II proposes to examine the meaning of the formulation of the Mishnah passage with its emphatic reference to *all*. What follows is that a range of such usages come under discussion. The passage at hand is so arranged as to serve M. Ar. 1:1, but, as we see, it serves equally well, if rearranged for the purpose, any other passage in which the emphatic language is used and then subjected to discussion such as is at hand. Accordingly, it is the traits of the formulation of the Mishnah over all that comes under discussion, and not the passage at hand in particular. The formulation of such an interchangeable discussion of Mishnah language therefore is prior to the composition of an exegesis of the present passage in particular.

Unit III repeats the same exercise, with exactly the same result, four times, for the dwelling in the tabernacle and the taking up of the palm branch, the use of the religiously significant articles of show fringes and phylacteries. The shift at the fifth entry marks the beginning of a new discussion, violating the strictly formal rules of the foregoing. Unit IV then conducts its own quite separate inquiry into an *all*-formulation. It fully spells out the several possibilities at hand. Units V-IX take up the problems of interest to other passages as well, none of them having the slightest point of contact with M. Ar. 1:1.

The same sort of exercises proceed at units X-XVI. Clearly, XVI contains some duplicated passages, excised. As usual, I have translated the printed text that the reader is likely to have in hand. Units XVIIff. proceed to a secondary exercise. Now we wish to explain not the inclusionary language, *all,* but the explicit reference to three classifications of persons. The problem, as we see, is that in each case, there is no reason to make explicit reference to one or another of these classifications, since if that category is not included by definition, then no category would be. The reasoning then flows from that problem. We have to show why one might have supposed a given category – the priesthood – should be excluded. The secondary expansion obviously bears no close relationship to the language of the Mishnah. The entire construction at hand follows its own logic of aggregation, explaining two different types of inclusionary formulations, first the general one, *all,* second, the specific one, consisting of specifications of obvious categories. The whole then is an exercise in the logic of list-making. That none of this bears any close relationship to the Mishnah passage at hand not only is self-evident but proved, also, by the utilization of the same construction, whole or in part, at other passages of the Mishnah at which the same sort of inclusionary language is used.

We note that units XX-XXIII go over exactly the same ground, in precisely the same order, as V-VIII. I suppose the entire set originally formed a single composition, broken up by the intervening materials.

But the whole – the total affect of the entire construction – hardly is spoiled. The unitary character of discourse, on the level of logic, is unimpaired by the shifts away from a merely formal unity such as the linkage of V-VIII to XX-XXIII would have accomplished. XXV-XXVI take up the exegesis of the pertinent verses, in particular Lev. 27: 2-4. The passage begins with the indication that subject to exegesis will be the language of the Mishnah. But in fact the whole is a ready-made discussion, which only later on reaches the question that accounts for inclusion of the entire construction. In fact, XXV.E is not explained until much later, at XXVII. Meanwhile we have a systematic testing of propositions, in the manner of the framers of Sifra [cf. Neusner, *Judaism and Scripture: The Evidence of Leviticus Rabbah*]. The type of discussion is continuous at XXV-XXVI; I break up the two only because the subject changes. Continuing the process of secondary amplification of materials already introduced, units XXVII-XXIX take up statements made earlier, as indicated. While XXX makes reference to XXIX.E, I treat it as an essentially autonomous construction, since it does go its own way.

The relationship of the materials at XXX to those at XXIX is not really clear. XXX is generally read as a discussion continuous with the foregoing, but that requires us to interpolate the conception that "assessment in accord with one's value" refers not to the person but to the limb. Then we understand XXIX to speak of one's pledging the worth of a limb, and the assessment is made in terms of the worth of that limb. But I see no reference throughout XXIX to that consideration. It seems to me that what is at issue, if we do not interpolate the stated consideration, can only be how we assess the value of one whose sexual status is not clearly established, and the theory is that such an assessment depends upon the standing or worth of the person. Abayye's answer, then, is that, as we demonstrated above, such a person is not subject to the law of Valuations anyhow. What makes this interpretation, which adequately serves what I designated as XXIX, difficult is that XXX.H explicitly refers back to Abayye's position in the foregoing. Now the consideration of the assessment of a limb is made explicit. What follows at XXX, however, flows from the issues introduced at the opening formula, A-G, and the moving argument never reverts to XXIX. In any event the discussion of the dispute of Meir and Judah and Simeon, XXX.Mff., clearly pertains to considerations other than those under discussion here. XXXI presents three theoretical questions of principle, with the possibilities spelled out, but no conclusion proposed.

Does this unit talk about "everything" or some few things? As I have pointed out, there is a rather carefully planned program that characterizes the Talmud. We move from Mishnah exegesis to a broader theme altogether. There is a clear plan that governs the formation of Unit III as well. There is some repetition in this program. But no on can doubt that a rather rigorously executed plan characterizes the whole. This Talmud does not talk about "everything" but about some few things. It does not call upon the Tosefta to explain the Mishnah at every point, but only at those points that, for whatever reason, the authorship at hand find the Tosefta's reading important. Consequently, not only does the Talmud not talk about everything in general, it also does not talk about everything particular to its task of Mishnah exegesis. Can we explain why the Talmud includes everything that is before us – and therefore can we postulate that the authorship of the Bavli has excluded what it found irrelevant and included only what served its purpose? We can certainly account for pretty much every line in the four folios that are covered here.

1:1H

H. One who is less than a month old is subject to the vow [of payment of worth by another], but is not subject to the pledge of Valuation.

I.

A. Our rabbis have taught: "He who pledge the Valuation of an infant less than a month old –

B. R. Meir says, "He pays his value [since there is no Valuation specified in Scripture]."

C. And sages say, "He has not made a statement of any consequence at all [and pays nothing]."

D. Concerning what underlying principle do they dispute?

E. R. Meir maintains the theory that, in general, a person does not make a statement that is to begin with null. [On the contrary,] the person knows that vows of Valuation do not apply to an infant younger than a month old, so he made the decision to make a statement for the sake of Heaven [and thereby deliberately pledged, not the Valuation, but the assessed market value].

F. Rabbis maintain the theory that a person will make a statement that is to begin with null. [Thus, Rabbis and Meir dispute the intention of the man who offered the statement.]

G. In accord with which of the foregoing positions is the following statement that R. Giddal said Rab said, "He who says, 'The Valuation of this utensil is incumbent on me' [while Valuations pertain only to human beings], pays the monetary worth of the utensil"?

H. It accords with the view of R. Meir [since Meir maintains that a person never makes a statement that is to begin with null].

I. Obviously, the statement may accord with the position of R. Meir. [Who needs to be told that!] But the issue is whether or not you may claim that, even in accord with [the principle of] rabbis [at C, above], [the framer of the statement at hand may concur].

J.   [How so? By what principle may we distinguish the case at A+C from the case at G]? In the former case [at C], the person who made the statement erred, thinking that, just as Valuations apply to someone from a month of age and older, so also Valuations may apply to an infant even less than a month of age. [So one made the statement in error, and it was null and void. It was made on the base of a false supposition as to the facts.]

K.   But here, where there is no possibility of making such a mistake [since Scripture explicitly speaks only of human beings, not of objects,] a person most certainly knows that a vow of Valuation does not apply to a utensil. Yet he deliberately made his statement for the sake of Heaven. [So in the present case, we might suppose, even rabbis can concur that the man pays the monetary value of the object.]

L.   Accordingly, we are informed that that is not the case [and rabbis do not profer the proposed distinction. Under all circumstances in their view the person's statement is null.]

M.   [5B] But [since Rab is merely explaining] the view of R. Meir, for what purpose [did Rab find it] necessary [to make such a statement? Surely Meir's position encompasses the case at hand. What possible consideration can have led Rab to the view that, within Meir's principle, one might err and suppose that the pledge of the Valuation of a utensil would produce no consequences? Surely Meir is clear at A+B.]

N.   What might you have said? The reason for the view of R. Meir in the former case is that [scriptural law has included by] decree an infant less than a month old on account of the [case of the infant] a month old, [who indeed is subject to a vow of Valuation. That is, if a man did not have to pay for an infant less than a year old, he may become confused and not pay when he vows to pay the worth of an infant one month old even though in the latter case he is liable. Thus, Meir forces him to pay even for the child younger than a month.] But here, [where we have] no [grounds to include] by decree [the case of the utensil], I might have maintained the view that no such liability is incurred [when a person says 'the Valuation of this utensil is encumbent on me].'

O.   [In making his statement, Rab therefore] informed us that the principle behind R. Meir's position is that, in general, a person does not make a statement that is to begin with null. There is then no difference whatsoever between the present case and the former case [such as is proposed at N].

P.   In accord with which position is the following statement, which Rabbah bar Joseph said Rab said, and there are those who state the matter in terms of the authority of R. Yeba bar Yosé in citing Rab: "He who sanctifies a beast belonging to his fellow pays the value of the ox." [The man cannot sanctify the ox itself, for one cannot sanctify a thing which is not his own possession to begin with. But the man in making his statement validly pledged the value of the ox, since he presumably possesses sufficient means to make such a statement of consecration of funds.]

Q. In accord with whose view is that statement? It [obviously] accords with the view of R. Meir. [Sages surely should not concur that an invalid statement of consecration bears any consequences whatsoever. But Meir can agree that the statement is not made without intent, and hence we impute the intent to consecrate the value of the beast.]

R. Now lo, Rab made that statement already [in the familiar matter above].

S. For R. Giddal said Rab said, "He who says, 'The Valuation of this utensil is incumbent on me' pays the monetary worth of the utensil." [Accordingly, the statement would surely cover the case of the cow as much as that of the utensil, and why should it have proved necessary to develop the foregoing discussion, P-Q, at all?]

T. [It indeed was necessary to do so. For] what might you have concluded? In the former case, in which a person knows that there is no vow of Valuation for a utensil, the person has intended to pay its value for the sake of Heaven.

U. But in the present case, we deal with a cow, which indeed is subject to an act of sanctification [since one can offer the beast itself on the altar].

V. Accordingly, there is the possibility of maintaining that this is what the person who made the statement was thinking: "If I report the matter to its owner, he will sell it to me. Let the beast then be deemed effectively consecrated as of this moment, and later on I shall offer it up." But it never entered the man's mind to consecrate the mere value of the beast.

W. [In stating the matter in the present context, the author] thus informs us [that Rab made no such distinction].

X. Said R. Ashi, "But that entire conception pertains only if the person used the language, "...it is incumbent on me." But if he had said only, "Lo, this [beast is consecrated, without specifying that its value is incumbent upon him,] it is not in such a case [that Meir would deem a consequential statement to have been made. In this latter instance, in which the man has said, 'Lo, this beast is consecrated,' no consequence ensues. The man has not taken a pledge to pay the value of the beast at all.]"

M.1:1H simply restates the scriptural specification that Valuations apply to one more than a month old. It links M.1:1 to M.1:2, building upon the distinction between M.1:1A and B, the pledge of a Valuation as against the vow of one's worth. The Talmud sustainedly and at length discusses not the Mishnah passage at hand but the secondary issues of a teaching bearing tannaitic authority. The issue, then, is systematically worked out, first, the debate between Meir and sages, and, second the secondary implications of Meir's and sages' views, possible distinctions between the case at hand and other matters. The discussion is fluent and uninterrupted, beginning to end.

Does this unit talk about "everything" or some few things? No, the Talmud executes a very well-defined program of analysis of problems. Can we explain why the Talmud includes everything that is before us – and therefore can we postulate that the authorship of the Bavli has excluded what it found irrelevant and included only what served its purpose? There can be no doubt of the facts of the matter. What Steinsaltz and Wieseltier describe as "about all things" really is about some few things, and we can always say what they are. So we know choices have been made and can answer the question: Why this, not that? It follows that the Talmud before us contains not "everything" or even everything in hand on the topic before us (such as we might claim to find in Tosefta, as we saw in Chapter Two), but only those few things that served the authorship's program – whatever that program was. But, I hardly need state, at this moment we have not got the slightest idea of the definition of that program, let alone its purpose.

1:2

A   The gentile - [printed text: idolator]

B.   R. Meir says, "He is subject to the pledge of Valuation [by others], but he does not pledge the Valuation [of others]."

C.   R. Judah says, "He pledges the Valuation [of others] but is not subject to the pledge of Valuation [by others]."

D.   And this one and that one agree that they vow and are subject to the vow [of payment of worth].

I.

A   Our rabbis have taught: "Israelites make a pledge of Valuation, but idolators do not make a pledge of Valuation.

B.   "Is it possible to suppose that they also are not subject to a pledge of Valuation?

C.   "Scripture states, '[When a] man [makes a special vow of persons]' (Lev. 27:2)," the words of R. Meir.

D.   Said R. Meir, "Now since one verse of Scripture has so stated matters as to broaden the coverage of the law, while another verse of Scripture serves to limit the coverage of the law, on what account do I maintain that [a gentile] is subject to a vow of Valuation but may not make a vow of Valuation?

E   "It is because the framing of Scripture serves to include a broader classification of persons who are subject to Valuations than in the case of those who make a pledge of Valuations. [How so?]

F.   "For lo, a deaf-mute, idiot, and minor may be subject to a vow of Valuation, but they may not make a vow of Valuation [as at M. Arakh. 1:1]."

G.   R. Judah says, "Israelites are subject to a vow of Valuation, but idolators are not subject to a vow of Valuation.

H.   "Is it possible to suppose that they also are not able to make a vow of Valuation?

I.   "Scripture says, '...man...' (Lev. 27:2)."

J. Said R. Judah, "Now since one verse of Scripture has so stated matters as to broaden, while another verse of Scripture serves to limit [the coverage of the law], on what account do I maintain that [a gentile] may make a vow of Valuation but is not subject to a vow of Valuation?

K. "It is because the framing of Scripture serves to encompass a broad classification of persons who are able to make vows of Valuation than those who are *subject* to vows of Valuation.

L. "For lo, a person of undefined sexual traits and a person who bears the sexual traits of both genders are able to make vows of Valuation, but they are not subject to vows of Valuation [as at M. Arak 1:1]."

M. Said Raba, "The practical decision of R. Meir is well-founded, but the reason that he gives for it is not, while the reason of R. Judah is well-founded, but the practical decision is not.

N. "The practical decision of R. Meir is well-founded, for it is written in Scripture, 'You [refering to gentiles] have nothing to do with us in the building of the house of our God' (Ezra 4:3), [and funds deriving from the vow of Valuation go to support the upkeep of the Temple buildings].

O. "The reason that he gives for it is not, for lo, he introduces the analogy of the deaf-mute, idiot, and minor. But they are distinct [from others in question], for they are not assumed to exercise mature judgment [and so they cannot take vows anyhow, while the gentile does exercise mature judgment].

P. "The reasoning behind the decision of R. Judah is well founded, for he derives proof from the analogy of the person of indistinct sexual traits or dual sexual traits. That indeed is a pertinent parallel [to the gentile], for even though they are assumed to be able to exercise intelligent judgment [still, they are not subject to a vow of Valuation], for Scripture itself has excluded them from consideration, [and since the gentile falls into their category, he too may not be subjected to a pledge of Valuation].

Q. "But [Judah's] practical decision is not well-founded, for it is written in Scripture, 'You [refering to gentiles] have nothing to do with us in the building of the house of the Lord, our God' (Ezra 4:3)."

R. As to this statement, "You have nothing to do...," how does R. Judah deal with it?

S. Said R. Hisda said Abimi, "[It is not that the funds received from the gentile who pledged a Valuation are actually used for the Temple. Rather, such funds as are paid in by reason of his Valuation are left on deposit ['hidden away', and not used for any purpose whatsoever.]"

T. But if that is the case, then the laws of sacrilege should not apply to those funds [which would create an anomaly in the law, since what is dedicated to the Temple's service is ordinarily subject to the protection of the laws of sacrilege].

U. Yet we have learned [at T. Meilah 1:8 A-G]: Animals set aside for sin-offering under five classifications are left to die, and the funds received in their connection go to the Dead Sea, so that one may not derive benefit from those funds, but the laws of sacrilege do not apply to them. [Since the animals will not serve as sacrifices, the laws of sacriledge no longer apply. Therefore one cannot say that the laws of sacriledge apply to the money given by a gentile since the money will never serve for maintaining the Temple.]

V. Therefore it has been taught with respect to Holy Things declared consecrated by gentiles: 'Under what circumstances [do the laws of sacriledge apply]? With respect to Holy Things consecrated for use on the altar. But as regards Holy Things consecrated for use in the upkeep of the Temple house the laws of sacrilege *do* apply to them.' [Accordingly, the proposed explanation is contrary to the explicit law at hand.]

W. "Rather," said Rava, "It is on account of the possibility of weakening the resolve [of the Israelites that the gentiles' contribution is excluded], for it has been written in Scripture, 'Then the people of the land weakened the hands of the people of Judah and harmed them while they were building' (Ezra 4:4). [Judah then understands the cited verse to refer to the conditions prevailing at that time and not to the law that would govern for all time.]"

II.

A. [6A] One Tanna taught: As to a gentile who offered a voluntary contribution for the upkeep of the Temple building, they accept it from him.

B. Another Tanna taught: They do not accept it from him.

C. Said R. Ila, said R. Yohanan, "There is no contradiction [between the two teachings]. One refers to [accepting a contribution] at the initial [stages of building the Temple], the other to [accepting a contribution for the maintenance of the Temple once the initial construction] is finished." [This explanation is now spelled out.]

D. For R. Assi said R. Yohanan said, "At the beginning [of construction], even water or salt do they not accept from the [gentiles]. But after the fact, while an identifiable object [to which a gentile may point as his contribution] they do not accept from him, an object that is not readily identified they do accept from him." [Thus, if he changes his mind he cannot ask for its return.]

E. What would fall into the category of an object that is readily identified?

F. Said R. Joseph, "It would, for instance, be a pointed cubit used to fend off ravens [from the Temple precincts]."

G. R. Joseph objected [citing a verse of Scripture that indicates gentiles indeed did make contributions of identifiable objects]: "'And a letter to Asaph, keeper of the king's park, that he may give me timber to make beams' (Neh. 2:8)."

H. Said to him Abayye, "The case of a gift from a [gentile] government is different, for the monarch [government] will never retract [and so may be relied upon to make a contribution that will permanently remain in the Temple].

I.   "That is in line with what Samuel said, 'If the monarch [government] says, 'I shall uproot mountains,' the monarch will uproot mountains and not retract.'"

III.

A   Said Rab Judah said Rab, "A gentile who set apart a portion of his crop, designating it as priestly rations – those who know him examine his [motives in doing so]. If [when he did so] it was to accord with the intention of an Israelite that he set apart a portion of the crop, then it is to be given to a priest [as his rations].

B.   "But if it is not [the case that it was simply to accord with Israelite practice, but that the gentile himself proposed to contribute to the upkeep of the cult], then the crop that he has set apart requires permanent deposit [and may not be used]. [How so?]

C.   "We take account of the possibility that he intended [to set apart the crop] for the sake of Heaven, [which he may not do]."

D.   They objected [by citing an authoritative teaching, now at T. Meg. 2:16:] **A gentile who sanctified a beam for use [T. adds: in a synagogue] and on it is written, "For the Name [of God]"** –

E.   **they examine him. If he said, "I set it apart to accord with the prevailing intention of Israelites, they plane it off [the Name] and make use of the remainder. But if not, it must be left on permanent deposit, lest it was in the intention of his heart to [contribute the beam] for the sake of Heaven.**

F.   Now the operative criterion at hand is that on the beam was written the Name [of God]. That is why the beam has to be left on permanent deposit. Lo, if there is no Name written on it, then it does not require permanent deposit. [So the operative criterion is not merely that the gentile has given the beam, but a further consideration is involved.]

G.   [No, that is not the case.] The same law applies, for even though the Name is not written on an object, the requirement of leaving the object on permanent deposit still applies [when he intends it for the sake of Heaven].

H.   But the law just now cited informs us that even though the Name is written on the beam, one has to plane the beam [and reimbue the Holy Name] and only then may make use of the beam. For when the name of God is written not in its appropriate place it is not holy.

I.   For we have learned: [If the Name of God] was written on the handles of utensils or on the legs of beds, lo, one should plane the name off and leave it on permanent deposit. [Therefore, there are two operative criteria in the law at E. It cannot be used because of the improper intention and it must be planed because of the use of God's name.]

IV.

A   Said R. Nahman said Rabbah bar Abbahu, "He who says, 'This coin is to serve for philanthrophy' is permitted to use it for some other purpose."

B. The assumption in the foregoing statement is that he may make use of the coin for his own need. But for the need of a third party [he may] not [utilize the coin].

C. [Rejecting the gloss at B,] said R. Ammi said R. Yohanan, "Whether it is for his own purposes or for the purposes of a third party, [he may make use of the coin at hand]."

D. Said R. Zeira, "The foregoing teaching applies only in the case of one who said, 'Lo, incumbent on me [is a *sela* for charity.]' But if the man had said, 'Lo, this [*particular* coin is incumbent on me to donate to charity],' he certainly has to give [that coin and may not use it either for himself or another]."

E. Raba objected to that statement, "Quite to the contrary, exactly the opposite conclusion is more reasonable. If the man had made explicit reference to *this* coin, he may make use of it, since he thereby accepts upon himself liability to replace the coin should it be lost. But if he said, 'Incumbent on me...,' [he has already accepted upon himself liability to pay no matter what, therefore] he may not [use it for other purposes] may he not do so? [Since both arguments are logical D-E,] there really is no difference [in the two situations]."

F. It was taught in accord with the position of Raba: A vow is in the category of philanthropy, but an act of consecration is not in the category of philanthropy.

G. What is the meaning of this statement? Neither a vow nor an act of consecration in fact falls into the category of charity.'

H. But is not this the meaning of the cited statement: A pledge to donate to philanthropy, lo, it is subject to the admonition not to delay [paying off just like a vow] [stated at Deut. 23:22].

I. [But philanthropy] is not in the category of an act of consecration. For in the case of what has been subject to an act of consecration it is forbidden to make use of such an object, while in the case of something designated for philanthropy, it is permitted to make use of such an object [until it is handed over for the purpose for which it has been designated].

J. Said R. Kahana, "I stated this tradition before R. Zebid of Nehardea. He said, 'As to you, that is how you stated the matter. But as to us, this is how we repeat it:

K. "'Said R. Nahman said Rabbah bar Abbahu said Rab, "He who says, 'This coin is for philanthropy' – he is permitted to make use of it for some other purpose, whether for his own benefit or for the benefit of a third party, whether he used the language, 'Incumbent on me' or whether he used the language, 'Lo, this...'"'"

V.

A. Our rabbis have taught [at T. Meg. 2:15 E-F]: [if someone said,] **"This coin is for philanthropy," before the coin has actually reached the possession of the charity collector, it is permitted to make use of the coin for some other purpose.**

B. Once the coin has reached the possession of the charity collector it is forbidden to make use of it for some other purpose.

C. [6B] Is that so? But lo, R. Yannai [who himself was a charity collector] would make use of funds for his own purposes and then pay them back.

D. The case of R. Yannai is different, for it was acceptable to the poor [that he postpone paying over the funds he had collected for them], for so long as he delayed, he continued to collect and bring them [more money].

VI.

A. Our rabbis have taught: As to an Israelite who contributed a candelabrum or a candle to the synagogue – it is forbidden to [make use of these objects for some purpose] other [than that for which they were originally contributed, e.g., disposing of them.]

B. R. Hiyya bar Abba [in considering the passage at hand] considered ruling that there is no difference between [one's using the object for some purpose other than the original one, whether the new purpose is] optional or religiously required.

C. Said to him R. Ammi, "This is what R. Yohanan taught: 'The teaching at hand applies only [to using the object for a new purpose] that is an optional matter. But as to a matter of carrying out a religious duty, it is permitted to make use of the object for some matter other than that for which it was originally contributed.'"

D. This is implicit in what R. Assi said R. Yohanan said, "As to an idol worshipper who donates a candelabrum or a candle to a synagogue, as long as the name of the donator is not forgotten it is forbidden to alter its use. But once his name is forgotten it is permissible to alter its use."

E. Now for what purpose has the object been changed from its original one? Shall we say that it is an optional matter? On what basis, then, would one specify the case of idolator [who donates]? Even [in the case of a gift from an] Israelite it would be forbidden to do so.

F. So it must involve altering its use for the purpose of a religious duty.

G. Then the applicable consideration is that the donor was an idolator, who would complain about the matter [for he would not want his gift being used to fulfill an Israelite religious obligation]. But in the case of an Israelite, who would not complain about the matter, it would be acceptable. [Hence, so far as Yohanan is concerned, even when the new purpose is optional, the object indeed may be used for some purpose other than the original one.]

VII.

A. Shaazeraq, a Tai [Arab] contributed a lamp to the synagogue, of Rab Judah.

B. Rahba used it for another purpose [than that for which it had been contributed], and Raba took it amiss [Jung].

C.   Some report that Raba changed [the use of the object], and Rahba took it amiss.

D.   Some report that the sextons of Pumbedita changed [the use of the object], and Rahba and Rabbah took it amiss.

E.   The one who changed [the use of the object from the original purpose] maintained that the donor was not often about, and the one who took it amiss reasoned that there are times that the donor does happen to come by.

The dispute at M.1:2 is perfectly balanced, with the point at issue expressed in the reversal of word order, B/C. Meir's position is that an Israelite may pledge the Valuation of a gentile (B.'s text: idolator), but a gentile may not pledge the Valuation either of himself or of anyone else. Judah's view is the opposite. Both parties have to figure out how the gentile is excluded from the law of Valuations (Lev. 27:2: speak to the children of Israel). In Meir's view, the matter rests upon the action of the person who takes upon himself to pay the Valuation; hence others may pledge the Valuation of the gentile, but the gentile may not pledge the Valuation of others. In Judah's view, the matter rests upon the status of that which is subject to Valuation. Hence the gentile may pledge the Valuation of an Israelite, but not of himself. Both parties agree that vows are permitted in all cases.

Unit I provides an extended amplification of the logic and exegesis behind Meir's and Judah's positions, together with a secondary analysis and expansion. Because of the introduction of gentile gifts to the upkeep of the Temple buildings, we proceed at unit II to take up aspects of that broader question. Unit III then moves us on to a broader question, beginning with where or not a gentile may designate a portion of his crop to serve as priestly rations, hence may consecrate part of his crop. The rule given before now applies. This leads to a tertiary discussion triggered by a parallel case. The remainder pursues tangential matters.

Does this unit talk about "everything" or some few things? We amplify the Mishnah. We then pursue a topic introduced within that amplification. We finally broaden the question under discussion – a perfectly reasonable program. Can we explain why the Talmud includes everything that is before us – and therefore can we postulate that the authorship of the Bavli has excluded what it found irrelevant and included only what served its purpose? True, some tangential matters do make their appearance. But in the aggregate, these prove episodic and random. The document over all is entirely cogent, and it clearly omits much that it finds of no relevance to its task, including, needless to say, not only the bulk of the Tosefta pertinent to this passage, but also pretty much everything "out there" that cannot have served.

1:3

A He who is on the point of death or he who goes forth to be put to death

B. is not subject to the vow [of payment of his worth by others] nor subject to the pledge of Valuation [by others].

C R. Hananiah b. Aqabya says, "He is subject to the pledge of Valuation,

D. "because its [a Valuation's] price is fixed.

E "But he is not subject to the vow [of payment of his worth by others],

F. "because its [a vow's] price is not fixed."

G. R. Yosé says, "He may vow [the value of another] and may pledge a Valuation [of another] and may declare something sanctified.

H. "And if he caused damage, he is liable to make restitution."

I.

A There is no problem [in understanding why] *he who is on the point of death is not subject to the vow [of payment of his worth by others]*, because he no longer possesses a money value at all [that is, since he is about to die he would not be worth any money if he was sold in the market as a slave. It is also understandable why he is...*subject to the pledge of Valuation [by others]*, for he cannot be set up [before the priest, as Scripture requires, since he is not free to go where he wishes (cf. Lev. 27:8)].

B. But as to him who goes forth to be put to death, while he is not *subject to the vow [of payment of his worth by others]*, because he no longer possesses a money value at all, why should he not *be subject to the pledge of Valuation [by others]?*

C For it has been taught [in a teaching in the authority of a Tanna]: How do we know that in the case of him who was being taken forth to execution and said, "My Valuation is incumbent on me," he has said nothing?

D. Scripture has said, "No devoted thing...shall be redeemed" (Lev. 27:28). [A condemned person falls into the category of *herem*.]

E Is it possible [that the same rule applies] even prior to the completion of his trial?

F. Scripture says, "...from man [in part]" and not the whole of a man [and before the end of the trial and the sentencing, he remains a whole man. Afterward he is no longer whole.]

G. Now in the view of R. Hananiah b. Aqabya, who holds, *"He is subject to a pledge of Valuation,"* because [in the case of a pledge of Valuation] there is a fixed fee [specified by Scripture, so the issue of the diminishing value of a person about to die does not enter],

H. how would one interpret this reference to "no devoted thing [shall be redeemed]?"

I.   It is to be interpreted [for a quite separate purpose] in line with that which has been taught by a Tanna: R. Ishmael, son of R. Yohanan b. Beroqah, says, "Since we find that those who are subject to the death penalty at the hand of Heaven are able to pay a monetary find and attain atonement for themselves, as it is said, 'If a ransom is laid on him' (Ex. 21:30), is it possible to suppose that the rule is the same for one who has been condemned to the death penalty to be executed by man?

J.   "[No, it is not possible, for] Scripture states, 'No devoted thing... shall be redeemed [and a man sentenced to death falls into that category]' (Lev. 27:28).

K.   "I know only that rule applies in the case of those who are condemned to death as guilty of a most severe crime, the inadvertent performance of which is not subject to atonement [such as blasphemy].

L.   "How do I know that the same rule applies to those who are put to death for lesser crimes, the inadvertent performance of which is subject to atonement?

M.   "Scripture states, 'No devoted thing....'"

II.

A.   *R. Yosé says, "He vows [the value of another] and pledges a Valuation [of another and declares something sanctified, and if he has caused damage, he is liable to make restitution]"* [M. 1:3G-H].

B.   Now did the authority behind the contrary opinion, stated at the outset [A-F] maintain that he does not [vow or pledge a Valuation? No one has raised the issue at all!]

C.   Thus in respect to his making a vow [of someone else's market value] or pledging a Valuation or declaring something to be consecrated, all parties concur.

D.   Where there is a point of difference, it concerns a case of [the condemned or dying man's] causing damage [to a third party, through his own chattels, e.g., his cow].

E.   The first party [to the Mishnah passage] maintains that if he caused damage, he is not liable [to pay] monetary compensation, while R. Yosé holds that if he caused damage, he is liable to pay monetary compensation [as M. 1:3H makes explicit. Since H makes such a statement, the exegete reasonably assumes that a contrary position is to be imputed to the party with whom Yosé at H differs.]

F.   What is the point at issue?

G.   Said R. Joseph, "At issue is the case in which there is a debt of the status of an oral debt [not secured by a bond] to be collected fom the condemned man's estate. [If, for example, the condemned man's chattels caused damage, but the injured party did not bring the case to court prior to the man's own trial. The assumption is that, since the Torah has secured for the injured party restitution for his damages, what is owing is in the status at least of an oral debt. Can the injured party collect from the estate of the condemned man?]

H. "The first party [to the dispute] maintains that an oral debt may not be collected from the estate [of the condemned man], while R. Yosé maintains that an oral debt may be collected from the estate."

I. Raba said, "All parties [to the dispute at hand] concur that an oral debt is not collected from the estate [of the condemned man]. Here the dispute concerns a monetary penalty imposed by the law that is written in the Torah [for a person who causes damage.]

J. "The first party to the dispute maintains that a debt [i.e. this monetary penalty] that is imposed by law written in the Torah is not tantamount to one that is secured by a written bond. [Hence it cannot be collected from the estate, as a debt secured by a bond can be but may be collected only when the man is alive.] R. Yosé takes the view that it is in the status of a debt that is secured by a written bond, [and hence may be collected even after the man's death]."

III.

A. Now there are those who report the dispute at hand, II F-J, in connnection with another passage entirely.

B. **He who goes forth to be put to death – if he inflicted injury on others, he is liable [to make restitution]. If others inflicted injury on him, they are exempt from making restitution. R. Simeon b. Eleazar says, "Also in the case of his having inflicted injury on others, he is exempt, for he may not once again be summoned to court [so there is no possibility of a court action against him]"** [T. B.Q. 9:15, with slight revisions in the wording].

C. [7A] May we then infer that the first party to the dispute maintains the view that the man may be summoned a second time to court [under the present circumstances]?

D. R. Joseph said, "At issue is the case in which there is a debt in the status of an oral debt to be collected from the condemned man's estate. The first party to the dispute maintains that an oral debt may be collected from the estate, while R. Simeon b. Eleazar maintains that an oral debt may not be collected from the estate" [II.G-H].

E. Raba said, "All parties concur that an oral debt is not collected from the estate [of the condemned man]. Here the dispute concerns a debt imposed by the law that is written in the Torah. The first party to the dispute maintains that a monetary penalty that is imposed by law written in the Torah [for causing damages] is tantamount to one that is secured by a written bond. [Hence, it can be collected from his estate without taking him to court]. R. Simeon b. Eleazar takes the view that it is not in the status of a debt that is secured by a written bond [and hence, cannot be collected without a trial. Since he cannot be put into double jeopardy, the money cannot be collected.]" [II.I-J].

F. [To the view that at issue is the matter of the status of the debt imposed by the law that is written in the Torah] the following passage was raised as an objection: *He who dug a pit in the public domain, and an ox fell on him and killed him* – *[the owner of the ox] is exempt [from having to pay compensation,]* and not only so, but if the ox died, the state of the [deceased] owner of the pit is liable to pay compensation for the value of the ox to the owner [of the ox] [M. B.Q. 5:5]. [Clearly, all parties concur that a debt imposed by the law that is written in the Torah *is* treated as if it is secured by a written bond and can be collected after the man's death. How then can Raba maintain that that principle is what is subject to dispute?]

G. Said R. Ila said Rab, "The [foregoing] law speaks of a case in which the case had already been brought to court [and the man had been ordered by the court to pay compensation. That order is equivalent in effect to a written bond.]"

H. But lo, "killed him" is what has been stated [by the authority of the passage implying that he died before a trial took place]?

I. Said R. Adda bar Ahba, "The passage speaks of a case in which the injury was such as to be fatal [but the man died later after the trial had taken place.]"

J. But did not R. Nahman say that Hagga taught, "...died and buried him...." [That is, the ox killed the man and buried him. There is no possibility then to maintain that the injury was not fatal forthwith, so there also is no possibility that the one who dug the pit was ordered by the court to pay. The man who dug the pit, now wounded and lying inside, prior to death surely could not have been taken to trial and been instructed by the court to pay compensation for the beast. Accordingly, the explanation proposed by Raba for the earlier dispute is not possible, for clearly all parties here concur in the principle that he maintains is subject to dispute.]

K. The case involves the situation where the court was convened at the mouth of the pit [and instructed the dying man to pay for damages. Accordingly, the monetary penalty specified by Scripture is not treated as if secured by a written bond. Hence, it can only be collected from the dead man's estate if a trial had taken place before his death].

IV.

A. Our rabbis have taught: As to him who is going forth to be put to death, they sprinkle on him blood from a beast that he has offered up as a sin-offering or as a guilt-offering [on account of some prior infraction of the law.] But if he committed a sin at that very moment, [priests are not] obligated [to attend to] his [need for bringing a sin-offering]. [No further cultic procedures are to be inaugurated on account of the condemned man. Since he continues to disobey the law, no sin or guilt-offering may be made on his account.]

B. What is the reason for this principle?

C. Said R. Joseph, "It is because the court is not to delay the execution of the decree against the man [so inflicting on him further, needless suffering]."

D. Said Abayye to him, "If that is the operative principle, then even [in the case described in] the opening clause [he should not be sprinkled with blood. Here, too, you have the case of a delay in executing the court's penalty!]

E. "[No. The former case] deals with a case in which the animal that has been set aside for sacrifice was sacrificed at that very moment. [Hence, there was no delay.]"

F. But if his sacrificial animal had not been sacrificed [immediately], what is the law?

G. Is [the law] not as indicated in the second clause [at A]: "But if he committed a sin at that moment, [priests are not] obligated [to attend to] his need for bringing a sin-offering]?

H. [If that were so], then [instead of repeating the tradition in the language, "But if he committed a sin at that very moment, [priests are] not obligated [to attend to] his [cultic requirements]," the passage should be phrased differently and the distinction should be made with reference to the [sacrifice itself] [Jung], [phrasing matters as follows:]

I. "Under what circumstances? In a case in which the animal-sacrifice had been sacrificed at that very moment. But if the animal set apart for the sacrifice had not been sacrificed at that moment, [the rite is] not [carried out at all]."

J. That indeed is how the matter has been stated: "Under what circumstances? In a case in which the animal sacrifice had been sacrificed at that very moment. But if the animal set apart for the sacrifice had not been sacrificed at that moment, then the condemned man is treated as if he had committed the sin at that very moment, and [priests are] not obligated [to attend to] his need [for bringing a sin-offering," as at A].

M.1:3 consists of a dispute, A-B versus C-F; the form of the second opinion, C-F, follows that of M.1:1D-E, F-G, that is, the specification of a reason for a rule. One who is about to die is worth nothing if sold in a marketplace, so, too, the one about to be executed. Therefore he is not subject to the vow that others will pay his worth or the pledge of Valuation. Hananiah rejects this view for the stated reason. The pledge of Valuation certainly is fixed and payable; the worth to be paid by a vow is null. Yosé's saying is separate from the foregoing. The man's estate can be encumbered by these vows or other obligations. The Talmud's exegesis of the Mishnah paragraph follows a clear-cut program. Unit I undertakes to clarify the language of the Mishnah passage itself. Unit II does the same, now carrying out a close reading of the latter part of the same passage. Unit III, continuous with the foregoing but pursuing its own interests, takes over the thesis given in unit II about what is at issue and assigns the disputed principle to another case entirely. This moves in its own direction, as we see. Unit IV then introduces a secondary teaching on the same theme as that of

M., supplementing the topic but not treating the principle at all. The cited passage is given its own systematic exegesis.

Does this unit talk about "everything" or some few things? The program has already been clarified, for the Mishnah, then the Tosefta, then some passages continuous with the foregoing in theme or principle. Can we explain why the Talmud includes everything that is before us – and therefore can we postulate that the authorship of the Bavli has excluded what it found irrelevant and included only what served its purpose? Indeed we can.

1:4

A.   The [pregnant] woman who goes forth to be put to death –

B.   they do not postpone [the execution] for her until she will give birth.

C.   [If] she sat on the travailing stool, they postpone [the execution] for her until she will give birth.

D.   The woman who is executed – they derive benefit from her hair.

E.   A beast which is executed – it [the hair] is prohibited from benefit.

I.

A.   [The rule of A-B] is self-evident, for [the foetus] is [merely part of] her body [and not a separate creature, until labor pains begin. There is no reason to take account of the foetus.]

B.   [No, it was] entirely necessary [to state the matter explicitly. Why?] I might have proposed the thesis that, since it is written, "According as the woman's husband shall lay on him" (Ex. 21:22) [in paying the indemnity for the miscarriage], [the foetus] belongs to the husband and should not be taken away from him.

C.   Accordingly, we are informed [that that is not the case where a woman is going to be executed].

D.   And may I perhaps maintain the view that that is indeed the case?

E.   [No. For,] said R. Abbahu said R. Yohanan, "A verse of Scripture has said, '[If a man is found lying with the wife of another man,] they shall die, even both of them' (Deut. 22:22). [The word, even,] serves to include the foetus."

F.   But the cited verse serves to prove [a different proposition:] "Both of them [the man and woman offender] must be equivalent [in status, that is, as adults. If adultery is committed by a minor and an adult, the former is not put to death]," the words of R. Josiah, [so that is the point proved by the cited verse when it says "even."]

G.   That is in accord with what you have stated [and, indeed, the word serves to prove both propositions.]

II.

A.   *If she sat on the travailing stool* [M. 1:4C]: What is the reason for the stated rule?

    B.   Because once the foetus has begun parturition, it is deemed a separate human being.

III.

    A   Said Rab Judah said Samuel, "As to a woman who is going forth to be put to death, they hit her on the womb so as to kill the foetus first, in order that the woman may not be disgraced [by having the foetus come forth after she has died]."

    B.   [The foregoing statement therefore] implies that the woman [without doing this] would die first. But we have it as fact that the foetus dies first.

    C   For we have learned the following rule [at M. Nid. 5:3]: *An infant merely a day old may inherit an estate or cause [one of his legal heirs to] inherit an estate.* [The pertinence of this statement becomes clear presently.]

    D.   In this connected, R. Sheshet stated, "He inherits the estate of the mother, so as to cause his brothers on his father's side to inherit that estate. [That is, if the infant survives the mother and then dies, his brothers on his already deceased father's side inherit his deceased mother's estate. The estate then does not pass back to his mother's family, as it would if the infant died without surviving brothers on his deceased father's side.]

    E   "Now that is the rule specifically in a case in which the infant is a day old. But in the case of a foetus, that is not the case."

    F.   [And the reason, obviously, is that we assume that if the mother died her foetus would die first] and a male offspring may not [theoretically] inherit the estate of his mother when he already is in the grave [before she dies] so as to pass on that estate to his brothers on his father's side. [Accordingly, the assumption above, A-B, that the foetus dies after the woman is clearly not held in the present instance and is called into question.]

    G.   [No, that is really not the case. Why not?] The rule just now given [assuming that the mother dies first] applies to natural death, for, since the infant is small, the poisonous drop [of death] given by the angel of death goes in very quickly and destroys the vital organs [so the infant dies first].

    H.   But in a case in which the woman is put to death, she dies first.

    I.   Now there was a case, in which [the foetus] moved three times [thus indicating that it survived the execution of the mother].

    J.   [No.] It was comparable to the case of the tail of a lizard, which twitches [after death even though the lizard is already dead].

IV.

    A   Said R. Nahman said Samuel, "In the case of a woman who sat down on the travailing stool and died, [even] on the Sabbath people may bring a knife and cut open her belly and remove the infant [even though cutting is normally forbidden]."

    B.   That rule is self-evident [and hardly requires articulation], for what has one done? [7B] He has only cut into meat [which one may do on the Sabbath, e.g., even in eating a meal. Why therefore was it found necessary to make such a self-evident statement?]

C.   Said Rabbah, "No, [it is not self-evident, and] it was necessary to
      state matters to indicate that one may bring a knife even through
      public domain."

D.   Yet what does he wish to tell us [in so stating]? Is it that in a case
      of doubt [as to the saving of life] one may violate the sanctity of
      the Sabbath?

E.   We already have learned that very point: In the case of one upon
      whom debris has fallen [on the Sabbath], in which case there is
      doubt whether he is there or not, whether he is alive or dead,
      whether he is a Canaanite or an Israelite, people may remove the
      mound [of debris] from on him. [So it is clear that, in a case of
      doubt, in order to save life one carries out an otherwise prohibited
      action.]

F.   [No,] it nonetheless was necessary to state the same principle in
      the *present* case. For] what might you otherwise have ruled? In
      that other case, the rule applies because there is the presumption
      that the man is alive [since he was alive before the debris fell], but
      here, in which there is no presumption that the infant is alive to
      begin with, I might have ruled that the rule does not pertain.

G.   Accordingly, we are informed [to the contrary, that that is not the
      case, and even in a case of doubt such as we have at hand, the
      same rule applies.]

V.

A.   *The woman who is executed* [M. 1:4D], and so forth:

B.   Why [in this case is it the rule that one may use the woman's
      hair]? [Is it not the case that her hair] is subject to a prohibition
      against deriving benefit?

C.   Said Rab, "The rule applies [however, only] in a case in which the
      woman herself has stated, 'Hand over my hair to my daughter'"
      [cf. T. Ar. 1:4D-F].

D.   But if she had said, "Hand over my hands to my daughter," would
      we have handed them over? [Of course not!]

E.   Said Rab, "The rule speaks of a wig made from the hair of a
      gentile woman. [In such a case, we do not regard the wig as part of
      her body and therefore prohibited for further utilization. Why
      not? Since she has spoken of the wig as separate from her body,
      we treat it as separate and hand it over to the daughter.]"

F.   So the reason is that the woman herself has stated, "Give [my wig
      to my daughter]." Lo, if she had *not* said, "Give...," [we should
      have regarded it as] part of her body and forbidden.

G.   But lo, this very principle [which you take for granted as valid]
      presents a problem to R. Yosé bar Hanina, for R. Yosé bar Hanina
      raised the question, "What about the hair of righteous women,"
      and in this very regard, Raba stated, "[In asking about the hair of
      righteous women, Hanina refers to the case of a righteous woman
      who is wearing] a wig made from the hair of a gentile woman."
      [Under discussion is the case of a rebellious city, which, in accord
      with Deut. 13:13 ff. is to be destroyed. The property of all residents
      is destroyed, and those who actually committed idolatry are put to
      death. Righteous persons are saved, but they too lose their

property. Is the wig of a righteous woman part of her body, therefore not destroyed, or is it mere property, therefore destroyed?]

H.　The reason that the problem troubled R. Yosé bar Hanina was that the wig was hung on a peg, [and so was not clearly part of the woman's body at any time]. But here [in the case of the woman who is put to death] we deal with a case in which the wig is permanently attached to the woman.

I.　The operative reason, then, is that the woman has stated, "Give...," but had she not said, "Give...," it would have been regarded as part of her body and therefore forbidden.

J.　[If the rule governing the woman refers to her wig when it says *"one may derive benefit from her hair,"* then that interpretation] poses a problem to R. Nahman bar Issac, [for he stated matters as follows]: "Lo, the rule at hand treats the woman as analogous to the beast. [Hence the reference of the framer of the Mishnah cannot be to the wig, which is not part of the woman's body. Why not?] Just as, in the case of the beast, we refer to its body [when we say one may not derive benefit from it], so here, too, we refer to the body of the woman [and not to her wig. So the wig would introduce an anomaly.]"

K.　"Rather," said R. Nahman, "[The cases are not analogous at all. For,] in the case of the woman, it is only when she actually dies that [her body] becomes prohibited, while in the case of the beast, it is at the conclusion of the trial [and not merely at the moment of execution] that the beast becomes prohibited. [That is the operative distinction explaining the Mishnah passage.]"

M.　Levi repeated the rule in accord with the view of Rab, and Levi repeated the rule also in accord with the position of R. Nahman bar Isaac.

N.　Levi repeated the rule in accord with the position of Rab [by formulating matters as follows]: "As to a woman who is going forth to be put to death and said, 'Hand over my hair to my daughter,' they hand it over to the daughter.

N.　"[Once she] has died, they do not hand it over to her, for what derives from a corpse is not given over for the benefit [of survivors]."

O.　[That second point] is self-evident [and hardly regards specification].

P.　"Rather," [repeat the tradition as follows:] *"the ornaments of the dead are not given over for the benefit of survivors."* [This version then must refer to the wig, just as Rab has said].

Q.　He further repeated the tradition in accord with the interpretation of R. Nahman bar Isaac: "As to a woman who has died, people may derive benefit from her hair. As to a beast who has been put to death, it is forbidden to derive benefit [from the corpse].

R.　"Now what is the difference between the one and the other? In the case of the woman, it is only when she actually dies that [her body] becomes prohibited while in the case of the beast, it is at the conclusion of the trial [and not merely at the moment of execution] that the beast becomes prohibited."

Does this unit talk about "everything" or some few things? Can we explain why the Talmud includes everything that is before us – and therefore can we postulate that the authorship of the Bavli has excluded what it found irrelevant and included only what served its purpose? The answers are self-evident. The Talmud systematically works out the explanation of the Mishnah's rules. Unit I explains why the rule of A-B must be made explicit. Unit II carries forward the exegesis of the same matter and completes it. Unit III raises the first of three secondary amplifications on the theme of the Mishnah paragraph, unit IV, the second, unit V, the third. This chapter contains nothing that lends support to the theories of Steinsaltz and Wieseltier on the character of the document. What they say may accurately describe some other tractates or chapters of the Bavli. But their descriptions prove wildly inappropriate to the highly disciplined and well-crafted writing before us. It begins to appear that, in taking their allegations so seriously and at face value, we may have done them an injustice; they, and many others who concur in their position, may simply be retailing hazy impressions of, not well-considered propositions about, the Bavli. Even though the results will begin to produce an embarassment for Steinsaltz's and Wieseltier's position, we nonetheless proceed to two more chapters of the same tractate, with the same issues in mind.

4

Bavli Arakhin
Chapter Four

As before, unit by unit, we ask these questions for the chapter at hand, in the language of Steinsaltz and Wieseltier:

1. Is it true that "The Talmud...deals with an overwhelmingly broad subject – the nature of all things according to the Torah. Therefore its contours are a reflection of life itself. It has no formal external order, but is bound by a strong inner connection between [sic!] its many diverse subjects"?

2. Is it true that "...the Talmud is, in truth, about all things. There is no corner of human life and no corner of Jewish life into which the fastidious rabbis did not peer"?

4:1

A. [17A] [The estimate of] ability to pay [is made in accord with the status of] the one who vows [Lev. 27:8].

B. And [the estimate of] the years [of age is made in accord with the status of] the one [whose Valuation] is vowed.

C. And [when this is according to] the Valuations [spelled out in the Torah], it is in accord with the status [age, sex] of the one whose Valuation is pledged.

D. And the Valuation [is paid in accordance with the rate prescribed] at the time of the pledge of Valuation.

E. [The estimate of] ability to pay [is made in accord with the status of] the one who vows: How so?

F. A poor man who pledged the Valuation of a rich man gives the Valuation required of a poor man.

G. And a rich man who pledged the Valuation of a poor man gives the Valuation required of a rich man.

4:2A-E

A. But in the case of offerings, [the rule] is not so.

B.   Lo, [if] one said, "The [obligation to bring] the offering of this person with skin disease (mesora') is incumbent on me," if the person with the skin ailment (mesora') was poor, he brings the offering of a poor man. [If the mesora' was] rich, he brings the offering of a rich one.

C.   Rabbi says, "I say, 'Also in the case of Valuations the rule is so.

D.   "And on what account does the poor man who pledged the Valuation of the rich man give the Valuation of a poor man? Because the rich man [under such circumstances, in any case] owes nothing.

E.   "But a rich man who said, 'My Valuation is incumbent on me,' and a poor man heard and said, 'What this one has said is incumbent on me [too],' he [the poor man] gives the Valuation of the rich one."

I.

A.   The estimate of ability to pay is made in accord with the status of the one who vows [M. 4:1A], as it is written [in Scripture], "According to the means of him who took the vow shall the priest value him" (Lev. 27:8).

B.   But is it the case that [payment according to the] years of his age is assessed only in respect to the one [whose worth has been] vowed? Is it not the case that it is only with regard to the one who has been subject to valuation? [Why then use the language of "vow" [at M.4:1B] when that language is inappropriate and inapplicable?]

C.   Since the framer of the passage has stated, *The estimate of ability to pay is made in accord with the status of the one who vows*, he also framed matters in respect to the assessment of years in the language of one concerning whom the vow is taken [rather than using the correct wording, the one concerning whom *the pledge of Valuation* is taken].

II.

A.   The estimate of ability to pay is made in accord with the status of the one who vows: How so? A poor man who pledged the Valuation of a rich man gives the Valuation required of a poor man [M. 4:1E-F]:

B.   What is the scriptural basis for this rule? As Scripture has said, "According to the means of him who took the vow."

C.   The All-Merciful thus had made the matter dependent upon the means of the one who took the vow.

III.

A.   But in the case of offerings, the rule is not so. Lo, if one said, "The obligation to bring the offering of this person with a skin ailment (mesora') is incumbent on me," if the person with the skin ailment (mesora') was poor, he brings the offering of a poor man [M. 4:2A-8B].

B.   But is that the case even though the one who took the vow was rich? [Surely not!]

C. "And if he is poor" (Lev. 14:21) is what the All-Merciful has stated, and this man is not poor!

D. Said R. Isaac, "[The rule speaks of a case in which] the one who took the vow was poor."

E. But perhaps the intent of the All-Merciful was to show mercy to the victim himself, but not to the one who took a vow in his regard, for has it not been written, "...if *he* is poor..."!

F. Said R. Adda bar Ahba, "[When Scripture states,] 'And his means not suffice,' it serves to encompass the one who takes the vow. But if the one who took a vow were rich, in such a case he would have to bring the offerings required of a rich man."

G. If that is so, why then does the Mishnah passage state, *But in the case of offerings, the rule is not so?*

H. [17B] The one [M.4:1E-F] refers to a person afflicted with the skin disease who was poor, and to one who took a vow concerning him who also was poor, and the other [M.4:2A-B] serves to exclude the case of a person afflicted with the skin disease who was rich, and the person who took the oath concerning him was poor.

I. You might have entertained the view that one might say, Since he was included, he was included for all purposes. [Jung, p. 101, n. 5: "One might have assumed that since on the basis of the Scriptural 'And his means suffice not,' we include the poor man vowing a poor leper's sacrifice in the consideration due to a poor man's dedicating a rich man, that therefore we might extend the same consideration even to a poor man's vowing a rich leper's sacrifice, therefore we need the exclusive meaning of, 'If he be too poor,' i.e., only a poor leper's sacrifice is reduced, but a rich leper's sacrifice, even if vowed by a poor man, is not reduced."]

J. Thus we are informed that that is not the case.

K. [To amplify:] Since we find in the case of Valuations that a poor man who pledged the Valuation of a rich man pays the Valuation owing by a poor man, we might have assumed that the same rule applies here.

L. Accordingly, Scripture states, "If *he* is poor...."

M. And in the view of Rabbi, who has said, "*I say, Also in the case of Valuations, the rule is so*" [M. 4:2C], here, too, we follow the obligation applying to the man in question [who is subject to the vow of Valuation, not the one who took the vow], there is no need for a verse of Scripture to exclude that possibility. So how shall we interpret that verse?

N. It serves as an exclusion.

O. What does it serve to exclude?

P. It serves to exclude the case of one afflicted by the skin ailment who was poor, while the one who took the oath concerning him was rich.

Q. I might have reached the conclusion that, since Rabbi has said that we assess matters in terms of the obligation pertaining to the person [subject to the vow of Valuation], here too the rule would be the same. Thus we are informed [that that is not the case].

When Scripture speaks of an ability to pay, it refers to the person who has to make the payment, the one who vows. When Scripture speaks of the age, it refers to the age concerning whom the vow is made, M. 4:1B, or the age or sex of the one whose Valuation is pledged, C. When a Valuation is pledged and the person to be valuated passes into another age category, D, the Valuation is owed as of the time of the pledge. Since B and C repeat one another (as M. 4:4 will show), the purpose clearly is to give us four remarkably succinct rules, built on the roots NDR and 'RK, respectively. The explanation, E-G, poses no problem of interpretation. M. 4:2A explicitly links M. 4:2 to M. 4:1E-G; then M. 4:2F-G to M. 4:3 (below) provide their own expansion of M. 4:1E-G, followed by their expected secondary development in terms of Temple offerings. Accordingly, we have a rather elaborate double expansion of M. 4:1E-G. The point of M. 4:2A-B is that while, in the case of Valuations, the estimate of the ability to pay is made in accord with the status of the one who makes the vow, in the case of offerings, it is made in accord with the status of the one who owes the offering, not the one who vows to pay it. This is spelled out at B. Rabbi then wishes to reject M. 4:1A and to impose the same rule as applies for offerings. His reasoning is spelled out at D-E. When the matter of Valuations is similar to that of offerings, there is no difference in the applicable rule. Does this unit talk about "everything" or some few things? Can we explain why the Talmud includes everything that is before us – and therefore can we postulate that the authorship of the Bavli has excluded what it found irrelevant and included only what served its purpose? The Talmud, for its part, systematically cites and glosses units of the Mishnah paragraph, providing a scriptural basis for each rule. Only unit III takes up matters of analysis of the operative principles at hand. Nothing is out of place; not a line is so irrelevant to its context as to justify the conception that the Talmud is about just anything, or about "everything" without order or sense.

4:2F-4:3

F.   [If] he was poor and got rich, or rich and grew poor, he gives the Valuation of a rich man.

G.   R. Judah says, "Even if he was poor and got rich and then became poor again, he gives the Valuation of a rich man."

A.   But in the case of offerings, the rule is not so.

B.   Even if his father [is about to] die and leave him ten thousand,

C.   [even if] his ship was at sea and [about to] arrive with ten thousand,

D.   the sanctuary has no claim whatsoever on them.

I.

- A. *If he was poor and got rich* [M. 4:2F]:
- B. "According to the means of him who took the vow" (Lev. 27:8).
- C. *Or rich and grew poor* [M. 4:2F]:
- D. "According to the means of him who took the vow" (Lev. 27:8).
- E. *R. Judah says, "Even if he was poor and got rich and then became poor again, he gives the Valuation of a rich man"* [M. 4:2G]:
- F. What is the scriptural foundation for the view of R. Judah? Scripture has stated, "But if he be too poor for your valuation" (Lev. 28:8).
- G. [The rule applies] only if he remains in his condition of poverty from the beginning to the end [of the transaction].

II.

- A. [By that same reasoning,] how do you deal with what follows: "If he be too poor..." (Lev. 14:19, 21). [The one afflicted with the skin ailment has to bring a guilt-offering, a sin-offering, and a whole offering. The latter two are of variable value, depending on the status of the one who is afflicted and now purified.]
- B. Would you hold the view that, in this case as well, the [person securing purification is subject to the offering for a poor person] only if he remains in his condition of poverty from the beginning to the end of the transaction?
- C. And if you wish to maintain that that is indeed the case, have we not learned [to the contrary, at M. Neg. 14:11, that we differentiate among the offerings required of the one who seeks purification from the skin ailment in accord with his condition at the moment at which each of the three required offerings is brought, so that, should his status change, he will bring a different offering in accord with his new status:] *A person who has suffered the skin ailment who brought his offerings as a poor man and suddenly got rich, or a rich man who became poor –*
- D. *"All is in accord with [the man's condition at the moment at which he brought] the purification-offering [among the three that are required]," the words of R. Simeon.*
- E. *R. Judah says, "All is in accord with [the man's condition at the moment at which he brought] the guilt-offering."*
- F. And it has further been taught on Tannaite authority: R. Eliezer b. Jacob says, "All is in accord with [the man's condition at the moment at which he brought] the bird-offerings."
- G. [By way of reply:] lo, it has been stated in regard to the problem at hand: Said Rab Judah said Rab, "All three authorities interpret the same verse of Scripture, namely, 'Whose means do not suffice for what is needed for his purification' (Lev. 14:32). [The dispute turns on the meaning of the words "what is needed."]
- H. "R. Simeon maintains the theory that at issue is that which effects purification, and what is it? It is the purification-offering.
- I. "R. Judah theorizes that it is the component of the offering which renders him fit once more, and what might that be? It is the guilt-offering.

J.   "R. Eliezer b. Jacob takes the position that it is the component that in fact causes the man to return to a condition of cleanness, and what is that? It is the bird-offering."

K.   Rather, why [does Scripture say] "[If] *he* [be too poor]" (Lev. 14:19, 21)?

L.   It is according to Rabbi (at M.4:2F, II.M), as he maintains, and to rabbis, as they do.

III.

A.   But [if *he* indicates that the person must remain in the same condition throughout the procedure, and if that is not the case, then he does not enjoy the remission accorded to the poor man,] how do you deal with the following, "And *he* being witness" (Lev. 5:1). [Does this mean] that he must be a valid witness from the beginning to the end of the process, [or otherwise the rule of Lev. 5:1 does not apply]?

B.   And should you say that that is indeed the case, lo, it has been taught in a Tannaite teaching:

C.   If someone had evidence that he might offer for another party, [which evidence he gained] prior to becoming the man's son-in-law, and then he became his son-in-law, [or if he acquired the evidence while] he had his sense of hearing, but then was struck deaf, or he could see and then became blind, or he was of sound senses and then became an idiot – lo, this one is invalid [to give testimony]. But if someone had evidence that he might offer for another party, [which evidence he gained] prior to becoming the man's son-in-law and he then became his son-in-law [18A] but afterward [he ceased to be his son-in-law because] the man's daughter died, [or] if he acquired the evidence while he had his sense of hearing but then was struck deaf and later on regained his sense of hearing, or if he could see and then became blind but regained his sight, or if he was of sound senses and then became an idiot but regained his senses – lo, this one is valid [to give testimony].

D.   This is the operative principle: In the case of anyone who at the outset and at the end was fit [to give testimony], such a one is fit to give testimony [even though at the intervening time he was not fit]. [This would contradict the supposition proposed just now.]

E.   The cited case is different, for Scripture has said, "...or if he saw [and was placed under oath] but he did not utter it, then he shall bear his iniquity" (Lev. 5:1). Accordingly, the All-Merciful has made the matter depend upon seeing [at the outset] and telling [at the end], and lo, [in the cases outlined above,] these [matters] are indeed present. [The intervening span is of no account.]

F.   In that case, why does Scripture state, "[If] *he* being a witness"? It accords with that which has been taught on Tannaite authority:

G.   If a bunch of people is standing, and those who were witnesses [for] his [case] were among them, and he said, "I impose an oath upon you people, if you have evidence to give in my behalf, that you come and give evidence in my behalf," –

> H.   Is it possible to suppose that [all of them] would be liable for the oath at hand?
> I.   Scripture says, "If he being a witness" (Lev. 5:1). [The oath applies only to specified persons but not to an amorphous group.]
> J.   And lo, the man has not specified which of the persons are to serve as his witnesses.
> K.   Is it possible to maintain that even if the man had said, "Whoever [knows testimony to serve in my behalf," without specifying whom he means], [the oath would still be valid?]
> L.   Scripture states, "And *he* being a witness..."
> M.   So lo, he must single them out. [A definite person must be specified as the witness who is to be subjected to the oath of testimony.]

IV.

> A.   *But in the case of offerings, the rule is not so. Even if his father is [about to] die and leave him ten thousand* [M. 4:3A-B].
> B.   [If that is the case], he is a rich man!
> C.   Said R. Abbahu, "I might say [the Mishnah passage means that the father] was going to leave him ten thousand [but had not yet done so]."
> D.   But that is self-evident.
> E.   [Indeed. We deal with a case] in which the father was dying [but had not yet died].
> F.   What ruling would you make in such a case?
> G.   Most of those who are dying actually do die.
> H.   Thus we are informed [that we do not decide on the basis of that supposition, but until the man actually has received his inheritance upon the father's death, we do not categorize him as a rich man].

V.

> A.   *[Even if] the ship was at sea and about to arrive with ten thousand* [M. 4:3C]:
> B.   [If that is the case], he is a rich man!
> C.   Said R. Hisda, "We deal with a case in which the man had rented, or hired out his boat to others."
> D.   But then there is the rental payment, [so he is not poor]?
> E.   Rental payments do not fall due until the end [of the period of rental, so while the boat is at sea, the rental payment is not owing and the man cannot be said to enjoy the ownership of what is owing in due course].
> F.   But you may derive the fact that he is rich because of his ownership of the boat, all by itself.
> G.   Lo, in accord with whose view is the passage at hand [which denies we take account of his ownership of the boat in assessing the man's worth]? It accords with R. Eliezer.
> H.   For we have learned: *R. Eliezer says, "If he was a farmer, they must leave him his yoke of oxen, and if he was an ass driver, they must leave him his ass"* [M. Ar. 6:3]. [Jung, p. 105, n. 1: Just as the farmer's yoke of oxen are his tools wherewith he earns his living, just as the ass driver's ass for that reason may not be taken in

pledge, so is this man's boat a tool wherewith he earns his living
and must not be taken either.]

M. 4:2F develops M. 4:1F-G. If a man was poor and got rich (M. 2:1),
or rich and grew poor, we impose the more stringent status. Judah does
not differ; he simply extends the rule. Then M. 4:3 again differentiates
Valuations from offerings. If a man was poor and he got rich (B, C), he
fulfills his obligation with the original offering required of him at the
moment at which he presented it. The Talmud first glosses, then
expands upon, the Mishnah passage. Does this unit talk about
"everything" or some few things? The Talmud deals with the
Mishnah, pure and simple. Can we explain why the Talmud includes
everything that is before us – and therefore can we postulate that the
authorship of the Bavli has excluded what it found irrelevant and
included only what served its purpose? The intent of the framer is
clearly to clarify the Mishnah paragraph; what serves, and what does
not, is readily discerned.

4:4A-J

A.   [The estimate of] the years [of his age is made in accord
        with the status of] the one [whose Valuation] is vowed:
        How so?

B.   A child who pledged the Valuation of an elder gives the
        Valuation of an elder.

C.   And an elder who pledged the Valuation of a child gives
        the Valuation of a child.

D.   And [when this is reckoned according to] the Valuation
        [spelled out in the Torah], it is in accord with the status of
        the one whose Valuation is pledged: How so?

E.   A man who pledged the Valuation of a woman gives the
        Valuation of a woman.

F.   And a woman who pledged the Valuation of a man gives
        the Valuation of a man.

G.   And the Valuation [is paid in accordance with the rate
        prescribed] at the time of the pledge of Valuation: How
        so?

H.   [If] one pledged the Valuation of another when the latter
        was less than five years old, and [that one] passed five,

I.   less than twenty years old and he passed twenty,

J.   he pays in accord with what is required at the time of the
        pledge of Valuation.

I.

A.   Our rabbis have taught on Tannaite authority:

B.   You have placed in the same classification vows of worth and
        Valuations, with regard to [the valuation of] a pearl for the poor,

C.   and with regard to the rule that the value of a limb be judged in
        accord with its importance. [Jung: If a poor man owned a pearl
        which is in his place of residence, for lack of demand, is worth but

thirty *selas*, whereas in a large town where there are many buyers, it would be worth fifty, one must assume that it is worth only what the poor man can get for it now, in his place of residence. The poor man who vowed his own valuation would hence not have to pay fifty *selas* (if he were between twenty and fifty years of age‸ although the pearl might fetch that price elsewhere. Now the same rule applies to the case of one who said, 'I take it upon myself to pay to the Sanctuary the value of this pearl." Here, too, since we compared valuation to vow of market value, the vower would have to pay the lower price....]

D. Is it possible that we should also place in a single classification pledges of Valuation and vows of the actual value [of an object, payable to the sanctuary], so that the donor must pay in accord with the price prevailing at the time he *actually* pays the funds?

E. [To forestall that conclusion], Scripture states, "According to your valuation it shall stand" (Lev. 27:17).

F. One pays only what the object was worth at the time of Valuation, [and not at the time of paying over what he owes, at which point a different value might attach to the object].

Does this unit talk about "everything" or some few things? Can we explain why the Talmud includes everything that is before us – and therefore can we postulate that the authorship of the Bavli has excluded what it found irrelevant and included only what served its purpose? The Talmud raises a separate question, based on the comparison of Valuations and vows of value, namely, why we do not invoke the rule of M. 4:4D-F for the case of M. 4:4G-J, that is, treating what is owing as relative to the price at the moment the funds are to be paid, as much as we treat what is owing as relative to the resources of the one who took the vow. The reason that that is not the case is neatly spelled out. Nothing is out of place; every unit, and nearly every line of every unit, is absolutely necessary to accomplish the framers' goals, which concern a limited topic and problem.

4:4K-R

K. [If a man pledged the Valuation of a child who on that day had reached his] thirtieth day [he is considered] less than that. [And if the person whose Valuation was pledged reached his] fifth year or twentieth year [he is considered] less than that. [That is, in order to fall into the category of a five year old or twenty year old he must be five years and a day or twenty years and a day.]

L. As it says, And if it be from sixty years old and upward, if it be a male (Lev. 27:7).

M. Lo, we derive the rule for all cases from that applicable to the sixtieth year.

N. Just as the sixtieth year is deemed equivalent to less than that age, so the fifth year or the twentieth year is deemed equivalent to less than that age.

O.   Is this so? If Scripture has treated the sixtieth year as less than it, it is to impose a more stringent rule. Shall we then treat the fifth year and the twentieth year as less than they, to impose a more lenient rule?

P.   Scripture says, Year...year..., for the purposes of establishing an analogy.

Q.   Just as *year* stated in connection with the sixtieth year is deemed equivalent to less than it, so year stated in connection with the fifth year and the twentieth year are deemed equivalent to less than they, whether this imposes a lenient or a stringent ruling.

R.   R. Eleazar says, "The foregoing applies so long as they are a month and a day more than the years [which are prescribed]."

I.

A.   [The use of the identical words cited at P for the exegetical purpose at hand is because] those [words] are free [for such usage, not serving any other interpretative purpose. That is why we may draw the comparison specified here.]

B.   If that were not the case, there would be the possibility of raising such a difficulty as we have raised [at M. 4:4.O]. But, as it happens, *Year...year...* do prove superfluous, [allowing the deduction specified at P-Q].

II.

A.   May we propose that the Mishnah rule at hand does not accord with the principle of Rabbi, for if it did, [it would present a contradiction] for has Rabbi not stated, "[When we find the word] 'up to' [used in the specification of a rule, e.g., covering age], the usage is inclusive [in which case 'up to such-and-such a year' means to include even the first day of that year]."

B.   For it has been taught in a statement of Tannaite authority: "From the first day until the seventh day" (Ex. 12:15) –

C.   May one suppose that the count begins from the first day, but does not include the first day, and likewise, goes up to the seventh day, but does not include the seventh day?" [18B]

D.   That would be in line with the statement, "From his head to his feet" (Lev. 13:12), in which "from his head" does not include his head, and "to his feet" does not include his feet.

E.   Scripture says, "Until the twenty-first day of the month, at evening" (Ex. 12:18). [Including the statement, "at evening," indicates that the seventh day is included in the count, likewise the first day. Accordingly, we can demonstrate that the first and seventh day are included in the Passover regulations specified at Ex. 12.]

F.   Rabbi says, "It is not necessary [to provide such a proof]. 'First' always means, 'including the first day,' and 'seventh' includes the seventh day."

G.   [No, the proposition that Rabbi does not concur here is not necessarily valid, for] you may even say that Rabbi [is in agreement]. But here the verses of Scripture are in balance.

H. [How so?] Since it is written, [From a month old even to five years old" (Lev. 27:6), why was it stated further, "From five years old even to twenty years old" (Lev. 27:5)? Therefore the verses are in balance [since the fifth and the twentieth years could belong to either of the two periods. Since the meaning of the verses is not determined, it is necessary to invoke the analogy provided at M. 4:4P. But under other circumstances, a framer in accord with Rabbi's principle would not find it necessary to do so.]

I. [Completing the exposition of the materials just now reviewed,] a master has said, "'His head,' not including the head, 'his feet,' not including the feet. How do we know [on the basis of Scripture that that is the fact]?

J. "If you wish, I shall state, 'Because the signs of the skin ailment that appear on the body differ from those that appear on the head [so we have to treat the two parts of the body as separate from one another].'

K. "If you wish, I shall state, [Scripture specifies], 'As far as the eyes of the priest can see' (Lev. 13:12). [A given part of the body is defined as a unit by the possibility of what the priest can see at a single glance. He could take in the body all at once, but not including the head or the feet, at which a more detailed inspection, e.g., of the hair of the head, of the space between the toes, would be required]."

III.

A. *R. Eliezer says, "The foregoing applies so long as they are a month and a day more than the years [which are prescribed]"* [M. 4:4R]. [From the passing of a month and a day beyond the fifth birthday, the child is in the status of the following span of time – fifth to twentieth – and so on, a qualification of M. 4:4K].

B. It was taught on Tannaite authority: R. Eliezer says, "Here it is said, 'and upward,' and there it is said, 'and upward' (Num. 3:43). [Any Levite more than a month old, even by one day, was included in the counting].

C. "Just as, in the latter case, 'From a month and one day' is the meaning, so here, too, the meaning is, a month and a day."

D. May I propose that just as there "one day" so here, too, "one day" [is the rule]? [Jung: Since here the addition is but one day, perhaps it ought to be exactly alike with the years in the case of valuations.] [Do we limit the argument at hand to the matter of the case before us, namely, the infant, or do we extend the same consideration to all the other cases.]

E. If that were the case, of what value would be the argument by analogy [proposed by M. 4:4P-Q]?

IV.

A. Our rabbis have repeated on Tannaite authority: "The year" stated with reference to Holy Things [animals set aside and sanctified for use in the sacrificial service], dwelling houses in a walled city, the two years of the field of possession, the six years of the Hebrew slave (Ex. 21:2), [and] the son or daughter, run from day to day [that is, from one day to the corresponding date in the following year. They do not follow the calendar: the count for the second year would not begin on the first of Tishri without regard to the point in the prior year at which the count began.]

B.   How do we know [from Scripture] that that is the case for the assessment of the age of Holy Things?

C.   Said R. Aha bar Jacob, "Scripture has said, 'A lamb in *its* first year' (Lev. 12:6) – thus its year and not the year as counted out from the creation of the world [at Tishri]."

D.   How do we know [from Scripture] that that is the case with reference to the dwelling houses in a walled city?

E.   For it is written, "Within a whole year from its sale" (Lev. 25:29) – its [year of] sale, and not the year as counted out from the creation of the world.

F.   The two years of the field of possession [during which the original owner may not redeem the field by repurchase]?

G.   For it is written, "According to the number of years of the crops he shall sell to you" (Lev. 25:15). There may be occasions on which a person may have usufruct of three crops in two years.

H.   How do we know [from Scripture] that that is the case for the six years of the Hebrew slave? As it is written, [Six years will he serve, and in the seventh" (Ex. 21:2). [This reference to the seventh year] implies that there may be times that, in the seventh year of his term of service, he will still be working.

I.   As to those for the son and the daughter – for what practical purpose do we require this rule?

J.   Said R. Giddal said Rab, "It is for use in regard to vows of Valuation."

K.   R. Joseph said, "It is with regard to our study of the chapter that deals with those born through Caesarean section [Jung: In that chapter the age is discussed at which a son or daughter is able to vow.]

L.   Said Abayye to R. Joseph, "Do you differ [from Rab]?"

M.   He said to him, "No. I say one thing, and he says a quite separate one." [We agree with one another.]

N.   That is a reasonable position, for if you maintain the view that the two are in conflict, so that the one who maintains the view that at issue are pledges of Valuation but not considerations raised in the chapter on Caesarean births, has not Rab stated that the practical decision in all cases in the cited chapter involves a full year reckoned from day to day. [So he clearly takes the same view in both categories.]

O.   Accordingly, what is the reason that the one who phrased matters in terms of reckoning the years for pledges of Valuation did not frame matters in terms of reckoning the years for the cases specified in the chapter on Caesarean births?

P.   Because [the cases of the son or daughter] are analogous to the cases cited earlier [e.g., the consecrated animals].

Q.   Just as the one set is written in the Torah, so the other refers to what is written in the Torah [that is, Valuations].

R.   And the other party [which makes reference to the cases specified in the chapter on Caesarean births, rather than to the matter of Valuations]?

S.   If it should enter your mind that the reference is to matters that are specified in Scripture, then the statement, "With a son or daughter" [19A] should be phrased, "male or female" [as is the case at Lev. 27].

V.

A.   Why is a female at old age valued at a third, while a man is not even at a third? [A woman under sixty is valued at thirty *selas*, above sixty, at ten; a man under sixty is valued at fifty *selas*, over sixty at fifteen *selas*, less than a third].

B.   Said Hezekiah, "People say, 'An old man in the house is a broken utensil in the house, an old woman in the house is a jewel in the house."

M. 4:4K + L-N form an appendix to G-J, and O-Q challenge the reasoning, but not the conclusion of L-N. Then R forms a further gloss of K. K therefore is the principal addition. A child five years old is deemed less than five; only when the sixth year begins (in contrast to R) do we charge the Valuation specified in Scripture, and so with twenty. The proof is at L-N. Scripture is explicit that one must be more than sixty years of age. O-Q indicate that the proposed analogy may not hold and provide a formal proof. Eleazar then states that the fifth, twentieth, and sixtieth years are deemed as equivalent to the preceding ones only for thirty-one days. From that point on, the fifth year is deemed equivalent to the following ones, down through the twentieth, and so for the twentieth and the sixtieth. His qualification, as is clear, goes right back to K and bears no relationship to the intervening materials. Unit I amplifies the exegetical discussion in the Mishnah paragraph itself. Unit II investigates the relationship between the formulation of the Mishnah paragraph and principles associated with the name of Rabbi [Judah the Patriarch]. Unit III amplifies Eliezer's position. Unit IV then moves from the Mishnah passage to a more general statement of the same principle. Now we cover a broad range of matters in which we measure by the passage of a year or more. May we say that the Talmud here covers just about anything, once it leaves the exegesis of the Mishnah? No, that is not the case. Mishnah exegesis having been accomplished, a range of well-defined questions is addressed: How the year is calculated – whether from the New Year or from the actual anniversary of the event at hand – is specified and then supported on the basis of scriptural evidence. Unit V leaves the present context and raises a more general question about the facts dictated by Scripture. True, I cannot account for inclusion of the unit of discourse here, though there may be some connection to the immediately preceding lemma. But it hardly follows that this unit talks about "everything." Can we explain why the Talmud includes everything that is before us – and therefore can we postulate that the authorship of the Bavli has excluded what it found irrelevant and included only what served its purpose? We can explain most things, and finding a purpose for the concluding unit seems to me not difficult.

When Steinsaltz claims to know that the Talmud "has no formal external order, but is bound by a strong inner connection between [sic!] its many diverse subjects," we must wonder on the basis of what tractate or chapter he has reached that conclusion. There clearly is a formal, external order, that is supplied by the Mishnah; and, in treating the Mishnah, there also clearly is a formal order of what comes first and what must follow. And when Wieseltier tells us that he thinks that "the Talmud is, in truth, about all things," his intent is equivalently obscure; so far as we examine a given tractate and its chapters, we see that the tractate is about the subject and the rules provided by the Mishnah, and, on that subject, all (available) "things" do not promiscuously enter in; some few things come to the fore. But if "all (available) things" are supposed to find a place, then we must wonder where are the whole of the Tosefta to this chapter and the whole of Sifra to this topic. Wieseltier's odd and specious allegation, "There is no corner of human life and no corner of Jewish life into which the fastidious rabbis did not peer," has to be revised, since, it is clear, there are certainly "corners" of the Tosefta and the Midrash-compilations into which, for the purposes of making the Talmud of Babylonia, the rabbis found it not at all necessary to peer. And as to the rest of all the corners of human life, who can make a judgment, without peering into Wieseltier's mind to discover what in the world he can have meant! What appears plausible or sounds impressive when announced with authority turns out to have remarkably slight substance when examined with care in the setting of the actual texts that these colleagues purport to know and to describe for a broad public. Still, a third go-around is required, to demonstrate that an entire series of chapters produces a uniform – equally disastrous – result for the allegations of Steinsaltz and Wieseltier.

5

Bavli Arakhin
Chapter Five

The analytical program is unchanged. After a sustained reading of the chapter, we shall once more ask whether what we have read conforms to the description of the Bavli that Steinsaltz and Wieseltier have given us. The questions remain as in the prior chapters – and the results are the same as well.

5:1

A. [19A] He who says, "My weight is incumbent on me [as a pledge to the sanctuary]" pays his weight –

B. If [he said], "Silver," [then he pays] in silver;

C. If [he said], "Gold," [then he pays] in gold.

D. It once happened that the mother of Yirmatyah said, "The weight of my daughter is incumbent on me." And she went up to Jerusalem, and weighed her [Yirmatyah], and paid her weight in gold.

E. [He who says], "The weight of my hand is incumbent on me [as a pledge to the sanctuary]" –

F. R. Judah says, "He fills up a jar and pokes it [his hand] in up to the elbow. And he weights out the meat of an ass, with the sinews and bones. And he puts it [the ass meat] into it [the jar] until it [the jar] is filled [to the brim as the water rises]."

G. Said R. Yosé, "And how is it possible to treat as equivalent one kind of flesh and another, and one kind of bones and another? But:

H. "They estimate how much the hand is likely to weigh."

I.

A. What is the meaning of, *If he said, "Silver," then he pays in silver, if he said, "Gold," then he pays in gold* [M. 5:1B-C]?

B. Said R. Judah, "If the man stated explicitly, 'silver,' then he pays silver, if he explicitly specified, 'gold,' then he pays in gold."

145

C.   That is self-evident!
D.   Lo, what it informs us is that the reason [one pays as specified] is that the man has made an explicit statement to that effect.
E.   But, if he had not made an explicit statement, he can ransom himself [paying off his obligation] in anything at all.
F.   That accords with Rahbah's view, for Rabbah said, "In a place in which people sell pitch by weight, one may redeem himself even with pitch.
G.   That, too, is self-evident.
H.   No, indeed, it is necessary to make that point explicit, for there are places in which people weigh pitch, and there are places in which they sell it by measure.
I.   What, then, might a person have held? Since it is not the case that all parties normally measure it, it may not serve. Thus we are informed that the opposite is the case.
J.   Said R. Pappa, "In a place in which people sell onions by weight, one may pay off his pledge even through onions."
K.   That is self-evident!
L.   No, it is necessary to make the point explicit, for when people weigh onions [for sale], the seller may toss in two or three more [and thus, he does not in fact sell them by weight].
M.   What might one have claimed? On that account, the onions fall out of the classification of what is sold by weight. Thus we are informed [that that is not the case].

II.

A.   *It once happened that the mother of Yirmatyah...* [M. 6:1D:]
B.   [Since the story makes clear that the mother did not specify she would pay in gold, yet she paid in gold,] does the inclusion of the precedent serve to contradict [the foregoing rule, that it is only when one specifies he will pay in gold that one pays in gold]?
C.   [No, that is not the case.] The formulation of the Mishnah rule lacks a necessary clause, and this is how it should be repeated: "And if it is an important person, even though he has not made it explicit that [he will pay in silver or gold,] we rule that [he must pay] in accord with his standing.
D.   [Then we introduce the precedent, as follows:] *It once happened that the mother of Yirmatyah said, "The weight of my daughter is incumbent on me." And she went up to Jerusalem and weighed her and paid her weight in gold* [M. 5:1D].

III.

A.   Said Rab Judah, "He who says, 'My stature is incumbent on me' must give a staff that cannot be bent [but is of thick metal].
B.   "'...the length of my stature is incumbent on me' gives a staff which can be bent [and is not necessarily thick metal, but thin and of less value]."
C.   They objected [by citing T. Arakh. 3:1]: *"[He who says,] 'My stature is incumbent on me,' [or] 'My full stature is incumbent on me' [in either case] pays over a staff that cannot be bent." [Accordingly, the distinction Judah has proposed is not validated in the formulation of the passage at hand.]*

D. [Judah] has stated matters in accord with the principle of R. Aqiba, who interprets [meanings imputed by the use of] superfluous words [in the formulation of a passage].

E. For we have learned: *[He who sells a house has not sold] either the cistern or the winepress, even though he wrote in the deed, "[the property's] depth and height."*

F. *"And the seller has to purchase from the buyer a right of way,"* the words of R. Aqiba.

G. *And sages say, "He does not have to do so."*

H. *And R. Aqiba concedes that, when the seller said to him, "Except for these," he does not have to buy himself a right of way* [cf. M. B.B. 4:9E-I].

I. Thus, since the man did not have to say a thing but did make the statement at hand, it serves to add an additional matter to the transaction.

J. Here, too, since the man did not have to say anything at all, but he did make the [qualifying] statement at hand, it serves to add an additional matter. [Jung, p. 113, n. 1: "Full" is a superfluous phrase, stature implies the full height. Hence the additional suggestion: It is only as to the full height that I assume obligation, but as to thickness, that may be as slender as possible.]

IV.

A. The following question was raised:

B. [If one said, "My stand" [19B], what is the meaning of that statement?

C. [If he said,] "My thickness," what is the meaning of that statement?

D. [If he said,] "My sitting," "My thickness," "My circumference," what is the meaning of those statements?

E. The questions stand, [there being no answer]. [All of these formulations prove ambiguous and may bear a number of meanings.]

V.

A. *"The weight of my hand is incumbent on me"* [M. 5:1E]:

B. Our rabbis have repeated [the following verse] on Tannaite authority [given in T.'s version, with slight differences from Bavli's:] **[He who says], "The weight of my hand is incumbent on me" gives [the equivalent of the weight] up to the elbow [M. Ar. 5:1E].**

C. [He who says], "The weight of my foot is incumbent on me" gives [the equivalent of the weight] up to the ankle.

D. How does he carry out [the measure]?

E. "He brings a jar full of water and puts his hand in it up to the elbow. He puts in his foot up to the ankle.

F. **"And he brings ass meat, sinews and bones. He weighs it out and puts into it [the water] meat equivalent in volume to his meat and bones equivalent in volume to his bones. [The amount of water displaced indicates that the meat equals the weight of his hand or foot.] [M. Ar. 5:1F].**

G. "Even though there is no proof for such a procedure, there is an allusion to it: Whose flesh is the flesh of asses (Ezek. 23:20)," the words of R. Judah.

H. Said to him R. Yosé, "How is it possible to treat as equivalent one kind of flesh and another, and one kind of bones and another? [M. Ar. 5:1G].

I. Said to him R. Judah, "They make a rough estimate of it.

J. Said to him R. Yosé, "While they are making a rough estimate of it, let them make a rough estimate of the hand – how much it weighs, and of the foot – how much it weighs!" [M. Ar. 5:1G-H]. [T. Ar. 3:2].

VI.

A Up to the elbow [of the foregoing]:

B. Now the following objection was raised:

C The washing for purposes of sanctification of hands and feet in the sanctuary is to be up to the joint [of the palm or foot, not all the way up to the elbow].

D. That indeed is the rule supplied by the Torah. But as to vows, you follow the normal usage of ordinary people [who make vows, interpreting what they are likely to mean by the language they use].

E And is it the case that, in accord with the rule of the Torah, one needs to wash only up to the joint [because this is what people mean when they refer to a hand]?

F. And lo, in regard to the placing of phylacteries, concerning which it is written in Scripture, "Your hand" (Ex. 13:9), it has been taught by the house of Manasseh, "'Your hand' means [the phylactery is placed] on the biceps muscle."

G. In the language of the Torah it indeed involves the whole of the biceps muscle. But in matters of vows, one follows the usage of ordinary people.

H. And as to the matter of the washing for purposes of sanctification of the hands and feet in the sanctuary, it is a practical law that has been handed on.

VII.

A The foot up to the knee [of the foregoing]:

B. The following objection was raised: "Feet" (Ex. 23:14) excludes people with wooden legs. [That is, in connection with making a pilgrimage, the use of the word, "feet," indicates that people with artificial feet are not required to make the pilgrimage. Thus, in context, the foot does not stretch up to the knee, but includes only the foot up to the ankle.]

C In matters involving vows, interpret what people say in terms of the ordinary usage.

D. And so far as the law of the Torah is concerned, does the term foot exclude people with wooden legs [Jung]?

E Now, lo, with respect to the rite of removing the shoe [in connection with freeing a deceased childless brother-in-law's wife from having to marry a surviving brother in line with Deut. 25:5-10], it is written, "From his foot" (Deut. 25:9), on which it has been taught, If she removed the shoe from the knee and below, her act of removing the shoe is valid. [Hence do we have a case in which, when the Torah uses the word, "foot," it means the leg from the knee and downward.]

F.   That case is different, for the language of Scripture is, "From off his foot," [which then encompasses a larger part of the leg than would normally be the case].

G.   If that is so, then if the woman unstrapped the sandal even above the knee, it should be a valid act of removing the shoe.

H.   Scripture states, "From upon...," and not "From over above the upper part...."

I.   Said R. Pappa, "From the foregoing discussion it is to be inferred that the *istawira* [the ankle] down to the ground [Jung: "The entire length of the foot from the ankle."] For if you think that it is treated as divided into two parts, then the *istawira* should be above the foot, and the thigh should be "over above the foot."

J.   R. Ashi said, "You may even maintain the view that it is divided into two parts. But whatever is horizontal with the foot [including the anatomical part called the *istawira*] falls into the category of the foot."

The point of M. 5:1A-C + D requires no comment. Since, D, the mother was rich, it was assumed she meant gold. E-H's problem is how to estimate the weight of the hand, in line with A-C. Judah proposes to figure out the volume and to weigh out an equivalent volume of ass meat. Yosé's objection is valid, but his solution is not impressive. The Talmud follows a kind of classic program in complementing and then expanding the range of discourse of the Mishnah paragraph. First we have a careful exposition of the meaning of the formulation given in the Mishnah, units I-II. We proceed, unit III, to introduce a complementary proposition relevant to the principle of the Mishnah, itself subjected to expansion. Unit IV then brings up further instances of ambiguous language. Unit V, systematically expounded by the parallel compositions at units VI and VII, presents Tosefta's supplement to the Mishnah. It would be difficult to imagine a more thorough confrontation with the Mishnah passage at hand. Does this unit talk about "everything" or some few things? One thing – the Mishnah paragraph before us, as read by the Tosefta. Can we explain why the Talmud includes everything that is before us – and therefore can we postulate that the authorship of the Bavli has excluded what it found irrelevant and included only what served its purpose? Not at all – unless we simply ignore the evidence in our hands.

5:2A-B

A.   [He who says], "The price of my hand is incumbent on me" – they make an estimate of him: how much is he worth with a hand, and how much is he worth without a hand?

B.   **This rule is more strict in connection with vows than in connection with Valuations.**

I.

A.   How do we make an estimate of his value?

B.   Said Raba, "They make an estimate of his value in the manner in which one makes an estimate for purposes of assessing damages [in personal injury cases. The man, then, is viewed as a slave on the block, assessed as to his value with, and without, a hand.]"

C.   Said to him Abayye, "Are the two cases parallel? There [in the case of assessing damages to be paid for injuries], the man [has been injured and so] is diminished in value, while here he is in good shape [since at issue is only assessing the value of a healthy man's hand]."

D.   [In answer to the question at A] Abayye said, "They make an estimate of how much a person is willing to pay for a slave who performs work with one hand only, as against one who works with both hands."

E.   With one hand? What is the sense, that the other is cut off? Then this is the same [case to which you objected just now at B, that is, where the estimates do not deal with parallel situations at all.]

F.   Rather, we deal with an estimate of the value of a slave who is sold when] one hand is written over to his original master [and not available for service to the purchaser, who gets work only with one hand. Then we have a slave in good shape, just as in the present case, and so a meaningful estimate can be reached.]

II.

A.   Raba raised the following question: "[If a court] made an estimate of a man for purposes of compensation for personal injury, and the man said, 'My value is incumbent on me [for the Temple],' what is the law?

B.   "Do we rule, lo, the man already has been assessed once [and that assessment remains valid]?

C.   "Or is it the case that an estimate of one's value made by a court of ten [such as is required for Valuations] is different from an estimate of value reached by a court of three [such as assesses damages for personal injury]?

D.   "If, further, you conclude that the case of an assessment reached by a court of ten is different from an assessment reached by a court of three, [then we deal with a further case, namely:] [If] the man said, 'My value is incumbent on me,' and they estimated him [and assigned a figure owing to the Temple], and he went and said again, 'My value is incumbent on me,' what is the law?

E.   "Here, on the one side, we most certainly have a case in which a court of ten has conducted the assessment.

F.   "Or perhaps the man has increased in value in the interval [so a new assessment is called for]?

G.   "[If, further, the man] said, 'My value is incumbent on me,' and [the court] did not make an assessment of his value, and then he went again and said, 'My value is incumbent on me,' what is the law?

H. "Here most certainly [20A] we assess the man's value one time only.

I. "Or perhaps, since the man took the vows one after another in two successive acts, do we also conduct two successive assessments of his value?

J. "And if, further, you should determine to rule that, since the man took the vows one after another in two successive acts, we also conduct two successive assessments of his value, [then what is done if the following occurred?]

K. "If the man said, 'Two assessments of my value are incumbent on me,' what is the law?

L. "Here the man most certainly has taken a vow [two times] simultaneously, so we assess him [for both vows] simultaneously.

M. "Or perhaps, since the man spoke of 'two [assessments],' it is as if he had said [his vows] in sequence, one after the other.

N. "And if you find reason to rule that, since the man spoke of 'two [assessments],' it is as if he had said [his vows] in sequence, one after the other, [then what is done if the following occurred]?

O. "If [a court] assessed his value quite *en passant* [and not with a vow in mind], what is the law?

P. "Do we rule, lo, it is an assessment made *en passant*, and it stands? Or perhaps do we require the explicit intention to conduct an assessment [for a particular purpose]?"

Q. One may solve one [of the stated questions] from that which we have learned:

R. *[He who said], "My worth is incumbent on me," and who died – the heirs do not pay off the vow, for corpses have no worth* [M. 5:2F-G].

S. Now if you wish to maintain the view that, in the case of an assessment conducted *en passant* [on its own and quite tangentially], we have a valid assessment, lo, in this instance the man's assessment stands. [How so?] Is there such a thing as a person who is not worth at least four *zuz* [when alive]? [So the answer to the question at hand is negative.]

T. [No, that is not necessarily so. Why not?] One who has been assessed in value has been assessed [in some way or another] but one who has said, "My worth is incumbent on me," has not yet been assessed at all.

Unit I clarifies the role of M. 5:2A by explaining how the estimate required by the Mishnah's law is reached. Unit II presents a sequence of successive questions, bearing no relationship at all to M. 5:2A-B. Had the unit occurred after M. 5:2F-G, it would make more sense. Perhaps, when the Talmud was printed not broken up by Mishnah paragraphs, the item fit in better. But the following Mishnah passage begins with a standard genre, namely, an extended complement taken out of the Tosefta. It would not have been likely for the Talmud's treatment of what is to come to begin with unit II in preference to the sort of material with which it in fact commences. Does this unit talk about "everything" or some few things? No, just the Mishnah and the Tosefta. Can we explain why the Talmud includes everything that is before us – and therefore can we postulate that the authorship of the Bavli has excluded what it found irrelevant and included only what served its purpose? The framers of the Bavli knew precisely what they wished to include, and it was not "everything" but only some things.

M.5:2C-J

C. More strict is the rule in connection with Valuations than in connection with vows.

D. How so?

E. He who says, "My Valuation is incumbent on me" and then dies – the heirs must pay [the Valuation].

F. [He who says], "My worth is incumbent on me" and then dies – the heirs do not pay [the vow].

G. For corpses have no price [worth].

H. [He who says], "The Valuation of my hand, or the Valuation of my foot is incumbent on me" has not said a thing.

I. [He who says], "The Valuation of my head," or "the Valuation of my liver is incumbent on me" pays the Valuation of his whole person.

J. This is the general principle: [If he refers to] something on which life depends, he pays the Valuation of his whole person.

M. 5:3

A. [He who says], "Half of my Valuation is incumbent on me" pays half his Valuation.

B. [He who says], "The Valuation of half of me is incumbent on me" pays the whole of his Valuation.

C. [He who says], "Half of my price is incumbent on me" pays half of his price.

D. [He who says], "The price of half of me is incumbent on me" pays the whole of his price.

E. This is the general principle: [If he refers to] something on which life depends, he pays the Valuation of his whole person.

M. 5:4

A. He who says, "The Valuation of So-and-so is incumbent on me" –

B. [If] the one who makes the vow and the one concerning whom the vow is made die –

C. the heirs [of the former] pay the pledge.

D. [If he said], "The price of So-and-so is incumbent on me" [and] the one who makes the vow dies, the heirs must pay the vow.

    E.   **[If] the one concerning whom the vow is made dies, the heirs do not have to pay.**

    F.   **For corpses have no price [value].**

I.

    A.   Our rabbis have taught: A strict rule applies to vows [to pay the value price] which do not apply to Valuations, and to Valuations which does not apply to [vows to pay] the price.

    B.   [For vows to pay] the price apply to man and beast, to live and slaughtered [beasts], to whole ones and to limbs,

    C.   And they apply without regard to ability to pay,

    D.   which is not the case for Valuations [T. Ar. 3:5].

    E.   A more strict rule applies to Valuations: How so?

    F.   For Valuations are subject to a fixed sum deriving from the Torah,

    G.   which is not the case of [vows to pay] the price.

    H.   He who says, "The Valuation of So-and-so is incumbent on me," and who dies, is liable [through his estate to pay the pledged Valuation] [M. Ar. 5:4A-C].

    I.   [He who says], "The price of this beast is incumbent on me" and who dies is liable.

    J.   [He who says], "The price of this beast is incumbent on me," and the beast dies – the one who vows is liable.

II.

    A.   If one said, "My Valuation is incumbent on me," and he died, his heirs [estate] must pay the pledge **[I.H. above].**

    B.   Does that statement imply that a loan made orally [not secured by a bond] is to be collected from the heirs? [That is ordinarily viewed as moot and not settled.]

    C.   The present case is to be distinguished from an ordinary one [of an orally secured loan], for in fact [what is owing] is in the status of a loan that accords with what is written in the Torah.

    D.   May we then infer that a loan in accord with what is written in the Torah is in the status of a loan that is written up in a bond?

    E.   With what sort of matter do we deal? It is a case in which one has gone to court [to make sure the payment is exacted].

    F.   Then along these same lines, in the case of him who said, "My value is incumbent on me," if he has gone to court, why should the heirs not pay [contrary to M. 5:2F]?

    G.   [If one has said,] "My value is incumbent on me," he has not yet been subjected to an assessment [as to his value], while if he has said, "My Valuation is incumbent on me," in no way has he not yet been subjected to an assessment [since the Torah has dictated his exact value for purposes of Valuations].

III.

    A.   *He who says, "The Valuation of my hand or the Valuation of my foot is incumbent on me" [has not said a thing]* [M. 5:2H].

    B.   Said R. Giddal said Rab, "But he still must pay its value."

    C.   But lo, the passage of the Mishnah is formulated as, *He has not said a thing,* [so why should he have to pay]?

D.   So far as the rabbis [who form the majority in the matter] are concerned, he has said nothing. But in the view of R. Meir, he has to pay the value [of the limb, since, as we recall, Meir maintains that people do not utter thoughts purposelessly, and so it was the man's intent to declare liability for such a gift, even though, in strict law, there is no such liability].

E.   Lo, this very matter has been stated once before, for R. Giddal said Rab said, "He who says, 'The Valuation of this utensil [which, of course, is not subject to Valuation at all] is incumbent on me' must pay the value of the utensil."

F.   [Why should the same point be made yet a second time]? What might you have said? In that other case [about the utensil] the ruling is that a person must pay because he knows that a Valuation does not pertain to a utensil. The donor, therefore, deliberately made the declaration [using the language of Valuations but] intending to pay the actual market worth [of the object].

G.   But in the present case, there was a genuine error, for the donor imagined that, just as there is the possibility of making a pledge of Valuation for one's head or liver [M. 5:2I], so there also is the possibility of declaring a vow of Valuation for the hands or feet. [That is why the donor made the statements at hand, but he was in error, and, in any event,] never made a declaration covering the market worth [of the hands or feet. Such a declaration never was in mind].

H.   Accordingly, we are informed that that is not the case.

IV.

A.   [*He who says,*] "*The Valuation of my head,*" *or* "*the Valuation of my liver is incumbent on me*" *pays the Valuation of his whole person* [M. 5:2I]:

B.   What is the scriptural basis for that rule? "[The Valuation of] souls" (Lev. 27:2) is what the All-Merciful has said, [covering what sustains the person's life].

V.

A.   *This is the general principle: If he refers to something on which life depends, he pays the Valuation of his whole person* [M. 5:2J].

B.   What does the augmentative language [of the general principle] serve to encompass?

C.   It includes [a statement referring to any part of the body] from the knee upwards.

VI.

A.   Our rabbis have taught: [He who says,] "Half of my Valuation is incumbent on me" pays half his Valuation [M. 5:2A].

B.   R. Yosé b. R. Judah says, "He is flogged and furthermore pays his entire Valuation" [T. Ar. 3:3D].

C.   Why is there a flogging?

D.   Said R. Pappa, "[It is not that he is actually flogged, but he is] penalized and pays [as an indemnity] a complete Valuation."

E.   What is the reasoning for such a view?

F.   It is a matter of a supererogatory decree [that one must pay a full Valuation for using the language, "a half-Valuation]," on account of the consequences of using the language, "The Valuation of half of me" [is incumbent, in which case the man pays the whole of his Valuation (M. 5:3B)], on account of the language's encompassing a matter on which life depends."

VII.

A.   *He who says, "Half of my Valuation is incumbent on me" pays half his valuation. He who says, "The Valuation of half of me is incumbent on me" pays the whole of his Valuation* [M. 5:3A-B].

B.   What is the scriptural basis for this rule?

C.   "[The Valuation of] souls" (Lev. 27:2) is what is written.

VIII.

A.   *This is the general principle: If he refers to something on which life depends, etc.* [M. 5:2]]:

B.   [The augmentative language] serves to encompass [a statement referring to any part of the body] from the knee upwards.

C.   Our rabbis have taught: He who pledges a half-Valuation –

D.   R. Meir says, "He pays the market value [of the person concerning whom one has made that pledge]."

E.   And sages say, "He has said nothing at all."

F.   Raba fell ill. Abayye and rabbis came to visit him and went into session [by his bedside] and engaged in discourse:

G.   [They observed,] "Now there is no problem with the view of R. Meir, for he maintains the principle that a person does not use language purposelessly.

H.   "He therefore sees no difference between [an obligation to pay] the whole [value of the body or half]. [Since the life depends upon half of the body its value is equivalent to the value of the whole.]

I.   "But in the view of rabbis, what theory can be at hand? If they maintain that a person does use language purposelessly, then even the whole of the Valuation one should not have to pay.

J.   "If they maintain that a person does not use language purposelessly then [he ought to pay even where at issue is a vow of] half of the valuation."

K.   Said Raba to them, "Rabbis in the present instance accord with the principle of R. Meir. But they also concur with the principle of R. Simeon.

L.   "They indeed accord with the principle of R. Meir, maintaining that a person does not use language purposelessly.

M.   "They accord with the principle of R. Simeon who has said that [The man is exempt because] the man has not made a voluntary donation in the way in which people usually make pledges. It is usual to make a pledge of a full, but not a half [donation, and hence in this case rabbis hold the man has not made an effective pledge at all.]"

IX.

A.   *He who says, "The Valuation of So-and-so is incumbent on me" – if the one who makes the vow and the one concerning whom the* vow is made die, the heirs [of the former] pay the pledge [M. 5:4A-C].

B.   What are the circumstances at hand?

C.   [If we theorize] that the [person subject to Valuation] has already stood in court, then that is the same as [the case above, II]. [So why repeat the rule?]

D.   It was necessary to present matters so as to lay out the concluding rule: *If one said, "The price of So-and-so is incumbent on me" and the one who makes the vow dies, the heirs must pay the vow* [M. 5:4D].

E.   [20B] What might you have said [to reach a contrary conclusion]?

F.   Since the man had not yet been assigned a specific value [prior to his death], the property [of the one who took the vow] has not yet been encumbered [so that, if he dies, his estate does not have to pay off the claim of the Temple].

G.   Accordingly, we are informed [that that is not the case. Why not?]

H.   Since he stood before the court, his property indeed has been encumbered, but as to the specification of the exact estimate of value, that is merely a post facto statement [of an obligation already automatically incurred].

We turn to a pledge of the price of the hand. The differing rules for pledges of Valuations as against those for vows of price are covered at M. 5:2E-J, M. 5:3, M. 5:4 (+ M. 5:5). The main point is that in the case of a Valuation, we have a fixed amount, which, once pledged, must be paid. In the case of a vow – for example, the pledge of one's price or value – the result is variable. E-F + G are clear as stated. The Valuation has a fixed definition and must be paid. But the price of the man depends upon the situation at the point at which the estimate is to be made, G. H of course contrasts to A, since someone can pledge the price of his hand, but not the Valuation of his hand. It is difficult, however, to claim that in the beginning were A, H, which then were separated and augmented. In fact, H goes together with I, and both are explained at J. If the man pledges the Valuation of his head, he has spoken of something essential to his life, therefore pays his whole Valuation. But there is no such thing as a Valuation of the hand. M. 5:3 goes over the ground of M. 5:2H-J. A person can pledge half his Valuation. But if he pledges the Valuation of half of himself, he must pay the whole, in line with M. 5:3E. Now the same rule applies to vows of one's price. Unit I presents Tosefta's complement to the Mishnah passage at hand, and unit II explores the secondary implications of the cited passage of the Tosefta, along with the Mishnah's rule. Units III and VIII introduce questions on the effect of using improper formulations, focusing upon the theory of Meir that people are careful about what they say. Unit III makes that point in connection with M. 5:2, and unit VIII goes over the same matter. Units

IV, V, VI, VII, and IX gloss cited passages of the Mishnah, working their way through the clauses in order. The framer of the Talmud thus presents a systematic exegesis of important clauses of the Mishnah. Does this unit talk about "everything" or some few things? The framer of the Talmud talks about the Mishnah. Can we explain why the Talmud includes everything that is before us – and therefore can we postulate that the authorship of the Bavli has excluded what it found irrelevant and included only what served its purpose? The purpose is Mishnah and Tosefta exegesis, and while there are talmudic discourses that vastly transcend the exegetical task, none of them is accurately captured in the claims at hand.

5:5

A.   [He who says], "This ox is a burnt-offering," "This house is qorban,"
B.   [if] the ox died or the house fell down,
C.   is not liable to pay.
D.   [If he said], "[The price of] this ox is incumbent on me for a burnt-offering," or "[the price of] this house is incumbent on me as qorban,"
E.   [if] the ox died or the house fell down,
F.   he is liable to pay.

I.

A.   Said R. Hiyya bar Rab, "[The rule at D] applies only if the man said, *'The price of* this ox is incumbent on me for a burnt-offering,' but if he had said merely, 'This ox is incumbent on me for a burnt-offering,' since the man has made explicit reference to *this* [ox] as owing for a burnt-offering, [if] the ox died, the man is not liable to make it up,

B.   "for he had indicated merely that it was incumbent on him to offer up that [particular ox]."

C.   People objected [by citing the following passage of Tosefta:]

D.   [He who says], "This ox is a burnt-offering" – the ox is deemed a burnt-offering. And it is subject to the laws of sacrilege. And they are not responsible for [replacing] it [if it should be lost] [if it dies or is stolen] [M. 5:5A-C].

E.   [He who says], "This ox is incumbent on me as a burnt-offering" – the ox is deemed a burnt-offering. And it is subject to the laws of sacrilege. And they are responsible for [replacing] it [if it should be lost] [M. 5:5D-F] [T. Ar. 3:11].

F.   [He who says, "The price of this ox is deemed a burnt-offering – the ox is deemed a secular beast and is not subject to the laws of sacrilege. And they are not responsible for replacing it if it should be lost] [T. Ar. 3:12].

G.   [We note that, in the latter case, the man has used the language, *incumbent on me.* Now the question is raised:] Is this statement any more authoritative than that of the Mishnah at hand? For, in the case of the Mishnah, I have interpreted the law to speak of a case in which the man has said, "The price [of the ox...]. Here likewise, we assume that the man has said, "The price..." Yet, since the concluding clause [at F] makes it explicit that the man has spoken of *the value of* the ox, it should follow that the beginning clauses [D-E] do not speak of a case in which he has used the language, "The value..."

H.   For in the concluding clause, we note that the Tanna repeats the language: **The price of the ox is a burnt-offering, in which case the [corpus of the] ox remains unconsecrated [in itself], so the laws of sacrilege do not apply to it. If it should die or be stolen, the man is not liable to make it up. But he *is* liable to make up the price of the ox [and that he must pay over to the Temple].**

I.   [Dealing with the supposed contradiction, we reply:] Both the first and the second clauses speak of a case in which the man has said, *"The value..."*

J.   In the former case, however, the man indicated that he intended [by his statement] to consecrate the ox as to its value [so the corpus of the ox itself is subject to the pledge].

K.   In the latter case, by contrast, it was the man's intent to indicate that, *when* proceeds of the ox come to hand, they will be consecrated [in which case the corpus of the ox itself is not consecrated].

L.   Then lo, [that latter statement contradicts the principle that] a person cannot consecrate something which has not come into existence [and the funds are not yet in hand]!

M.   Said Rab Judah said Rab, "In accord with whose principle is the matter formulated? It accords with the view of R. Meir.

N.   "For he has said, 'A person does indeed consecrate something which has not yet come into existence.'"

O.   There are those who state the matter as follows:

P.   Said R. Pappa to Abayye, and some say that it was Rami bar Hama who said it to R. Hisda, "In accord with whose view does the matter rule? It is in accord with R. Meir, who has said, 'A person does indeed consecrate something which has not yet come into existence.'"

Q.   He said, "And who else might it be! [It is obvious that that famous principle is associated in particular with Meir's name.]"

R.   There are those who assign the [entire debate about the principle at hand to a different topic entirely, as] follows:

S.   **He who rents a house to his fellow, and the house was smitten with a plague [such as is described at Lev. 14], even though the house was certified [as afflicted] by a priest, may say to him, "Lo, there is yours before you."**

T.   **If the house was torn down [as part of the purification process], he is liable to make it up to him [by supplying another] house.**

U.   **If [21A] [the owner] consecrated the house, the one who lives in the house pays the rent to the Temple [cf. T. B.M. 8:30A-E, with some variations].**

V.   If the man consecrated the house, the one who lives in the house – how under these conditions can one have consecrated the house at all [since he is not living in it]? "When a man shall consecrate his house" (Lev. 27:14) is what Scripture has said!

W.   Just as "his house" falls entirely within his domain, so whatever remains with his domain [is subject to consecration, excluding a case in which the man does not control the property, as is the case here, where he has rented it out].

X.   This is the intent of the cited language: If the one who rents the house consecrates it, then the one who lives in the house pays the rent to the sanctuary.

Y.   What sort of case is possible, in which the one who rents the house consecrates it? How could he live in the house? [If he did so,] he would, after all, be subject to violating the laws of sacrilege!

Z.   Furthermore, how is it the case that "he pays the rent to the sanctuary"? Since the man has committed sacrilege, the fee for the rent is regarded [by definition] as unconsecrated [for that is the automatic result of the act of sacrilege!]

AA. [We deal with a case in which] the man has said, "When the rent for the house comes to hand, it *will be* consecrated."

BB. But lo, a person cannot consecrate something which has not yet come into existence [and the funds are not yet in hand]!

CC. Said Rab Judah said Rab, "In accord with whose principle is the matter formulated? It accords with the view of R. Meir.

DD. "For he has said, 'A person does indeed consecrate something which has not yet come into existence.'"

EE. There are those who state the matter as follows:

FF. Said R. Pappa to Abayye, and some say that it was Rami bar Hama who said it to R. Hisda, "In accord with whose view does the matter rule? It is in accord with R. Meir, who has said, 'A person does indeed consecrate something which has not yet come into existence.'"

GG. He said, "And who else might it be!"

If the man specifies a particular ox, then he is liable only to hand over that ox. If he specifies the value of the ox, then he has to pay that value, whatever happens to the ox. Once the Talmud cites the passage of the Tosefta at hand, the real issue is how someone can consecrate what does not yet exist. Then we identify the framer of the passage(s) at hand with Meir's principle. I do not see how anyone is interested in the Mishnah paragraph, and it is clear that the entire discussion takes off from the introduction of the Tosefta's statement. So, in this case, the Talmud has been framed to serve the Tosefta. Does this unit talk about "everything" or some few things? One thing: the Tosefta. Can we explain why the Talmud includes everything that is before us – and therefore can we postulate that the authorship of the Bavli has excluded what it found irrelevant and included only what served its purpose? The purpose is to develop the analysis of the Tosefta's passage and move in a direct path from that starting point.

5:6

A.   Those who owe Valuations [to the Temple] – they exact pledges from them.

B.   Those who owe sin-offerings or guilt-offerings – they do not exact pledges from them.

C.   Those who owe burnt-offerings or peace-offerings – they exact pledges from them.

D.   Even though he does not make atonement [that is, atonement is not effected for him] unless he acts of his own will, as it is said, At his good will (Lev. 1:3), [nonetheless], they compel him until he says, "I will it."

E.   And so do you rule in the case of writs of divorce for women:

F.   They compel him until he says, "I will it."

I.

A.   Said R. Pappa, "There are occasions on which they exact pledges from those who owe sin-offerings, but do not exact pledges from those who owe burnt-offerings.

B.   "They exact pledges from those who owe sin-offerings in the case of the sin-offering of the Nazirite.

C.   "For a master has said, 'If [a Nazirite, completing his purification rite,] shaved off his hair on the occasion of the offering of any one of the three required offerings (Num. 6:14), he has carried out his obligation properly, and if the blood of one of the offerings has been tossed onto the altar on his account, the Nazirite is permitted to drink wine and to contract corpse uncleanness [his spell as a Nazirite having ended properly].'

D.   "[If he happened to have brought the required burnt-offering or peace-offering first, instead of the sin-offering, and] neglected it and did not bring it, [he would have no motive to do so, and on that account the Temple officials exact a pledge for what is owing].

E.   "[But] those who owe burnt-offerings are not required to put up a pledge. That is the case, in particular, for the burnt-offering brought by a woman who has given birth [in line with the requirement of Lev. 12]. Why so? Because Scripture listed it first [at Lev. 12:6: burnt-offering, then sin-offering]."

F.   But has not Raba said, "It was only as to reciting the text that Scripture gave preference [to the burnt-offering, but it need not be brought first. Hence the thesis offered at E is not sustained.]

G.   Rather, [a pledge is not exacted from] one who owes the burnt-offering brought in purification by one afflicted with the skin disease (described at Lev. 13).

H.   For it has been taught (at T. Nazir 4:8): R. Ishmael, son of R. Judah b. Beroqah, says, "Just as the sin-offering and guilt-offering [brought in the purification rite] are essential [and omission disqualifies the process], so the burnt-offering is essential [and since that is the case, the person securing purification is not likely to omit it." [So this exemplifies A.]

II.

A. *Even though he does not make atonement unless he acts of his own will...* [M. 5:6D]:

B. Our rabbis have taught on Tannaite authority: "He shall offer it" (Lev. 1:3) – that statement teaches that [the officials] compel [the beneficiary of the sacrifice (*sacrifier*) to perform it].

C. Is it possible to suppose that it may be even by force?

D. Scripture says, "At his good will" (Lev. 1:3).

E. How so?

F. *They compel him until he says, "I will it"* [M. 5:6F].

III.

A. Samuel said, "A burnt-offering requires concurrence [of the person in whose behalf it is offered], as it is said, 'At his good will' (Lev. 1:3)."

B. Of what does Samuel thereby inform us? We have learned in Tannaite teaching: Even though he does not make atonement unless he acts of his own will, as it is said, "At his good will"?

C. To the contrary, [what he has said] is indeed necessary, to deal, specifically, with a case in which one's fellow set aside [a beast for the burnt-offering to be brought] by the person himself.

D. What might one have ruled? Where we require the person's own knowledge and consent, it is in the case of [a beast that belongs to] himself, but in the case of a beast provided by his fellow, [we do not impose the same condition.]

E. Accordingly we are informed that there are occasions on which one is not willing to effect atonement through something that does not belong to himself [and so he, too, must consent to what the fellow has done in designating a beast in his own behalf].

F. The following objection was raised: [If someone said,] "The sin-offering and the guilt-offering owing by Mr. So-and-so are incumbent on me [21B]" –

G. If this was with the knowledge and consent [of the beneficiary, the latter has] carried out his obligation.

H. But if it was not with the knowledge and consent of the beneficiary, he has not carried out his obligation.

I. [If he said,] "The burnt-offering owed by Mr. So-and-so or the peace-offerings owed by Mr. So-and-so are incumbent on me," whether or not this was with the knowledge and consent of the other party, the beneficiary has carried out his obligation. [This contradicts the thesis imputed to Samuel by D-E, for there is no such distinction among types of offerings.]

J. Samuel may reply to you, Where the present teaching applies is to the time of the actual achieving of atonement [the sacrifice itself], for [the beneficiary of the rite] already has given his agreement [to the entire procedure], at the time of the designation of the animal for that purpose.

K. But the occasion to which what I have stated applies is the time of the actual designation of the beast [which must be done with the knowledge and consent of the beneficiary of the rite].

L. [What Samuel has said, then,] differs from the view of Ulla.

M. For Ulla has said, "There is no distinction between the sin-offering and burnt-offering, except that at the time of the designation of an animal as sin-offering, the beneficiary must give his knowledge and consent, while at the time of the designation of a burnt-offering, the beneficiary of the burnt-offering need not give his knowledge and consent.

N. "But as to what is done on the occasion of the actual atonement rite [when the beast is sacrificed and the blood sprinkled, for both sorts of offering, if it was with the knowledge and consent of the beneficiary, he has carried out his obligation, and if it was not with the knowledge and consent of the beneficiary, he has not carried out his obligation.

O. An objection was raised [to what both Ulla and Samuel have said], [If someone said,] "The sin-offering, guilt-offering, burnt offering, and peace-offerings of Mr. So-and-so are incumbent on me," – if this was with the beneficiary's knowledge and consent, he has fulfilled his obligation.

P. If it was not with his knowledge and consent, he has not fulfilled his obligation. [Samuel has maintained that there are occasions in which, even without the beneficiary's knowledge and consent, he has carried out his obligation. Ulla's distinctions, too, are ignored.]

Q. Samuel interprets the teaching to speak of the occasion on which the beasts are designated for use, while Ulla interprets it to speak of the occasion on which the actual rite of atonement is carried out.

R. Said R. Pappa, "The two teachings on Tannaite authority [first, if one undertook to pay for someone else's burnt-offering and peace-offering, the beneficiary has carried out his obligation whether or not he knew it; and, second, in every instance the beneficiary's knowledge and consent are required if he is to gain the benefit of a sacrifice] do not contradict one another.

S. The one speaks of the occasion on which atonement is achieved, the other of the occasion on which the beast is designated for its purpose.

T. The amoraic masters at hand also do not differ from one another. Samuel interprets the first of the two teachings to speak of the occasion on which atonement is accomplished and the second to speak of the occasion on which the beast is designated, and Ulla interprets matters in exactly the opposite way.

U. Then the Amoraim obviously do differ.

V. That statement is self-evident! What might you have said?

W. When Samuel spoke of the time at which the beast was designated, knowledge and consent are required, meaning that *also* at the time at which the beast was designated, that is the case [but it most certainly *is* the case for the time at which atonement is effected], [and he would be alleged to maintain that view] even though the first of the two teachings would contradict him.

X. Thus we are informed that that is not the case. [Samuel most certainly does not require agreement at the time of atonement.]

IV.

A. *And so do you rule in the case of writs of divorce for women: They compel, etc.* [M. 5:6E-F]:

B. Said R. Sheshet, "If someone makes an announcement at the time of the issuing of a writ of divorce [that he does not concur in what is done in his name], that protest is valid."

C. That statement is self-evident.

D. No, indeed, it was necessary to make it. For we take up the case in which he was made to agree and then did agree.

E. What might you have ruled? That in his later concurrence [his earlier protest] was nullified.

F. Thus we are informed that that is not the case.

G. If, after all, it were the case, the teaching should be repeated in this language: *[He is coerced] until he gives* [the writ of divorce].

H. What is the force of the language: *Until he says...* [M. 5:6F]?

I. It means, until he explicitly nullifies the protest [that he originally made].

The point of M. 5:6A-B is that, in the latter case, a person will surely want to expiate his sin and bring the necessary offerings, so we do not exact a surety. But in the matter of merely fulfilling a pledge (A), a person may be less zealous, so he must lay down a surety that he will pay the Valuation. C carries the matter forward, with its augmentation at D (+E-F). Burnt-offerings and peace-offerings fall into the category of A, since people may be slothful about bringing them. D then raises the question of forcing someone to bring an offering. The man does not carry out his obligation to bring a burnt-offering or a peace-offering if he is forced to do so against his will, so, D explains, there is a procedure to compel him to *want* to do so. Does this unit talk about "everything" or some few things? Can we explain why the Talmud includes everything that is before us – and therefore can we postulate that the authorship of the Bavli has excluded what it found irrelevant and included only what served its purpose? The Talmud does a fine job of explaining and then expanding upon the details of the Mishnah. Unit I presents in a rather subtle way the reason behind the law at hand. Unit II complements M. 5:6D, as indicated. This serves as an introduction to the protracted and thorough discussion of unit III. Here we have the Babylonian Talmud at its best. Unit IV clarifies M. 5:6E-F with a secondary detail. At this point, it should be clear to the reader, any further analysis of this tractate will turn up precisely the same evidence to refute the impressions and opinions – one cannot any longer dignify them with the title, "hypotheses" less still "characterizations" – put forth by Steinsaltz and Wieseltier. The only open question seems to be, what led them to such false and obviously confused perceptions of matters? Answers to that question will not be found in the Talmud of Babylonia. Let us now go on to Halivni's claims.

Part Three

"THE JEWISH PREDILECTION FOR JUSTIFIED LAW"
Halivni

TRUE FOR SIFRA AND (THEREFORE) ALSO
FALSE FOR BABYLONIAN TALMUD TRACTATE
ARAKHIN CHAPTER SEVEN

6

The Midrash and Scripture: Sifra's Program for Leviticus 27:16-25

> There is a Jewish proclivity for vindicatory law, for law that is justified, against law that is autocratically prescribed...a Jewish inclination for the vindicatory.
>
> David W. Halivni

Halivni's proposition is somewhat more difficult to grasp than that of Steinsaltz and Wieseltier, since it is cast in terms that are not readily defined. "Jewish proclivity," "vindicatory," "justified," being terms that seem for him to bear a very technical, and not a commonly known, meaning. What he seems to discern is a preference on the part of the Bavli's framers for presenting law tied to prooftexts of Scripture. If that is all he wishes to say, then it is trivial and commonplace, and we need not draw from that observation grand conclusions about proclivities and predilections. Everyone knows that the Mishnah's framers omit prooftexts even when presenting scriptural law. The tractates, Pesahim and Yoma, for instance, scarcely cite the pertinent verses of the Pentateuch and yet are quite incomprehensible without constant reference to those verses. Halivni treats the Mishnah as an aberration and maintains that the Talmud of Babylonia reverted to a long-standing "proclivity." If this is all that Halivni wishes to allege, then it is self-evident, but bears no urgent implications I can identify. That is to say, what Halivni wants to claim is that later authorities, those who received the Mishnah, wished in general to link rulings of the Mishnah to verses of Scripture. Anyone who opens a page of the Talmud of Babylonia knows that fact, which is simply a commonplace. Before proceeding, let me show why I maintain that if this is his main point, it is surely beyond serious objection, but not very

consequential. To give one minor example among many, let me cite M.
Arakhin 9:8 and its associated Talmud, 106B-107A:

9:8

A.   He who leases a field from his fellow
B.   to sow barley in it
C.   may not sow it with wheat.
D.   [If he leased it to sow] wheat,
E.   he may sow it with barley.
F.   Rabban Simeon b. Gamaliel prohibits [doing so].
G.   [If he leased it to sow] grain he may not sow it with pulse,
H.   [to sow] pulse, he may sow it with grain.
I.   Rabban Simeon b. Gamaliel prohibits [doing so].

I.1   A.   Said R. Hisda, "What is the scriptural basis for the ruling of R.
           Hisda? As it is written, 'The remnant of Israel shall not do iniquity
           nor speak lies; neither shall a deceitful tongue be found in their
           mouth' (Zeph. 3:13)."

      B.   An objection was raised [to the rule of M. 9:8D-F]: The collection
           of alms for Purim must be distributed on Purim. And the
           collection of alms for a given town must be distributed in
           that town. They do not investigate too closely to see
           whether or not the poor are deserving. But they buy calves
           for the poor and slaughter them, and the poor consume
           them. And what is left over should not fall to the fund for
           charity. "Out of funds collected for Purim a poor person
           should not make a strap for his sandal, unless he so
           stipulated in the council of the citizens of that town," the
           words of R. Jacob stated in the name of R. Meir. But
           Rabban Simeon b. Gamaliel [107A] imposes a lenient ruling
           in this matter. [The passage continues: But they should be
           used only for food for the holiday." R. Meir says, "He who
           borrows money from his fellow to purchase produce with it
           should not purchase utensils with it. If he borrowed money
           for the purchaser of utensils, he should not buy produce
           with it, for he thereby deceives the lender." (T. Meg. 1:5A-
           K)]

      D.   *Said Abayye, "The reason of R. Simeon accords with the position
           of the master [Rabbah b. Nahmani], who has said, 'If one wishes
           to let his land become sterile, let him sow it one year with wheat,
           the next with barley, one year lengthwise, the next crosswise.
           [Freedman: Therefore if he leased it for wheat, he may not sow it
           with barley, in the opinion of R. Simeon b. Gamaliel, lest wheat
           have been sown there the previous year.]' But that is the case
           only if one does not plow after the harvest and again before
           sowing. If he does so, there is no harm."*

Now if by a Jewish proclivity, all Halivni means is that it is routine in
the Talmud to cite prooftexts for mishnaic rules, then his extended

proof of what is spread out on virtually every page of the Talmud seems witless.

But what if he means that a critical concern, a generative and precipitating interest of sages is in deriving from Scripture whatever there is to say about the Mishnah's rules? Then he will find difficulty adducing evidence for his opinion in passages such as the one above. Once we distinguish, as we must, between a formality of adducing prooftexts and a generative problematic deriving from Scripture and dictating the shape and structure of a sustained discussion – and that would indicate, for a given authorship, a "proclivity" and a "predilection" indeed – then Halivni will find slight satisfaction in the numerous passages that are like the one just now cited. For what provokes the discussion at hand is not the prooftext that is cited, let alone the issue of whether, and how, Scripture has imposed the rule at hand. It is, rather, whether or not it is the fact that under all circumstances the assumed or stipulated conditions are to be observed; some say that is so, some deny it. Simeon b. Gamaliel denies it. Then the operative consideration turns out to be the practicalities of preserving the fertility of the soil or renewing it.

The reason I think Halivni gains no support from this passage is now to be made explicit. It is very simple. Scripture does not stand behind this passage; the content of Scripture has not precipitated the thought that is set forth here; a variety of established truths has to be sorted out, and that is what the framer of the passage accomplishes. Accordingly, we have to differentiate formal appeal to prooftexts from the substantive formation of an exegetical program out of Scripture. If Scripture were to predominate, then the requirements of exegesis would be dictated by the program, the order, the details and propositions of Scripture. If Scripture does not predominate, then it takes a subordinated and essentially ancillary role in the pursuit of an inquiry that finds its generative problematic and its energy elsewhere. Halivni's language strongly suggests that he thinks that, in the period beyond the Mishnah, Scripture framed the Judaic hermeneutic, precipitated its program, and defined its problematic. The pages of the Talmud of Babylonia provide a fine opportunity to test what it appears he wishes to say as his proposition: the paramount position of Scripture in the Judaic hermeneutic.

As I understand his position, he wishes further to maintain that the law originated in exegesis and only later on was re-presented as free-standing and not – in form – as the product of the reading and interpretation of verses of Scripture. That further supposition transforms what is a perfectly self-evident observation as to the form in which legal propositions are given into an allegation concerning the origins of the law. We cannot test this second proposition of Halivni's, since there is no evidence prior to the Mishnah about the form and substance of the law of the Judaism that reaches its initial literary formulation in the Mishnah. But there is, at least, a way of testing his conception of a "Jewish proclivity." If, as he maintains, "Jews," presumably (again for the sake of charity) meaning (at the very least) the sages of the Talmud of Babylonia, do prefer exegetical to apodictic formulation of law, – which in any event is a mere observation of a mostly formal order of facts, not a substantive insight into the inner structure of law – then we should find in that Talmud evidence to sustain that characterization. What sort of evidence should we find? It is evidence that, where sages can re-present rules in the form of exegeses of legal passages of the Pentateuch, they will do so. Not only so, but – still more to the point – where they are able to frame discourse in an exegetical form, they will do so. And, finally, when they discuss a topic on which Scripture is rich in information, they will systematically lay out their ideas in the manner of exegetes of Scripture.

This set of hypotheses about the anticipated traits of mind of sages who are supposed to exhibit a proclivity for vindicatory law, for law that is justified, against law that is autocratically prescribed, and who are alleged to embody in their writing a Jewish inclination for the vindicatory may as a matter of fact be tested. The reason is that we do have a document that most certainly does sustain Halivni's characterization. I refer to Sifra, which, in its reading of the book of Leviticus, does set forth all ideas within the simple form of a citation of a verse of Scripture followed by a comment on that verse. And still more important, Sifra does deem Scripture to form the sole reliable source of law.[1] If, then, we wish to see how an authorship that conforms to Halivni's description presents its ideas, we have a fine example in that document. Since tractate Arakhin goes over scriptural law, moreover, we can then turn to the Talmud of Babylonia's reading of the Mishnah on precisely the same matters as are treated in Sifra in its "vindicatory" manner. We then ask whether the framers of the Bavli also exhibit a predilection to "law that is justified, meaning, by appeal to prooftexts. What we shall now see is that the framers of Sifra persistently try to show that rules of the Mishnah derive from Scripture. They cite the verbatim formulation of Mishnah-tractate

---

[1]It would simply carry me too far afield to rehearse the argument of my *Uniting the Dual Torah: Sifra and the Problem of the Mishnah.* Cambridge and New York, 1989: Cambridge University Press. It suffices to state that everything Halivni says about "the Jews" is true of Sifra.

Arakhin Chapter Seven and link that formulation to verses of Scripture. So when Halivni insists that that is the norm, and free-standing analysis the aberration, Sifra assuredly sustains his point. In Chapter Seven we shall consider whether or not the Talmud of Babylonia identifies as its principal concern the same task of "vindication," meaning, discovering prooftexts for free-standing propositions. If it does, then we find some basis for concurring in Halivni's characterization (if not within the rather broad terms in which he expresses his conceptions), and if not, then we must wonder just how he knows about this "Jewish proclivity for vindicatory law, for law that is justified, against law that is autocratically prescribed" and this "Jewish inclination for the vindicatory."

The passage in Scripture that is discussed in both Sifra and tractate Arakhin Chapter Seven is as follows:

> If a man dedicates to the Lord part of the land which is his by inheritance, [then your Valuation shall be according to the seed for it; a sowing of a homer of barley shall be valued at fifty *sheqels* of silver. If he dedicates his field from the year of Jubilee, it shall stand at your full Valuation. But if he dedicates his field after the Jubilee, then the priest shall compute the money-value for it according to the years that remain until the year of Jubilee, and a deduction shall be made from your Valuation. And if he who dedicates the field wishes, redeeming, to redeem it, then he shall add a fifth of the Valuation in money to it, and it shall remain his. But if he does not wish to redeem the field, or if he has sold the field to another man, it shall not be redeemed any more; but the field, when it is released in the Jubilee, shall be holy to the Lord, as a field that has been devoted; the priest shall be in possession of it. If he dedicates to the Lord a field which he has bought, which is not a part of his possession by inheritance, then the priest shall compute the Valuation for it up to the year of Jubilee, and the man shall give the amount of the Valuation on that day as a holy thing to the Lord. In the year of Jubilee the field shall return to him from whom it was bought, to whom the land belongs as a possession by inheritance. Every Valuation shall be according to the *sheqel* of the sanctuary; twenty *gerahs* shall make a *sheqel*.
>
> Lev. 27:16-25

The reading of these lines in Sifra is in two chapters, given in sequence. First comes Sifra 273. Parashat Behuqotai. Pereq 10, which shows us what a document that takes as its problematic the exegesis of Scripture, its hermeneutic, its program, its problematic:

CCLXXIII:II
1.   A.   "If a man dedicates to the Lord part of the land which is his by inheritance:"
      B.   I know only that the law covers a field received by inheritance from one's father.

C.   How do I know that it covers also a field received by inheritance
      from one's mother?
D.   Scripture says, "If a man dedicates...."

Here the statement of Scripture is clarified so as to encompass a
field inherited on the maternal side. This, too, is covered by the law.
Then the details of the law as given in Scripture are exemplary of a
principle and general – a field inherited, whether from father or
mother – and not prescriptive and specific – a field inherited only from
the party named, the father.

2.   A.   "Then your Valuation shall be according to the seed for it:"
      B.   Not in accord with its dimensions [but rather, its productive
            capacity].
3.   A.   "A sowing of a homer of barley shall be valued at fifty *sheqels* of
            silver:"
      B.   Lo, this is by decree of the King [without further explanation]:
      C.   **All the same are he who sanctifies a field in the desert of
            Mahoz and he who sanctifies a field among the orchards of
            Sebaste:**
      D.   **[If he wants to redeem it], he pays fifty *sheqels* of silver for
            every part of a field that suffices for the sowing of a homer
            of barley [M. Arakhin 3:2B-C, 7:1].**
4.   A.   How do we know that a person is not permitted to sanctify his field
            at the time of the Jubilee, though if one has done so, the field is
            sanctified?
      B.   Scripture says, "If he dedicates his field from the year of Jubilee."
5.   A.   Why does Scripture say, "his field"?
      B.   **How do you know that, if in the field were crevices ten
            handbreadths deep or rocks ten handbreadths high, they
            are not measured with it [M. Arakhin 7:1G]?**
      C.   Scripture says, "his field," [and these are not reckoned as part of
            his field forming domains unto themselves].
6.   A.   "it shall stand at your full Valuation:"
      B.   **[For a Jubilee of forty-nine years,] one pays forty-nine *selas*
            and forty-nine pundions [T. Arakhin 4:10B].**
      C.   What is the value of this *pondion*?
      D.   It is at the rate of exchange of a *pondion* and some change
            [Hillel].
7.   A.   "[But if he dedicates his field] after the Jubilee:"
      B.   Near the Jubilee.
      C.   How do we know the rule for the period some time after the
            Jubilee?
      D.   Scripture says, "But if he dedicates his field after the Jubilee."
8.   A.   "His field:"
      B.   What is the point of Scripture here?
      C.   **How do you know that, if in the field were crevices ten
            handbreadths deep or rocks ten handbreadths high, they
            are not measure with it [M. Arakhin 7:1G]?**
      D.   Scripture says, "his field," [and these are not reckoned as part of
            his field forming domains unto themselves].

9. A How do we know that **they do not declare a field of possession sanctified less than two years before the year of Jubilee nor do they redeem it less than a year after the year of Jubilee [M. Arakhin 7:1A-B]?**

B. Scripture says, "then the priest shall compute the money-value for it according to the years that remain until the year of Jubilee." [Hence there must be at least two years].

C. Scripture says, "But if he dedicates his field after the Jubilee, then the priest shall compute the money-value for it according to the years that remain until the year of Jubilee" [T. Arakhin 4:8A-B].

10. A And how do we know that **they do not reckon the months against the sanctuary, but the sanctuary reckons the months to its own advantage [M. Arakhin 7:1C-D]?**

B. Scripture says, "But if he dedicates his field after the Jubilee, then the priest shall compute the money-value for it according to the years that remain until the year of Jubilee."

11. A And how do we know that **if one said, "Lo, I shall pay for each year as it comes," they do not pay any attention to him, but he pays the whole at once [M. Arakhin 7:1J-K]?**

B. Scripture says, "But if he dedicates his field after the Jubilee, then the priest shall compute the money-value for it according to the years that remain until the year of Jubilee."

12. A "Years that remain:"

B. Years does one reckon,

C. and one does not reckon months.

13. A And how do we know that if the sanctuary wanted to treat the months as a year, it may do so?

B. Scripture says, "[the priest] shall compute."

14. A "until the year of Jubilee:"

B. [But no part of the year of the Jubilee] shall enter the calculation.

15. A "and a deduction shall be made from your Valuation:"

B. even from the sanctuary['s claim,]

C. so if the sanctuary had the usufruct for a year or two prior to the Jubilee, or did not exercise the right of usufruct but had access to it [cf. T. Arakhin 4:10B],

D. one deducts a *sela* and a pundion for each year.

16. A "And if he who dedicates the field wishes, redeeming, to redeem it:"

B. The duplicated verb serves to encompass a woman.

17. A "And if he who dedicates the field wishes, redeeming, to redeem it:"

B. The duplicated verb serves to encompass an heir.

18. A "The field:"

B. What is the point of Scripture here?

C. One might have thought that subject to the law is only one who sanctifies a field that can take a *kor* of seed.

D. How do I know that if one sanctified a field that can take a *letekh* of seed, a *seah* of seed, a *qab* of seed, the same rule applies?

E. Scripture says, "the field."

19.   A   "He shall add a fifth of the value in money to it, and it shall be his:"
       B.   If he paid the money, lo, it is his.
       C.   And if not, it is not his.
20.   A   "But if he does not wish to redeem the field:"
       B.   This refers to the owner.
21.   A   "Or if he has sold the field to another man:"
       B.   This refers to the temple treasurer.
22.   A   "To another man:"
       B.   And not to his son.
       C.   May one say, "to another man" – and not to his brother?
       D.   When Scripture says, "man," it encompasses his brother.
       E.   How come you include the son but exclude the brother [in the present rule]?
       F.   After Scripture has used inclusionary language, it has gone and used exclusionary language.
       G.   I include the son, who takes the place of his father as to a betrothal of a bondwoman {Ex. 21:9: "And if he designated her for his son, he shall deal with her as is the practice with free maidens"], and as to control of a Hebrew slave [Ex. 21:6: "He shall then remain his slave for life" – but not the slave of his heir, meaning his brother (Hillel)].
       H.   But I exclude the brother, who does not take the place of the deceased brother either as to the betrothal of a bondwoman or as to control of a Hebrew slave.
23.   A   "It shall not be redeemed any more:"
       B.   Might one suppose that one may not purchase it from the Temple treasurer and it then will enter the status of a field that has been acquired through purchase [not inheritance]?
       C.   Scripture says, "It shall not be redeemed any more:"
       D.   In its prior status, it will not be redeemed, but one may purchase it from the Temple treasurer and it then will enter the status of a field that has been acquired through purchase [not inheritance].

The exposition is inclusionary, Nos. 1, 2. No. 3 begins a long sequence of passages, proceeding through No. 11, drawn from, or dependent upon, the language and the rules of the Mishnah and the Tosefta, as indicated. From No. 12 to the end we work out a familiar type of low-level exegesis, this, not that, or this, and also that. If we ask ourselves whether the passage at hand can have been composed without the Mishnah's rules, the answer is clear. Nos. 3-11 take for granted the rules of the Mishnah or Tosefta, which are cited verbatim and then given appropriate support in a cited verse. The issues of these compositions derive from the Mishnah and the Tosefta, because they concern the vindication of those document's formulations of the rules by appeal to Scripture. Then the authorship of Sifra in the cited compositions, and in the composite overall, responds to and draws for its generative conceptions upon the Mishnah and the Tosefta.

We proceed to the second of the two pertinent chapters of Sifra, which is 274. Parashat Behuqotai. Pereq 11. At stake in what follows is the second part of the cited passage of Scripture:

> But if he does not wish to redeem the field, or if he has sold the field to another man, it shall not be redeemed any more;] but the field, when it is released in the Jubilee, [shall be holy to the Lord, as a field that has been devoted; the priest shall be in possession of it. If he dedicates to the Lord a field which he has bought, which is not a part of his possession by inheritance, then the priest shall compute the Valuation for it up to the year of Jubilee, and the man shall give the amount of the Valuation on that day as a holy thing to the Lord. In the year of Jubilee the field shall return to him from whom it was bought, to whom the land belongs as a possession by inheritance. Every Valuation shall be according to the *sheqel* of the sanctuary; twenty *gerahs* shall make a *sheqel*.

CCLXXIV.I

1. A. "But the field, when it is released in the Jubilee:"
    B. The reference to "when it is released" in the masculine form indicates that the word "field" is masculine.
2. A. "Holy:"
    B. Just as what is referred to elsewhere [e.g., Lev. 27:14: "If anyone consecrates his house to the Lord...if he who has consecrated his house wishes to redeem it...,"] leaves the status of consecration only through redemption,
    C. so "holy" in the present context means that what has been consecrated leaves that status only through redemption.
3. A. "But if he does not wish to redeem the field, or if he has sold the field to another man, it shall not be redeemed any more; but the field, when it is released in the Jubilee, [shall be holy to the Lord, as a field that has been devoted; the priest shall be in possession of it:"]
    B. **"This teaches that the priests enter into possession of the field and they pay its price," the words of R. Judah.**
    C. **R. Simeon says, "They enter but they do not pay."**
    D. **R. Eleazar says, "They neither enter nor pay, but it is called 'an abandoned field' until the second Jubilee. If the second year of the Jubilee came and it was not redeemed, it is called a twice-abandoned field. That is so up to the third Jubilee. The priests under no circumstances enter into possession until another has redeemed it" [M. Arakhin 7:4A-H].**
4. A. "As a field that has been devoted; the priest shall be in possession of it:"
    B. What is the point of Scripture here?
    C. In the case of a field that is to go forth into the ownership of the priests in the Jubilee year, which one of the priests redeemed, and lo, it is now in his domain, **might one say, he may say, "Lo, since it goes forth to the priests in the Jubilee, and since, lo, it is now in my domain, then lo, it is mine"?**

D.   How do we know that it goes forth to all his brethren, the priests [M. Arakhin 7:3D-E]?

E.   Scripture says, "shall be holy to the Lord, as a field that has been devoted; the priest shall be in possession of it" –

F.   As to field that is to go forth into the ownership of the priests in the Jubilee year, which one of the priests redeemed, and lo, it is now in his domain, this is not his, but **it goes forth to all his brethren, the priests.**

5.   A.   "If he dedicates to the Lord a field which he has bought, which is not a part of his possession by inheritance:"

     B.   What is the point of Scripture here?

     C.   "He who purchases a field from his father, if his father died and afterward he sanctified it,

     D.   "might one suppose that it is in his possession merely as a field that one has purchased?

     E.   "Scripture says, 'If he dedicates to the Lord a field which he has bought, which is not a part of his possession by inheritance,' – thus excluding this case, since it is indeed a field received by inheritance, [lo, it is deemed a field which one has bought," the words of R. Meir.

     F.   R. Judah and R. Simeon say, "He who purchases a field from his father, then sanctified it, and afterward his father died,

     G.   "might one suppose that it should be in his possession as a field purchased by money?

     H.   "Scripture says, "If he dedicates to the Lord a field which he has bought, which is not a part of his possession by inheritance,' – thus referring to a field which is in no way suitable to being designated as a field that is gained by inheritance,

     I.   "thus excluding the present case, in which the field was suitable to become a field of inheritance" [with variations in the wording, M. Arakhin 7:5A-F].

     J.   A field which has been bought does not go forth to the priests in the Jubilee, for a man does not declare sanctified something that is not his own [M. Arakhin 7:5G-H].

6.   A.   "Then the priest shall compute the Valuation [for it up to the year of Jubilee, and the man shall give the amount of the Valuation on that day as a holy thing to the Lord]:"

     B.   The meaning of "Valuation" is only a calculation of the price.

     C.   This teaches that one pays the worth of the property.

7.   A.   Said R. Eleazar, "Here we find reference to reckoning the value, and in the discussion of the field received by inheritance, we find the same language.

     B.   "Just as in that case, 'then your Valuation shall be according to the seed for it; a sowing of a homer of barley shall be valued at fifty *sheqels* of silver,'

     C.   "so in this case, 'then your Valuation shall be according to the seed for it; a sowing of a homer of barley shall be valued at fifty *sheqels* of silver.'"

8. A. "and the man shall give the amount of the Valuation on that day:"
    B. One should not tarry.
    C. **For [in the wording of M. Arakhin 6:5F-G] even though if they bring a pearl to a city, it fetches a better price, the sanctuary nonetheless has a claim only in its own place and in its own time.**

9. A. "In the year of Jubilee the field shall return to him from whom it was bought, [to whom the land belongs as a possession by inheritance]:"
    B. Might one suppose that this refers to the Temple treasurer, from whom the field was purchased?
    C. Scripture says, "to whom the land belongs as a possession by inheritance."
    D. Why not say only, "to whom the land belongs as a possession by inheritance"? Why then add, "to him from whom it was bought"?
    E. A field which has gone forth to the priests at the time of the Jubilee, and the priest sold it, and the purchaser sanctified it –
    F. might one suppose that when the next Jubilee comes, the field returns to its original owner?
    G. Scripture says, "to him from whom it was bought."

10. A. "Every Valuation shall be according to the *sheqel* of the sanctuary; twenty *gerahs* shall make a *sheqel*]:"
    B. And Valuations are never less than a *sela*.

11. A. "According to the *sheqel* of the sanctuary:"
    B. What is the point of Scripture here?
    C. Since Scripture says, "and he shall redeem," one might suppose that this may be done even with slaves, bonds, or real estate.
    D. Scripture says, "according to the *sheqel* of the sanctuary"
    E. I know only that this is done with *selas* of the sanctuary. How do I know that the law encompasses movables?
    F. Scripture says, "and he shall redeem," so encompassing something movables.
    G. Then why does Scripture say, "according to the *sheqel* of the sanctuary"?
    H. This is meant to exclude slaves, bonds, and real estate.

12. A. "twenty *gerahs* shall make a *sheqel*:"
    B. This teaches you how much a *sela* is.

13. A. How do we know that if one wanted to use a larger *sela* than that, he may do so?
    B. Scripture says, "...shall...."

14. A. How do we know that if one wanted to use a smaller *sela* than that [it is not acceptable]?
    B. Scripture says, "according to...."

After some formalities, No. 3 brings us to the Mishnah's program, which predominates through Nos. 4, 5, 8 as well. The clarifications that follow, Nos. 6, 7, are particular to our topic. The remainder seems to me miscellaneous. But the exclusions and inclusions of Nos. 11-13 are noteworthy. Overall, then, the framers of Sifra wish us to read the verses of Scripture clause by clause and to link to them, in a systematic way, whatever we find in the Mishnah that pertains to the rule or subject at hand. What we now ask is whether the authorship of the Bavli has adopted this same program, or a program that in some important ways concurs that the principal task is to follow the program and issues of Scripture – in form at least, but, if possible, in substance as well. That question, and not the one of whether or not the authorities of the Bavli wish to show that the laws of the Mishnah may formally be linked to verses of Scripture – will elicit answers pertinent to what Halivni appears to wish to allege. Whether or not it is so, as Halivni states matters, that "there is a Jewish proclivity for vindicatory law, for law that is justified, against law that is autocratically prescribed"..."a Jewish inclination for the vindicatory," Sifra assuredly provides a fine example of a document that takes shape around Scripture and defines its program in response to the problem of showing how the law of Judaism is justified by, derives from, is vindicated within, Scripture. That is why Scripture forms the organizing principle of the document and defines its order and its structure. But the Bavli does not conform to this model, not at all, and as we shall now see, even when we consider the same subject matter as is before us, we do not find a parallel interest in organizing discourse around, and in response to, Scripture. Once more we remind ourselves that at stake is not merely the formality of providing prooftexts for the Mishnah's statements. It is the substantive exercise of framing entire discussions around Scripture and in response to the facts as Scripture lays them out and the problems of the subject matter as Scripture wishes to define them. That is something, we shall now see, that the framers of the Bavli did not do, even here, where they very well might have.

7

Has an Exegetical Program Defined the Generative Problematic of the Babylonian Talmud for Tractate Arakhin Chapter Seven in Such a Way as to Sustain Halivni's Claim? The Answer of Bavli Arakhin Chapter Seven

Unit by unit, we ask these questions for the chapter at hand, in the language of Halivni: has an exegetical program defined the generative problematic of Babylonian Talmud for tractate Arakhin Chapter Seven in such a way as to sustain Halivni's claim that "there is a Jewish proclivity for vindicatory law, for law that is justified, against law that is autocratically prescribed"..."a Jewish inclination for the vindicatory." Accordingly, at the end of my descriptive-analytical comments, I shall simply register this question and answer it: does this unit's authorship concur with the authorship of Sifra concerning what must predominate in our reading of the subject matter covered at Lev. 27:16-25 and treated by the Mishnah in tractate Arakhin Chapter Seven?

7:1A-D

A.   [24A] They do not sanctify [a field of possession] less than two years before the year of Jubilee.

B.   And they do not redeem it less than a year after the year of Jubilee.

C.   [In redeeming the field] they do not reckon the months against the sanctuary.

D.   But the sanctuary reckons the months [to its own advantage].

I.

A.   [To the rule at M. 7:1A-B, which states that an act of sanctification of a field cannot take place within two years of the Jubilee year,] the following objection was raised [from an authoritative teaching that indicates one *may* do so]:

B.   People may consecrate [fields] whether before or after the Jubilee year [without limit], but in the Jubilee year itself, one should not consecrate a field. And if one has declared a field to be consecrated, it is not regarded as consecrated. [There is a clear contradiction in the teaching at hand.]

C.   Both Rab and Samuel said, ["The meaning of the Mishnah passage is] people may not consecrate a field so that it is redeemed at a rate for less than two years. [No matter when the act of consecration takes place, the redemption fee covers two years of crops.]

D.   "And since people may not so consecrate as to redeem a field for the going rate of less than two years, a person should be mindful of his property and not consecrate a field in a span of time less than two years [prior to the Jubilee]."

II.

A.   It has been stated:

B.   He who consecrates his field in the Jubilee year itself --

C.   Rab said, "It is consecrated, and the man has to pay fifty [*sheqels* to redeem it]."

D.   Samuel says, "It is not consecrated in any aspect."

E.   R. Joseph raised the following objection, "Now in regard to the matter of sale, in which Samuel differs from Rab, one may construct an argument *a fortiori* [to support Samuel's view that one may not sell such a field, namely:] If a field that already has been sold reverts to its former owner [in the Jubilee year], a field that has not been sold – all the more so that it should not be subject to sale. [For if it were sold, it would simply revert automatically to the seller in the Jubilee year.]

F.   "But as regards the present case [of consecrating the field], is it possible to construct an argument *a fortiori*? [No. For as we shall see, the field does not always revert to the former owner in the Jubilee year. If the owner does not redeem it, then the priests must redeem it. Accordingly, one cannot infer as Samuel does that a field dedicated during the Sabbatical Year automatically reverts to the owner. On the contrary, the owner must redeem it.]

G.   "For surely we have learned in the Mishnah: *If the Jubilee year arrived and the field was not redeemed, 'The priests enter into possession of it but pay its price,' the words of R. Judah* [M. 7:4A-B]. [So there is no argument *a fortiori* at hand to sustain Samuel's position.]"

H.   Samuel concurs with R. Simeon, who has said [in the same passage:] *R. Simeon says, "They [priests] enter into possession of it but do not pay [the price of the field]."* [Here, the field automatically, without any redemption, passes to the ownership of the priests. Therefore we may construct the following argument *a fortiori*: One that already has been consecrated automatically goes forth in the Jubilee year. One that has not already been consecrated – is it not an argument *a fortiori* that it should *not* be subject to consecration at all?!]

I.   [24B] And Rab reasons that, ultimately does not the field return to the owner? [Surely not.] It returns to the priests, and the priests acquire possession from the table of the Most High. [So an act of consecration is valid, even in the Jubilee year, and contrary to Simeon's view, Rab maintains that this is not really an alienation of the field from the sanctuary at all, since the field never ultimately reverts to the owner anyhow.]

J.   What is the scriptural basis for Rab's view [at C]?

K.   It is because Scripture has said, "If from the year of the Jubilee he shall sanctify his field" (Lev. 27:17) – inclusive of the Jubilee year.

L.   And Samuel [replies], "Is it written, 'And if *in* the year of the Jubilee...'? '*From* the Jubilee year' is what is written, meaning, from the year after the Jubilee year."

M.   To be sure, in Rab's view, we find written, "If *from* the year of Jubilee" and also "and if *after* the Jubilee" (Lev. 27:17, 18). [Accordingly, if the field was consecrated in the Jubilee year, the full fifty *sheqels* are paid in the redemption price. If the redemption took place after the Jubilee year, then there is a reduction from the full price.]

N.   But in Samuel's view, what is the meaning of [the other verse:] "after the Jubilee"? It means, "After the year after the Jubilee" [thus accommodating his view of matters].

O.   An objection was raised [from I.B]: People may consecrate fields whether before or after the Jubilee year without limit, but in the Jubilee year itself, one should not declare a field to be consecrated. And if one has declared a field to be consecrated, it is not regarded as consecrated. [This surely contradicts Rab at II.C.]

P.   Rab will reply to you, "The meaning is that to be sure people may not consecrate a field so that it is redeemed at a rate governed by the rule of deduction. But the field indeed is holy so that one has to pay the full fifty *sheqels* [covering the entire fifty years]."

Q.   Does this then bear the inference that, if one consecrates the field before the Jubilee, it is sanctified so as to be redeemed at the deduction rate? But lo, Rab and Samuel both have said [I.C], "People may not consecrate a field so that it is redeemed at a [deduction] rate for less than two years."

R.   Rab may reply to you, "Now who is represented here? It is the rabbis, but I follow the view of Rabbi, who has said, 'When we speak of 'first,' the first day is included, so, too, when we speak of 'seventh,' the seventh is included. Here, too, when Scripture speaks of '*From* the year,' the Jubilee year is included [just as was stated above, K]."

S.   But if this is rabbis' view, where does the *pondion* come in? [Jung, p. 144, n. 7: If Scripture refers to the second year after the Jubilee [as Rab maintains], so that fifty *sheqels* are payable for forty-eight years, the redeemer must add one *pondion* to each *sheqel*. But according to Rabbi, Scripture speaks of the year of Jubilee itself, so that fifty *sheqels* are payable for fifty years, i.e., just a *sela* per year. How then does the *pondion* come in at all?]

T. And if you wish to propose that [Rabbi] does not require [the *pondion*], have we not learned: If one has sanctified the field two or three years before the Jubilee year, Rabbi says, "I maintain that one pays a *sela* and a *pondion*" [Cf. M. 7:2I].

U. Rabbi accords with the principle of R. Judah, who has said, "The fiftieth year counts on both fifty-year cycles. [Thus there are forty-nine years for each of which the redeemer has to pay a *sheqel* and a *pondion*.]

V. Does it follow that Samuel [who maintains that it is only after the Jubilee year that the redemption at a reduction takes place] takes the view that Rabbi concurs with rabbis? [Jung, p. 145, n. 1: That the Jubilee year is not included in the cycle of forty-nine years, so that there are a full forty-nine years between one Jubilee and another apart from the Jubilee year itself.]

W. For if [Rabbi's] view were to accord with that of R. Judah, he should read, "One *sela* and two *pondions*" [since we assign the year to both cycles, hence one *sela* covering the year, but a *pondion* for the preceding cycle and a *pondion* for the cycle now commencing].

X. Accordingly, we must conclude that, in Samuel's view, Rabbi [who demands only one *pondion*] concurs with rabbis [vis-à-vis Judah].

Y. Come and hear [reverting to II.B-D]: *And they do not redeem it less than a year after the year of Jubilee* [M. 7:1B].

Z. Now that statement poses no problem to the view of Samuel [that an act of consecration in the Jubilee year itself is invalid], so, it follows, people do not redeem a field less than a year after the end of the Jubilee year, [since there would be no field subject to redemption prior to that point, there having been no valid act of consecration during the year itself.]

AA. But as to Rab, what can be the meaning of *"less than a year after the year of Jubilee"*?

BB. Do you reason that the language means literally "after the Jubilee year"? What is the meaning of "after the Jubilee year"? [25A] It is "in the midst of the Jubilee, for so long as a year has not been completed, one does not deduct it [Jung, p. 145, n. 6: from the total of remaining years to the next Jubilee, and he who redeems must pay for the incomplete years a full *sheqel* with its *pondion*. The Mishnah thus means that after the Jubilee all redemptions must be made on the basis of complete years.]

CC. What, then, does he wish to tell us? Is it that they do not reckon with months so far as the sanctuary is concerned? But lo, that principle is explicitly expressed, as follows: *In redeeming the field they do not reckon the months against the sanctuary* [M. 7:1C].

DD. His intent is to indicate the reason for the rule. That is, what is the reason that *"They do not redeem it less than a year after the year* of *Jubilee* [M. 7:1B]? It is because *in redeeming a field they do not reckon the months against the sanctuary* [M. 7:1C].

III.

A.   *In redeeming the field, they do not reckon the months against the sanctuary.* [M. 7:1C]:

B.   Our rabbis have taught on Tannaite authority: How do we know that *in redeeming the field they do not reckon the months against the sanctuary?*

C.   As it is said, "Then the priest himself shall compute the money-value for it according to the years [that remain until the year of Jubilee]" (Lev. 27:18).

D.   It is years that you compute, and you do not compute months.

E.   And how do we know that if you wish to compute the months and treat them as a full year, you may do so?

F.   What would be an example of such a computation?

G.   For instance, if one consecrated the field in the middle of the forty-eighth year?)

H.   Scripture has said, "And the priest *himself* shall compute...." (Lev. 27:18) – in any way [advantageous to the Temple, along the lines of M. 7:1D].

The field of possession cannot be sanctified in the forty-eighth and forty-ninth year of the cycle, nor redeemed with a deduction in the first. Scripture speaks of years (Lev. 27:18), which must be at least two. If a person wants to redeem his field after the Jubilee, the reckoning in accord with the years remaining up to the Jubilee is made only at the end of a complete year. If he wants to redeem the field immediately following the Jubilee, he pays the full fifty *sheqels* (Lev. 27:17). The payment required for redeeming the field of possession at the outset of the Jubilee cycle thus is fifty *sheqels* for the specified area, that is, one *sheqel* per year (I). This sum, then, is diminished by one forty-ninth of the fifty *sheqels* as each year passes, one *sheqel* and one *pondion* (= 1/48th of a *sheqel*). The amount of money to be paid for redemption consists, therefore, of as many *sheqels* and *pondions* as the number of years up to the next Jubilee. The point of M. 7:1C-D is that two years and three months, for example, are not deemed as two years to the disadvantage of the Temple. One year and eleven months are reckoned as one year, not two full years. Units I and II form a single, continuous discussion, even though, as is clear, unit I may be read by itself. Since unit II refers back to it, however, we have to regard the entire construction as a sustained and brilliant exercise. The principles of the Mishnah paragraph are elucidated in all their complexity through the inquiry into the theories of the great amoraic masters, Rab and Samuel. Unit III clarifies M. 7:1C-D's scriptural foundations. does this unit's authorship concur with the authorship of Sifra concerning what must predominate in our reading of the subject matter covered at Lev.

27:16-25 and treated by the Mishnah in tractate Arakhin Chapter Seven? Unit I undertakes the comparison of the rule of the Mishnah with another rule on Tannaite authority. The issue is not pertinent to the verses of Scripture cited at the commencement of Chapter Six. The same is so at Unit II.

Only at the end of Unit II do we ask for a scriptural basis for Rab's view; that is hardly the centerpiece of the discussion. What is important is that both parties can show their principles derive from, or at least do not contradict, the law of Scripture. That is a quite different issue from the one that is raised by claims of a "proclivity," or allegations that discourse commences with the concern that everything be shown to flow from Scripture. Unit III does indeed ask "how do we know," cite Scripture, and then prove the point from Scripture. But has Scripture dictated the treatment of the Mishnah's topic, which derives from Scripture? The answer is entirely in the negative. It is one thing to maintain that authorities of the Talmud of Babylonia wish to show that a law of the Mishnah rests on scriptural foundations. They are pleased to do so. Let me state what I conceive to be the decisive issue: *it is quite another thing to demonstrate that Scripture has dictated the shape, structure, and direction of the treatment of the topic of Scripture in the Talmud of Babylonia's reading of the Mishnah.* That is manifestly not the case here. But it ought to have been the case, were Halivni's allegations to conform to the facts of the document.

Lest we forget Steinsaltz and Wieseltier, let us address their question as well. Does this unit talk about "everything" or some few things? Obviously, some few things. Can we explain why the Talmud includes everything that is before us – and therefore can we postulate that the authorship of the Bavli has excluded what it found irrelevant and included only what served its purpose? Certainly a very limited agendum has guided the framers to put things together as they have, and to select what they wished to include as well as what they wished to ignore (which, from our perspective, means only, everything in Tosefta that is not discussed in the Talmud of Babylonia).

7:1E-K, 7:2

E. He who sanctifies his field at the time of the Jubilee's [being in effect] [compare M. 8:1]

F. pays the fifty *sheqels* of silver [for every part of a field that suffices for] the sowing of a homer of barley.

G. [If] there were there crevices ten handbreadths deep or rocks ten handbreadths high, they are not measured with it.

H. [If they were in height] less than this, they are measured with it.

I. [If] one sanctified it two or three years before the Jubilee, he gives a *sela* and a *pondion* for each year.

J. If he said, "Lo, I shall pay for each year as it comes," they do not pay attention to him.

K. But he pays the whole at once.

A. The same rule applies to the owner [of the field] and every [other] man [in regard to what is paid (M. 7-1I-K) for the redemption of the field].

B. What is the difference between the owner and every other man?

C. But: the owner pays the added fifth, and no other person pays the added fifth [M. 8:1].

I.

A. A Tanna taught [with reference to M. 7:1F]: A field that will take a *kor* of seed, not one that yields a *kor* of produce.

B. Seed sown by hand, and not sown by oxen.

C. Levi repeated [the following teaching:] "Not [sown] too thick nor too thin but in an ordinary manner."

II.

A. *If there were there crevices ten handbreadths deep, and so on.* [M. 7:1G];

B. But let them be considered as sanctified as autonomous areas [of the field, since they are not regarded as part of the arable field for purposes of redemption, and let them be redeemed on their own].

C. And if you wish to propose that, since they do not take a *kor* of seed, they are not subject to consecration,

D. has it now been taught [to the contrary]: "A field..." (Lev. 27:16).

E. Why does Scripture say, "A field"?

F. Since it is said, "Fifty *sheqels* of silver for every part of a field that suffices for the sowing of a *homer* of barley" (Lev. 27:16), I know only that [the law applies] to a case such as is specified [in Scripture, that is, to a field of the specified size]. How do I know that the law encompasses a field suitable for sowing only a *letekh* of seed or a half-*letekh*, a *seah* of seed or a *tirqab* or a half-*tirqab*?

G. Scripture says, "A field" – of any dimensions. [Accordingly, the question phrased at B is a valid one.]

H. Said Mar Uqba bar Hama, "Here we deal with crevices filled with water, which are not available for sowing seed anyhow. You may closely examine the language of the Mishnah to see that point, since it speaks of things that are similar to rocks.

I. That does indeed prove it.

J. But then, if that is the case, smaller [areas than ten handbreadths] should be subject to redemption as well.

K. They are called small clefts of the earth or spines of the earth [and are taken into account as part of the field].

III.

A. *If one sanctified it two or three years before the Jubilee* [M. 7:11:]

B.   Our rabbis have taught: "And a deduction will be made from your valuation" (Lev. 27:18) – also from [the rate paid to the] sanctuary, so that, if the sanctuary had the usufruct of the field for a year or two years,

C.   or, further, if it did not enjoy the usufruct but it was in [the Temple's] possession,

D.   one deducts a *sela* and a *pondion* for a year.

IV.

B.   Our rabbis have taught: How do we know that if the owners said, "Lo, we shall pay for each year as it comes," one pays no attention to them?

C.   Scripture says, "The priest shall compute the money-value" (Lev. 27:18) – so that the money is all together.

V.

A.   *The same rule applies to the owner of the field and to every other man. What is the difference between the owner and every other man? But the owner pays the added fifth, and no other person pays the added fifth* [M. 7:2].

M. 7:1E-F brings us to the measurement of the field sufficient for the sowing of a *homer* of barley. When the Jubilee law is in force, the redemption price is paid as just now specified. (When it is not in force it is paid in accord with the value of the field.) All E-F say is what is stated by Lev. 27:16-17. G-H's point is that ridges or crevices do not go into the measurement of the specified area. I goes over familiar ground. The fifty *selas* are paid for forty-nine years from one Jubilee to the next, a *sela* per year. The fiftieth *sela* is added, by having the forty-eight pondions of which it is made up divided among the forty-eight years. Thus the man pays a *sela* and a *pondion* per year, just as we have seen. J-K add the further qualification that the full sum must be paid at one time.

M. 7:2 restates the rule of Lev. 27:19: *If he who dedicates the field wishes to redeem it, then he shall add a fifth of the valuation in money to it*. If, therefore, there are twenty years remaining in the Jubilee cycle, the man pays twenty *selas* and twenty *pondions,* plus five more of each, twenty-five *selas* and twenty-five *pondions* in all. M. thus reads the verse to exclude the person who has not dedicated his own field but who wishes to redeem a field dedicated by someone else; he does not pay the added fifth. The Talmud works its way through selected passages of the Mishnah and consistently supplies prooftexts for the Mishnah's rules. Only unit II undertakes a substantial inquiry. Does this unit's authorship concur with the authorship of Sifra concerning what must predominate in our reading of the subject matter covered at Lev. 27:16-25 and treated by the Mishnah in tractate

Arakhin Chapter Seven? Unit I's interest is in the clarification of the language of the Mishnah, not Scripture.

Unit II tests the law of the Mishnah against the law of Scripture; here we must regard Halivni's characterization as just. The same is to be said of units III and IV. So the composite assuredly wishes to read the Mishnah, or the rule before us, in dialogue with Scripture. Does this unit talk about "everything" or some few things? Some few things. Can we explain why the Talmud includes everything that is before us – and therefore can we postulate that the authorship of the Bavli has excluded what it found irrelevant and included only what served its purpose? Yes, we can say, with Halivni, that a limited program has guided the framing of the passage, and that program in the main is the interplay between the Mishnah and Scripture; whatever information that is adduced, of the larger store in hand (as we know from Tosefta) has been selected to respond to that one concern. So here we see a passage of the Talmud that conforms to the pattern we should have anticipated throughout, were the Talmud to sustain Halivni's broad generalizations. I cannot imagine more compelling evidence that Halivni is wrong; the evidence in his favor is paltry.

7:3

A.　[If] he sanctified it and redeemed it, it does not go forth from his domain on the Jubilee.

B.　[If] his son redeemed it, it goes forth to his father on the Jubilee.

C.　[If] someone else redeemed it, or one of the relatives, and he redeemed it from his domain, it does go forth from his domain in the Jubilee.

D.　[If] one of the priests redeemed it, and lo, it is in his [the priest's] domain, he may not say, "Since it goes forth to the priests in the Jubilee, and since, lo, it is in my domain, it is mine."

E.　But it goes forth and is divided among all his brethren, the priests.

I.

A.　[25B] Our rabbis have taught on Tannaite authority: "And if he will not redeem the field" (Lev. 27:20) [referring to] the owner.

B.　Or "if he has sold the field" (Lev. 27:20) [referring to] the treasurer [of the sanctuary].

C.　"To another man" (Lev. 27:20), [referring to] another man but not to [the seller's] son.

D.　You maintain that the meaning is, "to another man and not to the seller's *son*," but perhaps the meaning is, "to another man and not to the seller's *brother*."

E.　When Scripture states, "A man," lo, reference is made to the brother.

F.   How then am I to interpret the reference to "another"? It must mean," [Another] and not the son."

G.   And why do you include the son and exclude the brother?

H.   I include the son, because he stands in his father's stead in regard to designating [and betrothing a Hebrew handmaid to her master (Ex. 21:9), for the son automatically inherits the father's right] and in respect to the Hebrew slave [who owes seven years; if the father, who bought him died, the slave serves out the remaining years to the son].

I.   To the contrary, I should include the brother, who stands in his brother's stead for the purposes of Levirate marriage.

J.   [That hardly qualifies as an argument, for] the brother [only stands in his brother's stead] for the purposes of Levirate marriage in a situation in which there is no son. Lo, if there is a son, there is no place for the Levirate brother at all!

K.   Then derive the rule from the simple fact that the son [serves in his father's stead] for two purposes but the brother [serves in his brother's stead] for only one purpose. [May we conclude therefore that the Scripture refers to the son and not the brother?]

L.   [No, that will not do, for the matter of] the Hebrew slave ['s service to the son and not the brother] derives from the same refutation. [That is, Scripture does not specify whether the slave passes to the son or brother. But based on the same reasoning as above at J, namely that] the brother only stands in his brother's stead for the purposes of Levirate marriage. [When there is no son, the Talmud derives the son precedence over the brother in inheriting the slave.] [Both the brother and the son therefore have a single point.]

II.

A.   Rabbah bar Abbuha raised the question, "As to a daughter, what is the law on her preserving ownership of a field for her father [should she buy it? Do we regard this as a redemption of the field, as we do in the case of the son, M. 7:3B]?

B.   "Since as to the matter of the Levirate connection, the son and the daughter serve equally to exempt their mother from Levirate marriage, here, too, she should serve.

C.   "Or perhaps, since as regards inheritance, where there is a son, the daughter is considered as no different from an outsider [and does not inherit], she should not serve to preserve ownership."

D.   Come and hear, for a member of the house of R. Ishmael repeated [the following teaching:] "Whoever is considered as an outsider in a case in which there is a son [cannot preserve ownership of the field]."

E.   Now this [daughter] is considered an outsider in a situation in which there is a son, [so we opt for C.]

III.

A.   R. Zira raised this question, "As to a woman, who can preserve ownership of a field for her [as the son does for the father]?

B.   "[I may reason that] the husband should be able to preserve ownership for her, since he inherits her estate.

C. "And there are those who say that the son will preserve the ownership for her, since he may treat what is coming due to her estate later on as if it had already come into his possession [as part of her estate when she died, and he will inherit what she owns when she dies, as well as what will come due to the mother's estate even after she dies. The husband inherits only what she actually owns when she dies, but not what her estate is going later on to receive.]"

D. The question remains unresolved.

IV.

A. Rami bar Hama asked R. Hisda, "If someone consecrated a field less than two years prior to the Jubilee [during which the field cannot be redeemed], does the field go forth to the ownership of the priesthood [which would be the case if another man redeemed the field as is required, by paying the full fifty *sheqels*]?"

B. He replied, "What are you reckoning? [Do you interpret the statement of Scripture in this way:] 'A deduction will be made from your valuation...but the field when it goes out in the Jubilee' (Lev. 27:18, 21) means that a field which is subject to the deduction does go forth in the Jubilee, but when it is not subject to the stated procedure it does not to forth?

C. "[But that reasoning on the sense of Scripture is wrong.] Rather, 'And if he will not redeem the field, the field, when it goes out in the Jubilee year...' (Lev. 27:20, 21), and this field *also* is subject to redemption."

V.

A. *If one of the priests redeemed it* [M. 7:3D]:
B. Our rabbis have taught on Tannaite authority: "His possession [that is, of the field] shall belong to the priest" (Lev. 27:21).
C. What is the meaning of that statement?
D. How do we know that in the case of a field which is going to be turned over to the priests at the Jubilee year, but which one of the priests redeemed, that *he may not say, "Since it goes forth to the priests in the Jubilee, and since, lo, it is in my domain, lo, it is mine:"* [M. 7:3D]?
E. And surely it is logical that, since I can acquire ownership of what is in the hands of others, I should surely be able to acquire ownership of what is in my own hands *a fortiori!*
F. Scripture says, "His possession" meaning, "a possession which is his," and this is not his.
G. How so?
H. *It goes forth from his possession and is divided among all his brethren, the priests* [M. 7:3E].

The pericope is deceptively smooth, since M. 7:3A-C are not continued as to problem or principle by D-E. The first three rules do belong together. A is obvious, setting the stage for the others. The point is that if the original owner of the field redeems the field, he retains possession at the Jubilee. If the son redeems it, the father repossesses it. If the original owner, C, redeemed it from the person who redeemed it from the sanctuary, we invoke once more the rule of A. D's problem is separate. Scripture is clear that a field which has not been redeemed by the Jubilee year remains in the possession of the priesthood. D excludes the claim of a particular priest to acquire the field. What has happened is that the man has not redeemed the field. A priest has done so. The priest cannot claim the right to keep the field, D. That is, if an Israelite, not the owner, had redeemed the field, the priests would have received it in the Jubilee year; this particular priest – so it is claimed – possesses it and has the right to keep it. That is not acceptable. The Talmud at hand is rather inventive, since it raises a range of possibilities and asks some rather creative questions. Unit I asks for the basis for the son's special role, M. 7:3B. Units II, III, and IV follow a single plan of asking about some rather speculative matters. Unit V then moves on to the second part of the Mishnah pericope and provides an exegetical basis for the rule.

Does this unit's authorship concur with the authorship of Sifra concerning what must predominate in our reading of the subject matter covered at Lev. 27:16-25 and treated by the Mishnah in tractate Arakhin Chapter Seven? Unit I conducts an exegesis of Scripture. The issue of unit II is hardly required by Scripture's program on the topic at hand; it is speculative and concerns the analogy that governs the rule for the woman. Unit III is of the same sort; Scripture plays no role. Unit IV appeals to Scripture to supply an answer to a speculative question. Unit V adopts Scripture's program and links the Mishnah to Scripture. Here the results are mixed, of course; any claim of a powerful predilection to "vindication" of the law through appeal to exegesis seems plausible, if vastly overstated by Halivni's infelicitous word choices. Does this unit talk about "everything" or some few things? Again, the program is exceedingly well-crafted and economical. Can we explain why the Talmud includes everything that is before us – and therefore can we postulate that the authorship of the Bavli has excluded what it found irrelevant and included only what served its purpose? The exegetical program, as addressed to both Scripture and the Mishnah, is pointed and well focused. Halivni's satisfaction with the passage must, however, be restricted by the fact that the exegetical program in the end has not been dictated by Scripture alone or primarily.

7:4

A.   [If] the Jubilee arrived and [the field] was not redeemed,

B. "The priests enter into [the possession of] it but pay its price," the words of R. Judah.

C. R. Simeon says, "They enter, and they do not pay."

D. R. Eliezer says, "They neither enter nor pay.

E. "But: It is called an abandoned field until the second Jubilee.

F. "[If] the second year of the Jubilee came and it was not redeemed, it is called a twice-abandoned field,

G. "up to the third Jubilee.

H. "The priests under no circumstances [directly] enter into possession until another [party] has redeemed it."

I.

A. What is the scriptural basis for the position of R. Judah?

B. He appropriates the meaning of the word *holy* from the use of the same word in connection with the consecration of a house [at Lev. 27:14, 23. Both verses use the word when referring, respectively, to the consecration of a house and of a field of possession, one received by inheritance].

C. Just as, in the case of the consecrated house, [redemption requires] a money payment, so in the present case, a money payment is necessary.

D. And R. Simeon appropriates the meaning of the word *holy* in the present context from the use of the same word in connection with the lambs offered on the Feast of Weeks [specified at Lev. 23:20]. Just as, in that case, [the priest gets the beasts] free, so here too [priest gets the land] free.

E. And should not R. Judah derive the rule governing the case at hand from the case of the lambs brought on the Feast of Weeks?

F. [In his view,] we should compare Holy Things consecrated for the upkeep of the Temple house [as in the case of a field that has been consecrated] [26A] from the rule governing Holy Things consecrated for the upkeep of the Temple house [specifically, the house that has been consecrated, the value of which is given to the Temple.]

G. We should not compare Holy Things consecrated for the upkeep of the Temple house to Holy Things consecrated for use on the altar itself. [Accordingly, Simeon's reasoning involves the confusion of categories, so the analogy is improper.]

H. And should not R. Simeon derive the rule governing the case at hand from the rule governing the case of consecrating a house?

I. We derive the rule governing something that constitutes a gift to the priests from the rule governing another such object that is also a gift to the priests, but we do not derive the rule governing a gift to the priests from a case that does not involve a gift to the priests. [The consecrated house is a gift to the upkeep of the Temple house, while the field of possession and the specified lambs, Lev. 27:21 and 23:20, respectively, do not constitute gifts for the upkeep of the Temple house but for the priesthood, as Scripture specifies.]

II.

A.   *R. Eliezer says, "They neither enter nor pay"* [M. 7:4D]:

B.   Said Rabbah, "What is the scriptural basis for the position of R. Eliezer?

C.   "Scripture has said, 'And if he will not redeem the field.. it will not again be redeemed.... If he has sold the field to another man, [then]...the field, when it goes out in the Jubilee' (Lev. 27:20-21)."
[Jung, p. 152, n. 1: The two verses are combined to mean thus: If he does not redeem it, it shall not be redeemed any more, but if he (the treasurer of the Sanctuary) sells it, then the field is turned over on Jubilee to the priests. This implies that if the treasurer does not sell it, the priests do not enter into possession of the field.]

D.   Said Abayye, "[You are] a sharp knife, cutting up verses of Scripture [to suit your own convenience].

E.   "Rather, said Abayye, "The scriptural basis for the opinion of R. Eliezer accords with that which has been taught on Tannaite authority.

F.   "'It shall not be redeemed any more' (Lev. 27:20).

G.   "Is it possible to suppose that it may not be redeemed in such a way that the field will serve [the original owner] as a field acquired by purchase [until the next Jubilee]?

H.   "Scripture accordingly states, 'Any more,' meaning, it cannot be redeemed so as to restore it to its original status [as a field of possession], but it may be redeemed in such a way that the field will serve [the original owner] as a field acquired by purchase [until the next Jubilee].

I.   "Now [continuing the exposition] to what occasion [is reference made]? If we say, to the first Jubilee [after it was consecrated], why should it not be subject to redemption? It remains in the status of a field of possession up to that point! [That is by definition.]

J.   "But it is self-evident that reference is made to the second Jubilee [after it was consecrated].

K.   "According to which authority [is the exegesis presented by F-J]?

L.   "If we say that it accords with the positions of R. Judah and R. Simeon, [in their view] the field goes forth to the ownership of the priests [at the first Jubilee. How, then, can the statement refer to the second Jubilee?]

M.   "Accordingly, is it not in accord with the view of R. Eliezer? And it yields the scriptural basis for the position of R. Eliezer in the present context. [That is, at the first Jubilee after consecration, the field, not redeemed, belongs to the Temple. The priests do not gain ownership. The field then can still be redeemed from the Temple's ownership until the second Jubilee.]"

N.   Is that really your view? Then how do R. Judah and R. Simeon deal with the word *Any more*? [Surely they take the same view that Eliezer does about the meaning of that language.]

O.   Rather, in the present case with what situation do we deal? It is with a field that became a possession of the priests [at the Jubilee year]. A priest subsequently consecrated the field. Then the original owner came along to redeem the field [and regain ownership of it].

P. It might enter your mind to rule that the field may not be redeemed in such a way that it falls into the category of a field acquired through purchase.

Q. Scripture says, "Any more," meaning, the field may not be redeemed any more so as to return to its original status [i.e., as a field of possession], but it may be redeemed so that the field falls into the status, so far as the purchaser is concerned, of a field acquired through purchase.

R. Along these same lines have we not got the following teaching on Tannaite authority:

S. "In the year of the Jubilee the field [that has been purchased] shall return to him from whom it was bought (Lev. 27:24).

T. Is it possible to suppose that it reverts to the ownership of the Temple treasurer, from whom the purchaser bought it?

U. [To avoid that conclusion,] Scripture states, "Even to whom the possession [by inheritance] of the land belongs" (Lev. 27:24).

V. Why, then, should Scripture not simply say, "Even to whom the possession belongs"? Why is it necessary in addition to state, "To him from whom it was bought"?

W. [It is to deal with the following situation:] A field went forth to the priests. A priest sold it. The purchaser then consecrated it, and another party redeemed it --

X. Is it possible that the field should then revert to the original owner? [To forestall that conclusion,] Scripture states, "To him from whom it was bought." [It does not go back to the man who bought and consecrated the field. It goes back to the priest from whom the purchaser bought the field. In the case of a field of possession, once another party redeems the field and it reaches the ownership of a priest at the Jubilee year, the original owner, who had inherited the field as a field of possession, can no longer redeem it and recover it as a field of possession (Jung)].

Y. It was, moreover, necessary to make explicit, "It shall not be redeemed," and it also was necessary to write, "To him from whom it was bought."

Z. Had the All-Merciful [only] written, "It will not be redeemed," it would have indicated that [the law applies in such a way] that the field does not revert at all [to the one who consecrated it], but here, where the field does revert, let it revert to its original owner. Therefore it was necessary for the All-Merciful to write, "To the one who bought it." [Had Scripture said only that the field may not be redeemed anymore, I would have reached the conclusion that the field may not be redeemed in a case in which it does not go back to the one who consecrated it. That is, we have a case in which the priest consecrated the field after acquiring it in the Jubilee year. The original owner had not redeemed it. In this case, in the next Jubilee, the field goes out to all the priests. It does not revert to the priest who consecrated it. But Scripture would have indicated that the field reverts to the owner where the field reverts to the one who consecrated it. That is, the priest sold the field and the purchaser consecrated it, so it is a field acquired by purchase. If that field is redeemed, it reverts to the one who consecrated it, namely, to that priest who had received it in the preceding Jubilee year.]

AA.   If, furthermore, Scripture had written only, "To him from whom it was bought," [the law applies in a case in which] the original owner did not pay its value [to redeem it from the sanctuary. Someone else did so.] But here, where the original owner did pay the price of the field [and redeem it], I might have said that it should be restored to his possession. Therefore the All-Merciful has written, "It may not be redeemed."

BB.   And if the All-Merciful had written, "It may not be redeemed," but had not written, "Any more," I should have reached the conclusion that the field may not be redeemed under any circumstances.

CC.   Accordingly, the All-Merciful has written, "Any more," meaning, The field may not be redeemed any more in such a way that it will revert to its original condition, but it may be redeemed in such a way that it will be in the status of a field acquired by purchase [for the one who purchases it].

DD.   What is the upshot of it all [for our understanding of Eliezer's position that the priests cannot acquire the possession of the field until someone else has redeemed it]?

EE.   Said Raba, "Said Scripture, 'But the field, when it goes out in the Jubilee year...,' meaning, when it goes out of the possession of another party." [Jung, p. 154, n. 3: When it goes out of the possession of another who had redeemed it from the treasurer before the year of Jubilee, then shall it go out to the priests as their field of possession].

III.
A.   [26B] The question was raised: Is the original owner, in the period of the second Jubilee, in the status of an outside party or not? [The question flows from Eliezer's position. In his view, in the second Jubilee cycle the field is subject to redemption. What is the status during that cycle of the original owner, who had not redeemed the field in the first Jubilee? When he redeems the field, will the field go out to the priests in the third Jubilee? Or is he still regarded as the original owner so that, in the third Jubilee, the field will revert to him, as it would have reverted to him had he redeemed the field before the end of the first Jubilee (Jung)?]

B.   Come and hear [what has been stated at II.F-M:]
C.   "It shall not be redeemed any more" (Lev. 27:20).
D.   Is it possible to suppose that it may not be redeemed in such a way that the field will serve [the original owner] as a field acquired by purchase [until the next Jubilee]?

E.   Scripture accordingly states, "Any more," meaning, it cannot be redeemed as it had originally been [i.e., as a field of inheritance], but it may be redeemed in such a way that the field will serve [the original owner] as a field acquired by purchase [until the next Jubilee].

F. Now to what occasion [is reference made]? If we say, to the first Jubilee [after it was consecrated], why should it not be subject to redemption? It remains in the status of a field of possession up to that point!

G. But it is self-evident that reference is made to the second Jubilee [after it was consecrated].

H. According to which authority? If we say that it accords with the positions of R. Judah and R. Simeon [there is a problem, because in their view] the field in any event goes forth to the ownership of the priests [at the first Jubilee year. In their view, therefore, the original owner has no opportunity to redeem after this time.]

I. Accordingly, is it not in accord with the view of R. Eliezer?

J. And from the foregoing, we derive the conclusion that the original owner in the period of the second Jubilee is in the status of an outside party.

K. But is that your view? Then how do R. Judah and R. Simeon interpret the use of the word "any more"?

L. Rather, in the present case with what situation do we deal? It is with a field that was turned over to the priests [at the first Jubilee], and a priest consecrated the field, and the original owner came along to redeem the field [and regain ownership of it].

M. It might enter your mind to rule that the field may not be redeemed in such a way that it falls into the category of a field acquired through purchase.

N. Scripture says, "Any more," meaning, the field may not be redeemed any more so as to return to its original status, but it may be redeemed so that the field falls into the status, [so far as the purchaser is concerned,] of a field acquired through purchase.

O. Along these same lines, have we not the following teaching on Tannaite authority:

P. "In the year of the Jubilee the field [that has been purchased] shall return to him from whom it was bought" (Lev. 27:24).

Q. Is it possible to suppose that it reverts to the ownership of the Temple treasurer from whom the purchaser bought it?

R. [To avoid that conclusion,] Scripture states, "Even to whom the possession [by inheritance] of the land belongs" (Lev. 27:24).

S. Why does Scripture say, "To him from whom it was bought"?

T. [It is to deal with the following situation:] A field went forth to the priests. A priest sold it. The purchaser then consecrated it, and another party then redeemed it.

U. Is it possible that the field should then revert to the original owner? [To forestall that conclusion,] Scripture states, "To him from whom it was bought [even if that person is not the original owner]."

V. It was, moreover, necessary to make explicit, "It shall not be redeemed," and it also was necessary to write, "To him from whom it was bought."

W. Had the All-Merciful written, "It will not be redeemed," it would have indicated that the law applies in such a way that the field does not revert at all. Scripture therefore had to write, "To the one who bought it."

X.   If, furthermore, Scripture had written, "To him from whom it was bought," [the law would apply in a case in which] the original owner did not pay its value [to redeem it from the sanctuary. Someone else did so.] But here, where the original owner did pay the price of the field [and redeem it], I might have said that it should be restored to his possession. Therefore the All-Merciful has written, "It may not be redeemed."

Y.   And if the All-Merciful had written, "It may not be redeemed," but had not written, "Any more," I should have reached the conclusion that the field may not be redeemed under any circumstances.

Z.   Accordingly, the All-Merciful has written, "Any more," meaning, The field may not be redeemed any more in such a way that it will revert to its original condition, but it may be redeemed in such a way that it will be in the status of a field acquired by purchase [for the one who purchases it].

AA.   What is the upshot of the matter?

BB.   Come and hear: R. Eliezer says, "If the original owner redeemed the field in the second Jubilee [after the original consecration], it goes forth to the priests in the Jubilee [following]. [That would follow from an affirmative answer to the question raised at III.A.]

CC.   Said Rabina to R. Ashi, "Have we not learned to repeat the Tannaite statement as follows: *The priests under no circumstances enter into possession until another party has redeemed it* [M. 7:4H]?

DD.   He said to him, "The original owner during the second Jubilee [after consecration] is in the status of an outside party."

EE.   There are those who state matters as follows: R. Eliezer says, "If one has redeemed the field in the second Jubilee, it does not go forth to the priests at the Jubilee year."

FF.   Said Rabina to R. Ashi, "Have we not learned to repeat the Tannaite statement as follows: *R. Eliezer says, 'The priests under no circumstances enter into possession until another party has redeemed it* [M. 7:4H]'?"

GG.   He said to him, "If we derived the facts from the formulation of the Mishnah paragraph at hand alone, I should have concluded that the owner during the second Jubilee is in the status of an outside party. Accordingly, we are informed [that that is not the case. The owner is not considered an outsider during the second Jubilee, so that, if he redeems the field, it remains his possession at the upcoming Jubilee.]"

The issue at M. 7:4 is a field which has been dedicated, but not redeemed either by the original owner or by someone else. Judah assigns the field to the priests; but they pay the fifty *sheqels* for the specified area. Simeon says the priests take possession without paying. Eliezer's position is out of phase. He holds that the priests take possession of a field at the Jubilee *only* if someone already has redeemed it, H. Therefore, in the present case, A, the priests do not take possession and of course do not pay the price, D. E, F, and G simply spell out the status of the field for the next hundred years. Unit I provides a scriptural basis for the views of Judah and Simeon, and unit II proceeds to amplify and provide a basis for the position of Eliezer. Unit III develops the implications of Eliezer's position. It seems clear that the repetition of much of unit II's discussion in unit III (K ff.) is needless, and a critical text in time to come will give us a better view of what is at hand.

Does this unit's authorship concur with the authorship of Sifra concerning what must predominate in our reading of the subject matter covered at Lev. 27:16-25 and treated by the Mishnah in tractate Arakhin Chapter Seven? Scripture has not supplied the question to which the Mishnah paragraph addresses itself, "If the Jubilee arrived...," to the contrary, the Mishnah has defined the sustaining issue. Then and only then do we ask for a scriptural foundation for the answers. That is to treat Scripture (quite reasonably) as a source of authoritative law. The issue of whether or not Scripture has dictated the inquiry, defined the elements and order of the program of the Mishnah, is separate. In this case, facts of Scripture have suggested to the framers of the Mishnah a set of questions that require answers. The framers then propose answers and ask Scripture to sustain those answers through the facts it provides. So has Scripture defined the issues of the Talmud? No, the Mishnah has. The Talmud's fundamental program indeed is exegetical –in regard to the amplification and explanation of the Mishnah, that and not Scripture. In this characterization we can account for units I and II. The speculative question of unit III once more leads us to Scripture for information – but not for the question itself. This unit assuredly talks about some few things. We certainly can explain why the Talmud includes everything that is before us – and can postulate that the authorship of the Bavli has excluded what it found irrelevant and included only what served its purpose. It may by this point be unkind to observe that Wieseltier and Steinsaltz are wrong here too; the program is exceedingly well crafted, limited, purposeful; we find not "everything about everything" or even "everything about some one thing," but only a few things, the things that the framers of the passage have selected among a repertoire that encompasses, after all, Scripture, the Mishnah, Tosefta, and Sifra, on the subject before us.

7:5

A. He who purchases a field from his father, [if] his father died, and afterward he sanctified it, lo, it is deemed a field of possession (Lev. 27:16).

B. [If] he sanctified it and afterward his father died,

C. "lo, it is deemed in the status of a field which has been bought," the words of R. Meir.

D. R. Judah and R. Simeon say, "It is deemed in the status of a field of possession. Since it is said, 'And if a field which he has bought which is not a field of his possession' (Lev. 27:22) –

E. "A field which is not destined to be a field of possession,

F. "which excludes this, which is destined to be a field of possession [i.e., when his father dies]."

G. A field which has been bought does not go forth to the priests in the Jubilee,

H. for a man does not declare sanctified something which is not his own.

I. Priests and Levites sanctify [their fields] at any time and redeem them at any time, whether before the Jubilee or after the Jubilee.

I.

A. Our rabbis have taught: "How do we know [from Scripture] that in the case of one who purchases a field from his father and who consecrated it, afterward whose father died, the field should be regarded as his as a field of possession [= M. 7:5D]?

B. "Scripture states, 'And if a field which he has bought, which is not a field of his possession' (Lev. 27:22), – a field which is not destined to be a field of possession, which excludes this field, which *is* destined to be a field of possession," the words of R. Judah and R. Simeon [M. 7:5D-F].

C. R. Meir says, "How do we know that in the case of one who purchases a field from his father, and whose father died, and who afterward consecrated the field, the field should be his as a field of possession?

D. "Scripture states, 'And if a field which he has bought, which is not a field of his possession' (Lev. 27:22) – a field which is not [at this moment] a field of possession, excluding this case, which indeed *is* a field of possession."

E. May we then propose that it is in this principle that the parties differ:

F. R. Meir maintains [C] the theory that the acquisition of the usufruct of the field is equivalent to the acquisition of the capital [the field itself].

G. R. Judah and R. Simeon [A-B] take the position that acquisition of the usufruct of the field is not in the category of the acquisition of the capital [the field itself].

H. Said R. Nahman bar Isaac, "In ordinary circumstances, in the view of R. Simeon and R. Judah, acquisition of the usufruct of the field is equivalent to acquisition of the capital [ownership of the field itself].

I. "But [27A] in the present case, there is a verse of Scripture at hand, which they have interpreted as follows:

J. "Scripture might as well state, 'If it is a field acquired by purchase which is not a field of *his* possession,' or it might also have written, 'which is not a field of possession.'

K.   "What is the meaning of the explicit reference, to 'A field of *his* possession'? Not a field which is *not* going to become a field of possession under any circumstances.

L.   "That usage excludes the present case, in which it is destined to enter the status of a field of possession [in due course]."

II.

A.   *Priests and Levites sanctify their fields at any time* [M. 7:5I]:

B.   It was assuredly necessary to make explicit reference to their right to redeem the field at any time, to distinguish them from Israelites, who may redeem [their fields] only up to the Jubilee year [but not afterward].

C.   So we are informed that priests and Levites may redeem their fields at any time.

D.   But what purpose was there to include the reference to the fact that priests and Levites may consecrate their fields at any time? Even Israelites also may do so.

E.   And if you say that the reference is to the Jubilee year itself [that priests and Levites, but not Israelites, may consecrate their fields], then that thesis would pose no problem for Samuel, who has said that in the Jubilee year itself, a field may not be consecrated. So we would be informed that priests and Levites may consecrate their fields at all times [including the Jubilee year, when Israelites may not do so.]

F.   But in the view of Rab, what purpose is there in including such a detail about priests and Levites? Even Israelites also may do so.

G.   But, according to your own thinking, why should the framer of the passage have included the language, *whether before the Jubilee or after the Jubilee?* [In your reading of the passage, the meaning would then be that priests and Levites, but not Israelites, may consecrate fields before and after the Jubilee, but Israelites may not do so. [That reading is manifestly absurd.]

H.   Rather, since the framer of the passage stated in the former case [namely, that of the Israelites, M. 7:13] *whether before the Jubilee or after the Jubilee,* he recorded the same formulation in the latter case [priests and Levites], *whether before or after the Jubilee.*

I.   And since, along these same lines, he formulated the former case, *They may not consecrate...or redeem...,* he formulated the latter case in the same way, *They do consecrate...they do redeem.*

We recall (M. 3:2) that a field of possession differs from a field which has been purchased. The former is acquired by inheritance, the latter is bought. The former is subject to the fixed valuation of Lev. 27:16ff., the latter is evaluated in accord with its actual worth. The former if not redeemed by the Jubilee falls to the priests; the latter does not. Now we ask some secondary questions on the disposition of fields which may fall to one by inheritance but which also are purchased by the potential heir. A makes the basic point that if one purchases a field from his father but afterward will have inherited it in any case, then the field is deemed a field of possession. If after the father's death the man sanctifies the field, it falls into the category of a field he has acquired through inheritance, not purchase. B then asks the more interesting question: What if the man purchased it from the father and sanctified it. He has not then inherited the field. But he is *going* to acquire by inheritance what he already has acquired through purchase. Meir does not treat that which is going to happen as if it already has happened. Therefore if the man purchased the field and sanctified it before the death of the father, then at the time the field was sanctified, it is in the status only of a field which has been bought. Judah and Simeon take up the contrary position, for reasons which are specified nicely at E-F. G-H then tells us what difference is made between the field of possession and the one of purchase. Scripture, of course, states this same rule. I (= Lev. 25:32) is distinct from the foregoing construction. It excludes priests and Levites from the Jubilee rule. They may redeem a field even after the Jubilee year. I do not understand why it has been placed here. Unit I, as usual, provides a scriptural foundation for the positions of the authorities of the Mishnah passage. Unit II investigates the implications of the formulation of the rule as the Mishnah presents it.

Does this unit's authorship concur with the authorship of Sifra concerning what must predominate in our reading of the subject matter covered at Lev. 27:16-25 and treated by the Mishnah in tractate Arakhin Chapter Seven? We start, unit I, with the inquiry into the scriptural basis for a rule of the Mishnah. But if we examine the rule – one who purchases a field from his father and who consecrated it, afterward whose father died, the field should be regarded as his as a field of possession – we can hardly find in Scripture reason to raise such a question to begin with. It must follow that the question has originated elsewhere than in Scripture's account of the topic before us. Answering the question by appeal to Scripture is not the same thing as trying to justify every statement we make from Scripture; more to the point, a "proclivity" toward reading a topic as Scripture does, rather than (e.g.,) as the Mishnah does is hardly shown in this passage; the opposite "proclivity" is demonstrated. Unit II obviously works on a problem that Scripture has not precipitated. Does this unit talk about "everything" or some few things? The program is as usual economical and rigorously disciplined. Can we explain why the Talmud includes everything that is before us – and therefore can we postulate that the authorship of the Bavli has excluded what it found irrelevant and included only what served its purpose? The basis throughout is the same: the Mishnah's program. The Bavli represents an exercise in Mishnah exegesis, and, while scriptural exegesis plays its role, the interest in linking the law (of the Mishnah) to Scripture must be judged subordinate. Does Sifra's sustained interest in Scripture exegesis characterize the Talmud of Babylonia? No, the Talmud of Babylonia reads the Mishnah in the manner in which Sifra reads Scripture. To answer the question with which we began: has an exegetical program defined the generative problematic of the Babylonian Talmud for tractate Arakhin Chapter Seven in such a way as to sustain Halivni's claim? Very simply, no.

Part Four

CONCLUSION

8

Selectivity and the Question of Tradition

In *The Bavli and its Sources,* in the concrete and particular instance of tractate Sukkah I asked whether a system of applied reason and sustained, rigorous rational inquiry can coexist with a process of tradition. I argued that it cannot. In that book I further raised the question of whether and how – on literary grounds alone – the principal documents of the Judaism of the Dual Torah can be shown to exhibit continuities from one to the next. If they do, then, *on literary grounds alone,* we may claim that the writings constitute sources that all together form a tradition, a set of documents making a single unitary, continuous, and, therefore, also cogent, statement. If they do not, then we shall have to seek other than documentary evidence for the traditional status and character imputed to these same writings by the theology and law of formative Judaism. Again to state with emphasis: *I therefore want to know whether and how – again, in concrete, literary terms – a document makes its part of such a traditional statement, speaking, for its particular subject, in behalf of the entirety of the antecedent writings of the Judaic system at hand and standing in a relationship of continuity – not merely connection – with other such writings.* The answer to that question will tell me how a traditional writing is formulated. If the question has no answer, and in the Bavli it does not, then it must follow that the Bavli is a document that has been framed through a process of not tradition but selection. And that is how I see the Bavli.

Let me expand on the question before us. How does the authorship of a corpus of writings that unfold one after another take up sources and turn them from traditions into a systematic and cogent statement. To answer the question, for obvious reasons I turned to the document universally assigned canonical and official status in Judaism from antiquity to the present day, the Talmud of Babylonia. In the centuries beyond the closure of the Bavli in ca. A.D. 600, people would universally turn to the Bavli as the starting point for all inquiry into any given topic, and rightly so. Since the Bavli made the first and enduringly definitive statement, we impute to the Bavli canonical status. If, therefore, we wish to ask about how a variety of sources turned into a tradition, that is to say, about the status of statements of a continuous tradition of documents of the formative age of the Judaism of the Dual Torah, we inquire into the standing of a Bavli tractate as testimony on its subject within the larger continuous system of which it is reputed to form a principal part. What we want to know about that testimony, therefore, is how the Bavli relates to prior documents. The reason is that we want to know whether or not the Bavli constitutes a statement of a set of such antecedent sources, therefore a step in an unfolding tradition, so that Judaism constitutes a traditional religion, the result of a long sedimentary process. As is clear, the alternative and complementary issue is whether or not the Bavli makes its own statement and hence inaugurates a "new tradition" altogether (in that theological sense of tradition I introduced in the preface). In this case the Judaism defined by the Bavli is not traditional and the result of a sedimentary process but the very opposite: fresh, inventive, responsive to age succeeding age.

In studies such as this one on Arakhin and the prior one on Sukkah, therefore, I take up a Bavli tractate in particular for a simple reason. It is that, on any given topic, a tractate of the Bavli presents the final and authoritative statement that would emerge from the formative period of the Judaism of the Dual Torah. That statement constituted not only an authoritative, but also an encompassing and complete account. That is what I mean by the making of a traditional statement on a subject: transforming in particular the received materials – whatever lay at hand – into a not merely cogent but fixed and authoritative statement. What I wish to find out is the canonical status of the Bavli, insofar as the authorship of the Bavli transformed its antecedents, its sources, into traditions: the way things had been, are, and must continue to be, in any given aspect of the life and world view of Israel, the Jewish people, as the Bavli's authorship understood the composition of that Israel. Accordingly, I mean to investigate how a principal authorship in Judaism has taken up whatever sources it had in hand and transformed them into the tradition of Judaism: the canonical statement, on a given subject, that would endure. To state the result of that work, which precipitated the interests that have been continued in this one, very simply:

What earlier authorships – represented by the Talmud of the Land of Israel – wished to investigate in the Mishnah, the points they wished to prove by reference to verses of Scripture important in our tractate – these have little or nothing in common with the points of special concern systematically worked out by the authorship of the Bavli. The Bavli's authorship at ca. 600 approaches Mishnah exegesis with a program distinct from that of the Yerushalmi's authorship of ca. 400, and the Bavli's authorship reads a critical verse of Scripture within a set of considerations entirely separate from those of interest to the authorships of Leviticus Rabbah and Pesiqta deRab Kahana of ca. 450 and 500. Any notion that the Bavli's authorship has taken as its principal task the restatement of received ideas on the Mishnah topics and Scripture verses at hand derives no support to speak of from the sample we shall examine.

To broaden the range of discourse, let me underline what I conceive to be the results of that finding. So far as a process of tradition takes over the formation of a cogent and sustained statement, considerations extraneous to rational inquiry, decided, not demonstrated facts – these take over and divert the inexorable processes of applied reason from their natural and logically necessary course. And the opposite is also the case. Where a cogent statement forms the object of discourse, syllogistic argument and the syntax of sustained thought dominate, obliterating the marks of a sedimentary order of formation in favor of the single and final, systematic one. So far as an authorship proposes to present an account of a system, it will pay slight attention to preserving the indicators of the origins of the detritus of historical tradition, of which, as a matter of fact, the systemic statement itself may well be composed.

The threads of the tapestry serve the artist's vision; the artist does not weave so that the threads show up one by one. The weavers of a tractate of the Bavli make ample use of available yarn. But they weave their own tapestry of thought. And it is their vision – and *not* the character of the threads in hand – that dictates the proportions and message of the tapestry. In that same way, so far as processes of thought of a sustained and rigorous character yield writing that makes a single, cogent statement, tradition and system cannot form a compatible unit. Where reason governs, it reigns supreme and alone, revising the received materials and, through its own powerful and rigorous logic, restating into a compelling statement the entirety of the prior heritage of information and thought.

In this context, as we now have seen, Halivni's position has proven not so much erroneous as trivial and irrelevant, not because there is no interest in showing scriptural bases for the Mishnah's rules, but because not Scripture, nor even the Mishnah, but the autonomous program of logic – applied logic and practical reason – of the framers of the Bavli is what has made the Bavli what it is. So whether or not people look to Scripture for information is not a principal concern. We can prove that they constantly referred to Scripture where they could, and wanted to, where Scripture failed them. What we want to know is whether or not it is from Scripture that they derived the generative problematic, the governing inquiry, that has made their document what it is. And what we now see full well is the contrast between a document that does turn to Scripture for its structure and program, Sifra, and another that does not, the Talmud of Babylonia.

Steinsaltz's and Wieseltier's profound misunderstanding of the character of the Talmud of Babylonia matters not as a matter of mere fact but as an issue of talmudic hermeneutics. If they are right, then the Talmud is not only about everything in general. We reconsider their now-astounding language for one last time; they say: "The Talmud...deals with an overwhelmingly broad subject – the nature of all things according to the Torah. Therefore its contours are a reflection of life itself. It has no formal external order, but is bound by a strong inner connection between [sic!] its many diverse subjects....The authority of the Talmud lies in its use of this rigorous method in its search for truth with regard to the entire Torah – in other words, with regard to all possible subjects in the world, both physical and spiritual," "the Talmud is, in truth, about all things. There is no corner of human life and no corner of Jewish life into which the fastidious rabbis did not peer." The opinions they express, the language they choose – in light of the document we have examined, these appear simply out of all contact with the writing before us. If they were right, then we should have concluded that the Talmud is about nothing in particular. But we have seen that the Bavli is very much about some few things – in all their rich particulars. And that statement pertains not merely to the Bavli's topical program (defined though it is by the Mishnah and its agenda) but to its substantive propositions, the things that, through an infinity of details, the framers wish to show time and again.[1] So Steinsaltz and Wieseltier are wrong not merely because the Talmud's character contradicts their rather airy characterization of it, but because they massively miss the mark in their witless

---

[1]But that is not to suggest I claim at this moment to know what those things were. I can say with some certainty what I think were the very few, large points that the framers of the Mishnah said over and over again, in numerous ways. This I have specified in my *Judaism as Philosophy. The Method and Message of the Mishnah.* Columbia, 1991: University of South Carolina Press.

misunderstanding of the document. What they see as all-encompassing is a selective piece of writing; what they see as essentially pointless – the document as a whole – proves purposeful and well-crafted. That explains why they are wrong, and why vast stretches of the document, including every line in this book, proves they are wrong.

Why does it matter to my study of the formation of Judaism? The reason is that critical to that study are the correct classification and characterization of the Talmud of Babylonia. Is the story of the formation of Judaism in late antiquity the history of the sedimentary agglutination of a tradition? Or does the Judaism that through the Bavli comes out of late antiquity speak for some few people, who have formed a system pretty much within the outlines of their own plan? For whom, then, does the Judaism embodied in the Bavli speak, in what context, for what purpose, in response to what ineluctable problem, providing what self-evidently valid answer? Whether or not these questions are even to be addressed to the document depends upon whether we conceive the document to be traditional or systemic. That is why the issue of selectivity proves so preponderant: if choices, then who made the selections and why. If no choices, then for whom does the document speak, and why does it speak at all – as, by definition, it assuredly does?

In my judgment while the writing appears to be "traditional," because of its perennial reference to received traditions, it in fact is highly selective. The reason that judgment matters is that, in interpreting the character of the system adumbrated by the Bavli, my first step is to classify the system as a whole, and, as is now clear, I classify that system as not traditional but autonomous, not received but composed with a plan and a program particular to its authorship. In my hermeneutics, I therefore contrast thought received as truth transmitted through a process of tradition against thought derived from active rationality. This I do by asking a simple question: does what is the most rigorously rational and compelling statement of applied reason known to me, the Talmud of Babylonia or Bavli, constitute a tradition and derive from a process of traditional formulation and transmission of an intellectual heritage, facts and thought alike? Or does that document make a statement of its own, cogent and defined within the requirements of an inner logic, proportion, and structure, imposing that essentially autonomous vision upon whatever materials its authorship has received from the past? My mode of asking that question in these pages, we recall, is to test allegations that yield a picture of a traditional document against the character of three documents themselves: Tosefta, which is traditional in relationship to the Mishnah, having no structure but the Mishnah's;

Sifra, which is traditional in relationship to Scripture; and the Bavli, which to begin with selects what it wishes of the Mishnah (thirty-seven out of sixty-two usable tractates) and then imposes its plan and its questions upon the Mishnah. The first two are classified as traditional, the first as selective.

In *The Bavli and its Sources*, the answer emerged through a sequence of simple tests which concerned the framing of the program of inquiry and the character of the sustained discourse of the Bavli by comparison to the prior Talmud, the Talmud of the Land of Israel or the Yerushalmi. Specifically, I argued, if I can show that in literary terms the Bavli is not traditional, formed out of the increment of received materials, the form of the reception of which governs, but – in the sense now implied – systemic, that is, again in literary terms orderly, systematic, laid out in a proportion and order dictated by the inner logic of a topic or generative problem and, therefore, authoritative by reason of its own rigorous judgment of issues of rationality and compelling logic, then I can offer a reasonable hypothesis resting on facts of literature. Specifically I can contribute a considerable example to the debate on whether tradition may coexist with the practical and applied reason of utter, uncompromising logical rationality and compelling, autonomous order. The result was quite one-sided. The Yerushalmi turned out not to define the program of the Bavli; the Bavli emerged as a free-standing reading of the Mishnah. Its authorship chose the tractates that it found important – ignoring some treated by the Yerushalmi, treating others ignored by the Yerushalmi, and making up its own program for documents covered by the Yerushalmi as well. In the present volume, the test has concerned allegations about the traditionality of the Bavli, a broader and not so carefully delimited matter. But the result is still quite one-sided, for as we tested what Halivni, Steinsaltz, and Wieseltier have to say about a document they perceive as traditional and not autonomous and systemic, we time and again found their views not so much wrong as beside the point, and occasionally even grotesque in their ignorance; Wieseltier in particular proves guilty of exaggerations beyond all evidence, but Steinsaltz, too, emerges as something of an enthusiast.

In contrasting selectivity with traditionality, quite clearly, I use tradition in a literary sense, as referring to a process by which writings of one kind and not another take shape. So let me then define what I mean by tradition and place into the context of Judaism the issue I have framed, to begin with, in such general terms.[2] For if any noun follows

---

[2]Here I review the arguments of *The Bavli and its Sources*.

the adjective, "rabbinic," it is not "Judaism" but "tradition." And by "tradition" people mean two contradictory things.

First, when people speak of "tradition," they refer to the formative history of a piece of writing, specifically, an incremental and linear process that step by step transmits out of the past an essential and unchanging fundament of truth *preserved in writing,* by stages, with what one generation has contributed covered by the increment of the next in a sedimentary process, producing a literature that, because of its traditional history as the outcome of a linear and stage-by-stage process, exercises authority over future generations and therefore is nurtured for the future. In that sense, tradition is supposed to describe a *process* or a chain of transmission of received materials, refined and corrected but handed on not only unimpaired, but essentially intact. The opening sentence of tractate Avot, "Moses received Torah from Sinai and handed it on to Joshua," bears the implication of such a literary process, though, self-evidently, the remainder of that chapter hardly illustrates the type of process alleged at the outset.

The second meaning of tradition bears not upon process but upon content and structure. People sometimes use the word *tradition* to mean a fixed and unchanging essence deriving from an indeterminate past, a truth bearing its own stamp of authority, for example, from God at Sinai.

These two meanings of the same word coexist. But they are incompatible. For the first of the two places a document within an on-going, determinate historical process, the latter speaks of a single statement at the end of an indeterminate and undefined process, which can encompass revelation of a one-time sort. In this book I use only the first of the two meanings. When, therefore, I ask whether or not the Bavli is a traditional or a selective document, I want to know whether the present literary character of the Bavli suggests to us that the document emerges from a sedimentary process of tradition in the sense just now specified: an incremental, linear development, step by step, of law and theology from one generation to the next, coming to expression in documents arrayed in sequence, first to last. The alternative – which I believe has here once more proven the more likely of the two propositions – is that the Bavli originates as a cogent and proportioned statement through a process we may compare – continuing our geological metaphor – to the way in which igneous rock takes shape: through a grand eruption, all at once, then coalescence and solidification essentially forthwith. Either the Bavli will emerge in a series of layers, or it will appear to have formed suddenly, in a work of supererogatory and imposed rationality, all at once, perfect in its ultimate logic and structure.

When I maintain that the Bavli is not a traditional document, I issue a judgment as to its character viewed as literature in relationship to prior extant writings. Everyone of course must concur that, in a theological sense, the Bavli is a profoundly traditional document, laying forth in its authorship's terms and language the nature of the Judaic tradition, that is, Judaism, as that authorship wishes to read the tradition and have it read. But this second sense will not recur in the pages that follow. In framing the issue of tradition versus system, I sidestep a current view of the literature of formative Judaism. That view, specified presently, ignores the documentary character of each of the writings, viewing them all as essentially one and uniform, lacking all documentary definition. In a variety of studies I have argued precisely the opposite.[3]

---

[3]I began in 1972 with the Mishnah and the Tosefta, at first seeing them as Mishnah-Tosefta, only later on understanding that they are essentially distinct statements, each with its tasks and purpose. My *History of the Mishnaic Law* (Leiden, 1974-1986) in forty-three volumes and associated studies, worked on that matter, yielding *Judaism: The Evidence of the Mishnah* (Chicago, 1981: University of Chicago Press). Subsequent studies of the Yerushalmi, The Fathers According to Rabbi Nathan, Genesis Rabbah, Leviticus Rabbah, Pesiqta deRab Kahana, Pesiqta Rabbati, and the Bavli, have shown me that each of these documents is subject to precise definition in its own terms, as to both rhetorical and logical plan and topical program. Three works provide a good picture of the basic argument and method worked out in a variety of monographs and books: *The Integrity of Leviticus Rabbah: The Problem of the Autonomy of a Rabbinic Document* (Chico, 1985: Scholars Press for Brown Judaic Studies), *Comparative Midrash: The Plan and Program of Genesis Rabbah and Leviticus Rabbah* (Atlanta, 1986: Scholars Press for Brown Judaic Studies), and *From Tradition to Imitation. The Plan and Program of Pesiqta deRab Kahana and Pesiqta Rabbati* (Atlanta, 1987: Scholars Press for Brown Judaic Studies). In two other works, I have applied the results to specific allegations concerning the character of that same literature deriving from Orthodox-Jewish literary critics, who see the whole as uniform and interchangeable, lacking all documentary specificity. The systematic reply to these approaches, which restate in literary terms the received theology of Judaism and its hermeneutic, is in these works: *Canon and Connection: Judaism and Intertextuality* (Lanham, 1987: University Press of America), which addresses the propositions on the character of the canonical writings of formative Judaism currently set forth by Shaye J. D. Cohen, Lawrence H. Schiffman, and Susan Handelman; and *Midrash and Literature: The Primacy of Documentary Discourse* (Atlanta, 1987: Scholars Press for Brown Judaic Studies), which addresses the characterization of Midrash compilations deriving in their most recent, if not most felicitous or compelling version, from James Kugel. Elsewhere I go over some of the results of the former work. In all instances I lay forth sizable samples of the literature, and test the allegations of

What I have shown in this book for Tosefta's and Sifra's relationship to the Bavli – as in *The Bavli and its Sources* for the Yerushalmi's relationship to the Bavli – is a simple proposition. The prior writings were used when wanted, ignored when not; they provided valued, authoritative information; but they defined no program, provided no framework and order of inquiry, dictated no issues, determined no results. The heirs, in the Bavli, utilized these sources (or, materials later on collected and preserved therein) pretty much as they found them useful, meaning, for their reasons, in the realization of their program. With the Bavli as the literary realization of the system overall, we may then conclude that the Judaism of the Dual Torah knows not traditions to be recited and reviewed but merely sources, to be honored always but to be used only when pertinent to a quite independent program of thought. That is to say, the components of the Torah of that Judaism do not contribute equally and jointly to a single comprehensive statement, handed on from generation to generation *and from book to book,* all of them sources forming a tradition that constitutes the Torah.

Each has a particular message and make a distinctive statement.[4] In literary terms, the various rabbinic documents commonly (and, from a theological perspective, quite correctly) are commonly represented as not merely autonomous and individual statements, or even connected here and there through shared passages, but in fact as continuous and and interrelated developments, one out of its predecessor, in a long line of canonical writings (to Sinai). The Talmud of Babylonia, or Bavli, takes pride of place – in this picture of "the rabbinic tradition" – as the final and complete statement of that incremental, linear tradition, and so is ubiquitously described as *"the* tradition," par excellence. In this concluding monograph I shall demonstrate that, vis-à-vis its sources, the Bavli represents an essentially autonomous, fresh, and original statement of its own. How so? *Its authorship does not take over, rework, and repeat what it has received out of prior writings but makes its own statement, on its own program, in its own terms, and for its own purposes.*

---

the Orthodox-Jewish literary critics against that evidence. In my view the results prove somewhat one-sided, but, of course, the way forward lies through further dialogue on these interesting questions.

[4]Obviously, all fit together into a common statement, the Torah or Judaism. That fundamental theological conviction defines Judaism and cannot – and should not – give way before the mere testimony of literary evidence. But it is the fact that whatever traits join the whole of the rabbinic corpus together into the single Torah of Moses our Rabbi, revealed by God to Moses at Sinai, they are not literary traits of tradition.

Every test I can devise for describing the relationship between the authorship of the Bavli and the prior and extant writings of the movement of which that authorship forms the climax and conclusion yields a single result. Unlike Sifra and Tosefta, the authorship of the Bavli does not pursue anyone else's program – even that of the Mishnah. The Bavli's authorship selected thirty-seven tractates and therefore bypassed twenty-five. How traditional is an authorship that has attended to a little more than half of its received and authoritative writing? No less than 40 percent of the tractates of the Mishnah are simply ignored by the Bavli. And however sustained its exegesis of the Mishnah tractates that are taken up, the Bavli's authorship does not merely receive and refine writings concluded elsewhere. It takes over a substantial heritage and reworks the whole into its own sustained and internally cogent statement – and that forms not the outcome of a process of sedimentary tradition but the opposite: systematic statement of a cogent and logical order, made up in its authorship's rhetoric, attaining comprehensibility through the syntax of its authorship's logic, reviewing a received topical program in terms of the problematic and interests defined by its authorship's larger purposes and proposed message. The samples of the Bavli we reviewed – and any others I might have chosen! – constitute either composites of sustained, essentially syllogistic discourse, in which case they form the whole and comprehensive statement of a system, or increments of exegetical accumulation, in which case they constitute restatements, with minor improvements, of a continuous tradition. In my view, the reader is going to review sustained, directed, purposive syllogistic discourse, not wandering and essentially agglutinative collections of observations on this and that, made we know not when, for a purpose we cannot say, to an audience we can scarcely imagine, so as to deliver a message that, all together and in the aggregate, we cannot begin to recapitulate.

There is no denying that Halivni, Steinsaltz, and Wieseltier in their diverse characterizations have a point, since it is true that the authorship of the Bavli drew upon a sizable corpus of materials of indeterminate character and substance, which we assuredly do classify as traditions handed on from their predecessors. Hence the authorship of the Bavli made use of both sources, completed documents, and also traditions, transmitted sayings and stories, ordinarily of modest proportions, not subjected to ultimate redaction. But the authorship of the Bavli did whatever it wished with these materials to carry out its own program and to make its own prevailing statement. These received materials, undeniably formulated and transmitted in a process of tradition, have been so reworked and revised by the penultimate and ultimate authorship that their original character does not define the syntax of argument and the processes of syllogistic discourse, except by way of supplying facts for someone else's case. Whether or not we can still discern traces of received statements, even in wordings that point to an origin other than with our authorship, is beside the point. Proof of my case does not derive from the failure or success of scholars to identify the passages of the Bavli that antedate the penultimate or ultimate work of composition.

To be sure, I regard as ultimately unsuccessful the convoluted effort by Halivni, in his *Sources and Traditions*, to tell us not only the original form but also the latter (by them utterly undocumented) literary history, of these unredacted sayings.[5] Endless speculation on what may have been masks the simple fact that we do not know what was. But that is not much to the point anyhow. The point is what we have, not what we do not have, and we have the Bavli to tell us about the work of the penultimate and ultimate authorship of the Bavli. That suffices. The facts are what they are.

In its final, literary context defined by the documents or sources we can identify, the Bavli emerges as anything but the seal of "tradition" in the familiar sense. For it is not based on distinct and completed sources handed on from time immemorial, subserviently cited and glossed by its own authorship, and it does not focus upon the systematic representation of the materials of prior documents, faithfully copied and rehearsed and represented. We have, of course, to exclude the Mishnah, but this fundamental document is treated by the authorship of the Bavli in a wholly independent spirit. The upshot is that the Bavli does not derive from a process of tradition in the first sense stated above, although, as a faithful and practicing Jew, I believe that the Bavli truly constitutes "tradition" in that second, theological sense to which I referred: a new statement of its own making and a fresh address to issues of its own choosing. Viewed as literature, the Bavli is not a traditional document at all. It is not the result of an incremental and linear process; it does not review and restate what others have already said; its authorship does not regard itself as bound to the program and issues received from prior ages. By its selectivity, the Bavli's authorship shows us that their document constitutes a systemic and not a traditional statement.

True, the Talmud of Babylonia draws upon prior materials. It was not made up out of whole cloth by its penultimate and ultimate

---

[5]All the more so Halivni's student, Richard Kalmin. That is why I reprint in the appendix of this book my review of the Halivni-Kalmin theory of the redaction of the Talmud of Babylonia.

authorship, the generations that drew the whole together and placed it into the form in which it has come down from the seventh century to the present day. The Bavli's authorship both received out of the past a corpus of *sources*, and also stood in a line of *traditions* of sayings and stories, that is, fixed wordings of thought the formulation and transmission of which took place not in completed documents but in ad hoc and brief sentences or little narratives. These materials, deriving from an indeterminate past through a now-inaccessible process of literary history, constitute traditions in the sense defined in the preface: an incremental and linear process that step by step transmits out of the past an essential and unchanging fundament of truth and writing. The process of selectivity worked itself out in a review of these traditions. The document emerged out of those principles of selectivity that guided the choice. The next task in the description of the formation of Judaism therefore requires us to discover the principles that told people why this, not that. This distinction, then, between traditions and sources, between selectivity and tradition, has now to be spelled out, since others who may wish to pursue issues within the classifications or categories defined by Halivni will now require new definitions to replace his.

Traditions: some of these prior materials never reached redaction in a distinct document and come down as sherds and remnants within the Bavli itself. These are the ones that may be called traditions, in the sense of materials formulated and transmitted from one generation to the next, but not given a place in a document of their own.

Sources: others had themselves reached closure prior to the work on the Bavli and are readily identified as autonomous writings. Scripture, to take an obvious example, the Mishnah, tractate Abot (the Fathers), the Tosefta (so we commonly suppose), Sifra, Sifré to Numbers, Sifré to Deuteronomy, Genesis Rabbah, Leviticus Rabbah, the Fathers According to Rabbi Nathan, Pesiqta deRab Kahana, Pesiqta Rabbati, possibly Lamentations Rabbah, not to mention the Siddur and Mahzor (order of daily and holy day prayer, respectively), and various other writings had assuredly concluded their processes of formation before the Bavli's authorship accomplished their work. These we call *sources* – more or less completed writings.

To conclude: in contrasting tradition and selectivity, tradition as against system, I really want to know the answer to one question: is a document that is received as authoritative (in theological terms, "canonical") essentially a restatement of what has gone before, or is such a writing fresh and original? If the answer is that the Bavli restates a consensus formed through ages, then our conception of the literary definition of the canon of Judaism will take one form. I have shown once more that the Bavli's authorship makes an essentially new statement. When we know how that statement is – what I call "the Bavli's one voice"[6] – and what statement is intended, we shall understand the final stage in the formation of Judaism. The Bavli in relationship to its sources is simply not a traditional document, in the plain sense that most of what it says in a cogent and coherent way expresses the well-crafted statement and viewpoint of its authorship. Its authorship exercised an ongoing privilege of selectivity. Excluding, of course, the Mishnah, to which the Bavli devotes its sustained and systematic attention, little of what our authorship says derives cogency and force from a received statement, and most does not. The authorship of the Bavli selectively made up a tradition.[7]

---

[6]*The Bavli's One Voice: The Types of Discourse of the Talmud of Babylonia.* Atlanta, 1991: Scholars Press for South Florida Studies in the History of Judaism.

[7]In the following books I explain how the authorship of the Bavli imparted a traditional form to their free-standing system: *The Making of the Mind of Judaism.* Atlanta, 1987: Scholars Press for Brown Judaic Studies; and *The Formation of the Jewish Intellect. Making Connections and Drawing Conclusions in the Traditional System of Judaism.* Atlanta, 1988: Scholars Press for Brown Judaic Studies.

Appendix

The Halivni-Kalmin Theory of the Redaction of the Babylonian Talmud

The Redaction of the Babylonian Talmud: Amoraic or Saboraic? By Richard Kalmin. Monographs of Hebrew Union College 12. 215 pp. Cincinnati, 1989: Hebrew Union College.

Professor Richard Kalmin of Jewish Theological Seminary of America here addresses the question of the final stages in the redaction of the Talmud of Babylonia. He seeks knowledge of "who the redactors were, at what time period(s) they lived, and how they reworked their sources." Kalmin proposes to answer these questions in a way that will prove unfamiliar, even recondite, obscure, and eccentric, to scholars who work on the history of documents that lack clear evidence of authorship, text tradition, and the like. For ordinarily when people ask about the history of a document, they want to know where and when it is first attested by some external writing, for example, when we find the first references to, and citations of, the document under study. Furthermore, the manuscript tradition will be asked to lead us to the earlier representation of the writing at hand. Finally, traits of the document overall will be assessed as a first step in finding out whether the writing is a composite or unitary, and, if unitary, for whom the document speaks.

Kalmin rejects these universally accepted procedures, common in scholarship on anonymous writings in antiquity (whether the Pentateuch or the Mishnah or Midrash compilations or the Yerushalmi). He chooses, rather, a quite different approach to the problem, and, I have to say, his method is one that seems to me somewhat precious and idiosyncratic. Because of the work's obscurity and self-referential character, I am inclined to wonder whether his ideas will make much of an impact on others who investigate the same questions. For in the end, even if we were to concede every point Kalmin wishes us to accept, I am not clear as to why he thinks he has answered the question announced at the outset, nor do I know what, if anything, is at stake in his book.

A description of his program will explain why I find the work so alien to contemporary humanistic learning. The very layout of the work is daunting. The very opening pages validate my judgment that the man is simply talking to himself. For he begins not with a preface but with a chart of "characteristics of Talmud rabbis." This involves "group A Amoraim (ca. 390-501) [1] strong tendency to make prescriptive and interpretative or explanatory statements; [2] independent; no tendency to appear in connection with a small number of sages [3] multi-dimensional; active as both students and teachers [4] their statements are integrative into the core of the *sugya* [5] their statements do not refer to or respond to discussions by the *stam*. This kind of thing goes on for Group B Amoraim or Group 2 Amoraim and then Group 1 Amoraim, then Group 3 Amoraim; then the *stam* [anonymous sections of the Talmud; then The Saboraim (post-amoraic). His date for this last group is from 501. There follow three charts: theory of saboraic redaction; theory of continuous redaction; then theory of stammaitic redaction. All of this is given without a single definition, without the slightest interest in explaining the source of the characterizations, part of which I cited; without any introduction to what is at stake or at issue. I find puzzling just what Kalmin proposed to accomplish in these rather daunting charts.

His introduction then surveys regnant opinion on the redaction of the Babylonian Talmud. Such a survey goes over ground covered in *The Formation of the Babylonian Talmud. Studies on the Achievements of Late Nineteenth and Twentieth Century Historical and Literary-Critical Research.* (Leiden, 1970: Brill), but Kalmin's discussion is more comprehensive and better composed than those studies of individual scholars' opinions. Kalmin's main interest is in Halivni's "theory of stammaitic redaction," though in his behalf it must be said that he has read the work of others as well. Kalmin sets up his problem as follows. There are three basic theories on the redaction of the Bavli. Certain features, he claims, should characterize the document, if one or another of those theories pertains.

Thus he says, "According to the theory of saboraic redaction, we would not expect to discern evidence of a unique editorial role on the part of the late Amoraim. According to this theory the distinctive features we encounter among the final generations of Amoraim should be in line with discernible amoraic trends. We should observe a smooth transition from the generation of Rav Ashi's teachers to the generation of Rav Ashi and from that point to the generation of Rav Ashi's students and beyond." I am not at all clear on why Kalmin is so certain that these are the characteristics that "should" emerge, and it seems to me somewhat facile on his part so to define matters as to prove his point *a priori*. Kalmin claims to show that "the attributed material that survives from the late amoraic period conforms to clearly definable patterns, and that these patterns are the continuation and development of patterns exhibited by previous amoraic generations." It goes without saying that every line of his study then rests upon the premise that all attributions are sound and reliable; without that premise, nothing can be done along the lines he has taken in this book. Only if the attributions are valid can he know which saying or composite or composition is of "the late amoraic period," and which is not. But the fabricated argument, resting on an unsubstantiated "should be" thus and so, is true to the one important stream of talmudic exegesis, the pilpulistic, which manufactures questions and then makes up answers to them. Not a few of the reviewers of the books by David Halivni, on which Kalmin says he bases his entire work, have dismissed as pilpulistic the same kind of argumentation.

That is not the only way in which Kalmin has more or less made things up as he has gone along, inventing his own classifications and categories to suit the occasion. He divides amoraic statements into "prescriptive, interpretative or explanatory and argumentational categories. This then provides "the key to dividing the final generations of Amoraim into two major groups. The first group, which will be referred to as Group A, consists of the few late Amoraim who produced a significant amount of prescriptive and interpretative material and relatively little argumentation. The second group, which will be referred to as Group B, consists of the remainder...of late Amoraim, whose argumentational statements overwhelmingly outnumber their prescriptive and interpretative statements." Immediately following, in Kalmin's exposition, is this: "At first glance, the literature produced by the Group B Amoraim establishes a powerful link between these Amoraim and the *stam*, for the *stam* is likewise overwhelmingly argumentational in character. The *stam* took upon itself the task of composing an enormous commentary on the tannaitic and amoraic legacy to which it was heir, of supplying its argumentational underpinnings, and of recreating the logical arguments by which conclusions had earlier been reached when no account of these arguments survived from the Amoraim themselves."

Rather than tax the reader's patience with a précis of further stages in Kalmin's argument, let me give the center of matters in his own words, provided on the book flap (the most clearly expounded propositions in the entire book, alas): "Kalmin notes that in each case where a late Amora appears to respond to statements by the stam, it is possible, and usually preferable in the light of certain incongruities in the sugya as it presently stands, to detach the amoraic statement from its connection to the stam and restore its original connection to an earlier amoraic or tannaitic source. The simplest explanation for this phenomenon...is that late Amoraim do not respond to the earlier *stam* discussions because there were no earlier *stamot*. Composition of the stam...did not begin until after the conclusion of the amoraic period." All of this, I maintain, is simply a fabrication, which emerges when one has made up one's own definitions, invented one's own questions, and produced answers in accord with one's own program. Readers by this point will expect, in any event, a rather compendious treatment of texts, so that they may share in the inquiry that the author undertakes. Otherwise, how are we to know what it means to "detach the amoraic statement from its connection to the stam" or to know why that is required at all? A survey of the remainder of the book produces the following: Who lived during the final amoraic generations? "Rav Ashi and Ravina are the end of *horaah*, the theory of Hanokh Albeck; Mar bar Rav Ashi and his literary contribution, the theory of Avinoam Cohen; characteristics of the final generations of Amoraim; the final generations of Amoraim, transition or continuity? the relationship between the final generations of Amoraim and the *stam* and its impact on the question of redaction. That concludes the book: ninety-four pages, six chapters in all. There follow thirteen appendices. Only the first allows us to peer over Kalmin's shoulder as he reads a text: the analysis of *sugyot*. He treats all of five! He gives the Hebrew-Aramaic original, untranslated, and then, without telling us how he reads the passage, he proceeds to make observations about it.

Let me give his treatment of the first of the five examples of "*sugyot* which contain implicit *stam* commentary on statements by Group A or Group B Amoraim. Here is what he tells us about his untranslated, merely paraphrased paragraph (Ket. 69a):

> According to the *sugya* as it presently stands, Rav Yemar's dialogue with Rav Ashi is based on a *stam* discussion of R. Yohanan's opinion. According to the *stam*, the unmarried daughter loses her dowry because once she receives half of the inheritance and is amply provided for, the dowry is no longer necessary. The purpose served by the dowry has been achieved by other means, and the dowry can therefore be dispensed with. It is on this *stam* interpretation of R.

Yohanan that Rav Yemar's objection appears to be based. There is no reason to assume, however, that Rav Yemar and Rav Ashi could not have arrived at the above interpretation of R. Yohanan (most likely the simple meaning of his statement) without the *stam*. Rav Yemar could have independently arrived at this interpretation and assumed it as the basis for his objection. Only later, when the *stam* interpolated material into the *sugya*, was the impression created that the dialogue between Rav Yemar and Rav Ashi was dependent on the *stam*.

Now it appears to me that Kalmin has simply imposed upon the passage his own premises and proved his point merely by announcing it. The entire argumentation consists of "there is no reason to assume." And what we have to assume is that Yemar and Ashi could have arrived at their reading of Yohanan's statement without the intervening anonymous materials.

How does Kalmin know this, and why does he insist that what they could have done they did do? His proposed deconstruction of the text is all that his argument consists of: it might have been put together in some other way than the way in which we have it, specifically, in the way in which, as a matter of hypothesis, Kalmin thinks it was formed: "only later, when the stam interpolated material into the sugya, was the impression created that the dialogue...was dependent on the stam." The other four "examples," upon which the entire argument of the book rests, are similar exercises in begging the question.

A brief survey of a sample of his appendices will strengthen the impression that Kalmin is pretty much talking to himself. These are the other twelve: appearances with Rav Ashi and the later Ravina; objections ["the following is a complete list of the objections by Group B Amoraim]; questions [the following is a complete list of the questions by Group B Amoraim]; prescriptive statements [ditto]; interpretative or explanatory comments [ditto]; argumentational responses [the same as before], and so on.

So while Kalmin asks the right question, as he says, "who the redactors were, at what time period(s) they lived, and how they reworked their sources," he has not set forth a method that can answer that question, and, it must follow, as a matter of fact he has not even pretended to answer that question, nor has he answered any other. The book has no conclusion; it just trails off into a thicket of appendices. That is why his work is to be characterized as not merely obscure but obscurantist. Kalmin has contributed nothing to public discourse on the subject he has chosen. He has pursued a very private program of his own, and the result is a book that is unreadable and utterly idiosyncratic.

If this is the kind of solipsistic scholarship that the critical, scientific school at the Jewish Theological Seminary of America and Hebrew Union College-Jewish Institute of Religion aims at creating, then the rest of us will have to take our leave with no sense of having missed important and consequential learning. The yeshiva world will ignore this book because Kalmin concludes [again his book flap] "that the Talmud does not present us with an accurate picture of the rabbinic movement in Babylonia and that significant pieces are missing from the Talmud's account of the activity of most Amoraim." That conclusion will hardly win a warm welcome in the yeshiva world, which has slight patience, any more, for smart-aleck debunking.

But the academic world will ignore this book too. The reason is not because it is poorly argued and clumsily written and disorganized and incoherent, though it is, and not because the strategy of exposition utterly fails, though it does. It is that the results, if correct, are trivial and in no way help us to answer the important questions that Kalmin claims to address. If we want to know something about the redaction of the Babylonian Talmud, we shall have to describe the Babylonian Talmud and its paramount traits of rhetoric and logic and determine whether it is a compilation or a well-crafted composition, working our way from the outside to the inside. In starting from the smallest whole units of thought, the individual sentences, Kalmin has replicated an error of several generations' standing, and the utterly useless result, comprising made-up words that only the author and his six best friends use anyhow is yet one more charge exacted by the rather aimless and self-referential (not to say self-serving) program of academic isolates in rabbinical seminaries. This is what emerges when scholars talk entirely to themselves and listen to no one else. The difference between Kalmin's version of "the redaction of the Babylonian Talmud" and an academic reading of the same problem is the difference between Nintendo baseball and the kind you play on a real baseball diamond.

Index